gⁱeener One Shade at home

A Room by Room Guide to Reduce Toxins, Lighten Your Environmental Footprint, and Live Simpler

LORI SULLIVAN

One Shade Greener Publishing
Plymouth, Michigan

One Shade Greener at Home: A Room by Room Guide to Reduce Toxins, Lighten Your Environmental Footprint, and Live Simpler/ Lori Sullivan

First edition 2023

ISBN 979-8-9874018-0-4 (paperback)
ISBN 979-8-9874018-1-1 (eBook)

To everyone who wants to make a difference but doesn't know where to start.

CONTENTS

MY ONE SHADE GREENER JOURNEY

Fifteen years ago, I started on a journey to lessen my environmental impact. I knew very little of what that even meant at the time, but I was intrigued by the articles and content I was reading. I heard about toxins in the products we use every day, recycling was being introduced in my community, and there was a lot of conversation around slow living as a reaction to our fast-paced lives.

I dove in, reading everything I could find about green living, toxins, and sustainability. I started making changes in my home, from recycling more to trying household tips and techniques while also discovering a global community making green products that weren't boring or too expensive. I started to share what I was learning via a Facebook group and a blog called *One Shade Greener*.

A few years in, a busy family life with teenagers in the house had me step away from sharing my journey online. However, I continued to try things in my own home. Today, I'm greener than I was back in 2007 when I started my journey. Yet, there is still a long way I can go in reducing my impact. *One Shade Greener* is not just a company name or title of a book; the phrase articulates my philosophy:

To take steps day by day to become one shade greener.

These pages contain ideas I've personally used and ideas I haven't tried but have heard good things from others about. I wanted this book to become a resource for anyone beginning their journey. As I dove into my research, I realized that the brands and products to consider are unique in different parts of the world. As a result, this book took a turn to become a resource for people who live in the United States. While this is narrower than I had intended, I believe it will be more relevant.

I hope the book will provide you with ideas and inspiration to begin your journey to becoming one shade greener. What has worked for me may not be the right solution for you. However, every change we make matters, and if we all make changes together, we truly make an impact.

Two items to note before we get started:

1. Websites and products mentioned throughout the book are valid at publication but may change over time. Always do your own research to confirm.
2. The book contains brand and do-it-yourself ideas for personal care products. Always check with a doctor before using any new product or DIY recipe to ensure the ingredients won't adversely impact you.

INTRODUCTION

CHAPTER LAYOUT

THE DESIGN YOU CAN EXPECT AS YOU MOVE
THROUGH THE BOOK

This book is very flexible to adapt to your approach and style. Below are the highlights to be aware of before you dive in to tailor the experience of the book to you:

Chapter Structure: The chapters are divided into rooms of your home. You can follow the order I have provided or create a different order that makes more sense for your lifestyle and current situation.

Then, each chapter is divided into focus areas. Those will vary from chapter to chapter, depending on the products and considerations of the room.

Most chapters provide eco-friendly brands as starting points for product alternatives. There are three levels, as explained below:

- **Light Green** – These products have improved the ingredients and/or parts and are healthier for your home. However, they still have recycling challenges, typically from the packaging.

- **Dark Green** – These alternatives have improved the ingredients and have better or no packaging.

- **DIY Green** – This is what you would expect from DIY. There are recipes and alternatives that you can make on your own, using easy-to-obtain ingredients, many of which may already be in your kitchen cabinets. Always check with a doctor before using any new product or DIY recipe to ensure the ingredients won't adversely impact you.

There is no correct answer as to which level is best. You will make different choices depending on where you are in your journey, your current life stage, the input of members of your household, and your current budget levels. Any are good, and you need to find the one that is right for you right now. In a month, a year, or longer, you may revisit the choices and take a new direction—I know I have!

My Journey: Each chapter begins with a summary of how I've implemented changes in that room. My choices may not be the same as yours, but you can start to see how little movements make an impact over time.

Also, when I started the journey in 2007, our household comprised my husband, myself, and two children (seven and ten at the time). Today, my daughter is out of college and living on her own. My son is still in college and home during school breaks. This has changed the dynamic and choices I've made over the years. I'll note where it makes sense on some of the differences based on life stage.

Fast Five: Some of you might want to make a change quickly and don't have time to read the chapter right away to get started. For this reader, I've provided a "Fast Five" at the end of each chapter. These are the five steps in each room that you can take right away to make an impact and begin to celebrate some wins on your journey to become one shade greener.

THE 4PS FRAMEWORK

A STRUCTURE TO THINK ABOUT SUSTAINABILITY IN YOUR HOME

Before we start on the journey, I want to introduce you to my framework for thinking about sustainability in your home. Many believe sustainability is just about protecting the planet. While that is part of the equation, for me, there are three other considerations. This framework broadens your perspective from Planet to also include People, Pocketbook, and Process.

We make decisions every day. Many tie to products that come into our home. These decisions range from small things like a tube of toothpaste to large purchases like a new vehicle. Each of these decisions has an impact. Using the framework of the 4Ps, you can intentionally guide the decisions you make for the products coming into your home. Below is an overview of these four considerations:

PLANET – Starting with the planet, there are ways the products we purchase, and our habits impact the environment around us.

- **Natural Resources** – For any product in the home that uses electricity, gas, or water, we want to understand how efficient those products are and how our habits create an impact when using them. As we lessen our use, this is good for the planet, and, in turn, we will likely save some money on our personal energy bills.

- **Parts and Ingredients** – Understanding the components and ingredients that go into products is important to the environment

5

and the health of the people in our homes. When making purchases, we'll look to answer two questions: Are we bringing toxins into our house? How easy or difficult will disposal of this product at the end of its useful life?

- **Packaging** – We bring many disposable products into our home, from items in our pantry to those in our laundry, bathrooms, and more. Considering the packaging those items come in and determining if there is an alternative with fewer or better materials can lighten the impact on the environment while generating less trash and recyclables for you to manage.

- **Distribution** – The final environmental impact is the path a product takes to get to you. When you buy locally, this will have less impact than purchasing something created in a nearby state, neighboring countries, and across the globe. Becoming aware of where your products are being shipped from lessens the impact on the planet.

PEOPLE – When greening your home, I believe we must protect the environment and reduce the abovementioned impacts. However, as I dove deeper, I realized that the decisions that positively impact our environment almost always have an equally positive impact on the people in our homes. There are two positive impacts:

- **Health** – Each chapter of this book will cover ingredients in products that have the potential to negatively impact your health. Thus, removing toxins has the potential to literally make you feel better.

- **Peace of Mind** – There are many ways that the journey to green living can give you more peace of mind. Cleaner ingredients make you feel better about what you put on and in your body. The simple, intentional mindset of green living can help you feel like your home is full of the "right" number of things and not overflowing with items you don't need or use. In addition, removing the mental clutter of too much in your life is also effective in achieving peace of mind.

POCKETBOOK – Anytime I speak with someone about living a more sustainable lifestyle, chances are that the first thing I hear is, "Green products cost more money." I'm not going to argue with that; often, they do but not always. However, my challenge to you is this:

Where can you find savings to offset the minimal cost increase of greener products? Maybe it takes two weeks of not buying your morning coffee outside the home to save up the amount needed to make the incremental investment in eco-friendly products in your laundry room. Would you be willing to make the trade-off to remove the toxins from your environment?

Other ways green living can positively impact your finances include selling items you no longer use, reducing your energy consumption, evaluating the need to buy things (like clothing), and buying used instead of new. All of these are choices you can make. I hope this book gives you the information you need to make the right decisions for you. You may not decide to change something like your laundry detergent, but my goal is that you are doing it intentionally, knowing the pros and cons of your choice.

PROCESS – I would be remiss if I didn't mention the importance of the process in making changes. Making your home greener is not going to happen overnight, and some areas will have choices for you to make on how to do something differently compared to how you've always done it – essentially changing your habits.

For example, if you create a pile of electronics that are no longer being used, you'll need to choose what to do with them. In the past, you might have tossed them in the trash. Now, you might consider trying to sell them online, having a garage/yard/tag sale, donating them to a good cause in your area, or recycling them at a local recycler. All of these are good choices. Depending on the items and your trade-off for time vs. money, you can make the right choice for you and establish a new process or habit.

GETTING STARTED – STEP 1: CREATE A PLAN

Before we jump into the rooms of your home, it's good to spend just a little time thinking about why you are starting the journey and what your approach may look like. Below are some questions and thoughts to kick-start your green home project.

What are Your Goals? – When you think about greening your home, what goals do you have? Do you want to reduce energy use, choose healthier products, and/or relook at everything? Keeping your goals at the forefront will keep you on track when deciding what ideas to prioritize.

How Will You Approach Trade-offs? – Considering the 4Ps Framework, the elements can sometimes require you to make trade-offs. How would you rank order the importance of the four? There is no right answer here, just the right answer for you. You might be at a point in life where your pocketbook tops the list, and you will focus on changes that aim to save you money. For others, your top priority might be people, and you will be focused on getting the toxins out of your home. For others, lightening your environmental impact may be paramount.

Will You Go Solo or With Others? – Will you accomplish more on your own or in a group? If you are disciplined and self-directed, dive in! If you are concerned that you might not stick to a schedule and want some accountability, find some friends or co-workers to join you in overhauling their space. Think of it like a "Greening Your Home" book club.

Is this a Household Project or Your Own? – If you live with others, your family and/or roommates, you need to decide if and how you will involve them in the project. You might decide to partner on all aspects of the book. On the other hand, you may have a conversation that discusses the project and decide where others will and will not be involved. Maybe they are comfortable that you will make some new product decisions (soap, laundry detergent, etc.) that they will try but don't need to decide with you. For changes that require the entire household, you could have discussions as they come up. During my first wave of changes, my family was aware of what I was doing but had no interest in being involved. They didn't resist, but it really was my project in the beginning. You can figure out the level of involvement that works for you and those in your home.

Will You Follow the Order or Skip Around? – As mentioned earlier, the chapters are sorted by room in the home and can be addressed in any order you choose. Think about the order and determine if you want to follow the order of the book or create your own.

Is the Fast Five Right for You, or Will You Dive Deeper? – This one is straightforward. Do you want to take all the steps in each chapter or start with the fast five in each room and come back to make more changes later?

GETTING STARTED – STEP 2: OBSERVE

Before diving into the rooms, I recommend you spend a day or two observing your habits with sustainability in mind. We've all heard about reducing, reusing, and recycling. I'm also sure you are already doing things in each of those areas.

As we look at each room, we will consider two additional Rs – refuse and repurpose. Below is a quick summary of all five to put you in the mindset of observing current behaviors in your home and enabling you to identify changes you might want to make.

Refuse – Before getting to the well-known Rs, the best place to start is with Refuse. When deciding to buy anything, the concept of refuse is to take a moment to stop and think, "Do I need this?" before making the purchase. You should buy what you want, not just what you need, taking this moment of pause may have you reconsidering some purchases. If you don't bring things into your home, you don't need to worry about the other Rs. As purchases come up, start to ask the question, "Do I need to buy this?"

Reduce – This is the concept of "less is more." Reducing the amount of anything in your home—clothing, books, toys, Knick knacks, paper, electronics, and more—can not only clear the space and be environmentally friendly but can also give you peace of mind by helping you to live simpler with less visual clutter. Look around your house and see if there are areas where you want to reduce.

Reuse – Reuse can take a couple of different forms. The first is to ensure you aren't buying single-use products like disposable plates and silverware. The second is to consider "reusing" something someone else no longer needs. In other words, consider purchasing secondhand. This may not be right for everyone, but it will positively impact the Planet and your Pocketbook. To shift your mindset here, start to look at things in your life that are disposable and think, "Could I find a non-disposable alternative?". As you look to make purchases, ask, "Could I purchase this secondhand?".

Recycle – This is the R that most are familiar with. According to the EPA, about 32% of Municipal Solid Waste was recycled and composted. (*National Overview: Facts and Figures on Materials, Wastes and Recycling | US EPA*, 2017). The numbers have increased, but there is a long way to go. Instead of automatically putting items in the trash, the goal is to find a way to recycle them. As we go through the chapters, you will realize that some of the items you are likely throwing into your recycle bin may not actually be recyclable. Considering the recyclability of the parts and packaging of the items you purchase becomes the best way to make a positive impact. Start to think about what is going into your trash and determine if there is a way to recycle those items.

Repurpose – Repurpose is the concept of taking something that has lived out its intended use and shifting the purpose to something else. An easy example is to use old towels for cleaning or as rags in the garage. There are many creative ideas for repurposing that you can find online. Do you have items you are ready to throw out that could be used differently?

GETTING STARTED – STEP 3: DOWNLOAD / BOOKMARK RESOURCES

Throughout the book, there are several foundational websites and apps that will be very helpful resources as you embark on your journey. Many are offered as both a website and an app that can be downloaded on your phone for the times you are out shopping. By spending a little time bookmarking these on your computer and downloading the apps to your phone for reference, they will always be at your fingertips when you want to use them as a resource.

RECYCLING: Your Guidelines – The first resource to have on hand is the guidelines for recycling in your local municipality. I recommend bookmarking the recycling page online and printing a copy for easy reference around the house. This will ensure you aren't putting things into the recycling bin that can't be accepted. Take note of the plastics; all are marked with a number 1-7 on the bottom. My municipality only takes 1, 2, 4, 5, and 7. So, I need to make sure I don't put any 3s or 6s in the bin.

RECYCLING: Earth911 or iRecycle – This is a resource I have used since about 2011 and have found it SO helpful on a regular basis over the years. Just type in the item you want to recycle and your zip code. From there, you get a list of locations that will take the item in your area. On your computer, the resource can be found at www.earth911.com. In the app store, you can search Earth911 or iRecycle. The app is called iRecycle but is powered by Earth911.

RECYCLING: Plastic Bags – An important item to note is that many types of plastic wrap and packaging can't be recycled curbside because they will get caught in the curbside machines. You can find drop-off locations at www.how2recycle.info for items like plastic shopping bags, shipping packaging, and plastic wrap items like toilet paper are packaged in. They even take used plastic baggies! My local grocery store has a drop-off point, making it easy and convenient for drop-offs.

APPLIANCE PURCHASE: Energy Star – The Energy Star website – www.energystar.gov – has all the information you need to reduce home appliances' energy consumption. There are sections that review the efficiency of products, including water heaters, washers & dryers, laptop computers, ceiling fans, windows, and MUCH more. In addition to information on product efficiency, they also let you know if rebates are available.

CLEANING PRODUCTS/FOOD/PERSONAL CARE: Environmental Working Group (EWG) or Healthy Living – The Environmental Working Group focuses on evaluating products you bring into your home and provides certifications and ratings. They have been in this business since 1993, and I trust their evaluations. On your computer, you can find the ratings at www.ewg.org/guides. Scroll down on the left to see different product categories. I find their website a bit challenging to navigate and struggle to find the right location; hence, I prefer the app. Search EWG in the app store, and you will find two apps, EWG Healthy Living and EWG's Food Scores. I recommend downloading both.

CLOTHING: Good On You – This company provides ratings for clothing and accessory brands and can be found online at www.GoodOnYou.eco. They also have an app that can be downloaded for when you are out shopping. The site provides a five-point overall scale from Great to Poor. This rating is achieved by a combination of scores in three detailed areas: Planet, People, and Animals.

Now that we have a foundation of where to start, the book's remaining chapters will focus on the rooms of your home and how you can incorporate changes to make your spaces one shade greener.

THE FAMILY ROOM

The family room is where we gather to relax and have downtime, enjoying activities like watching television or playing games. As the first room chapter of this book, I'm using the family room to focus on areas that apply to the entire home—including overall energy efficiency, lighting, general home cleaning, and TVs/game systems—no matter what room they are used in. We will also cover what to look for when making home upgrades like painting, flooring, and furnishings.

The chapter will start with my story and then move into five focus sections: Energy Use, Family Room Cleaning Products, Entertainment, Home Improvements, and Furnishings & Home Décor. Each focus area will dive deeper into the impacts and provide ideas to lessen your environmental impact.

MY ONE SHADE GREENER STORY

As I thought about organizing my story for this room, the best approach seemed to be using the category areas of focus in the chapter. Below is a little glimpse into the priorities, updates, and transitions that have occurred over the years. I hope my personal stories help you realize that change doesn't happen overnight. However, consistent changes over longer periods can truly make an impact. You will also see that we made trade-offs like anyone else with our decisions. Sometimes, the choice is the greenest option, and at other times we are a lighter shade of green…or not green at all. We are all a work in progress. I've tried to learn and make decisions that feel right for our family. With that background, here is our evolution.

Energy Use: Nearly ten years ago, we started replacing all the light bulbs in our home as they burned out. We went from incandescent to CFL and are now in the process of switching over to LEDs as the CFLs reach the end of their life. Another change we made about seven years ago was to add a programmable thermostat that helps us regulate temperatures and keep them at reasonable levels in the summer and winter. We are better at not using the air conditioning as much in the summertime than keeping temperatures low in the winter and not using heat.

Cleaning: The cleaning in this chapter focuses on dusting and cleaning floors, so that is where I'll focus this summary. I've always used cloths or recycled t-shirts to dust. However, I haven't yet found an alternative to the dusting spray I grew up with. With window cleaning, I've switched the solution I use and try to use soft cloths instead of paper towels. Over five years ago, we replaced our bag vacuum with a bagless one to reduce waste and recently moved to a bagless automatic vacuum. Our wood and tile floors are mostly just cleaned with a broom and sometimes a bit of vinegar and water.

Entertainment: This area of our home is important to us. We tend to have newer televisions located in almost every room. They were on more than they probably should have been for many years. These days, we try to ensure TVs are turned off in rooms we aren't currently in. On the gaming front, our kids have always been into gaming systems. From connected systems to handhelds and more recently, computer and cloud based. We have had them all. Our children still use the gaming systems, but that is now an element of their homes and apartments and less a part of our current empty-nest environment.

Home Improvements: On the home improvement front, painting has been the most frequent activity we have undertaken over the years. I love painting and find it very relaxing. Our choices include brushes, tape, rollers, and the paint itself. When a project comes up, I've tried to look for paints without volatile organic compounds (VOCs) and have been better at this on some occasions than others. On the disposal front, I'm very good; I know the guidelines and ensure I'm getting rid of the paint properly. We'll discuss how to do this later in the chapter.

Just a few weeks ago, we made a significant home improvement, replacing the 25-year-old windows in the entire house. I expect (and hope) we will see a difference in energy costs as we had a lot of air gaps and leakage with the old windows. Other home improvements over the years have been when the HVAC, water heater, and roofing had reached the end of their life. We researched each of those replacements and tried to find the best solution for both the planet and our pocketbook at the time.

Furniture and Accessories: Unlike entertainment, furniture and accessories are areas where we are under buyers. We wait until we must replace a piece of furniture and have a lot of difficulties deciding to spend money on new vs. used. I enjoy the hunt of finding secondhand furniture and pieces that are unique and fit our style. That is how most items are selected and brought into our home.

I have also been known to do things to "refresh" furniture and prolong its life. One recent example is our master bedroom furniture. We purchased very good quality furniture a few years after we were married and have owned the set for about twenty years. I started to want something new and considered painting the pieces. In the end, I left the wood natural and painted the hardware (from light to dark). This solution provided a much lighter impact both on the planet and our pocketbook.

UP NEXT IN MY HOME: Some additional rooms need a fresh coat of paint, and some furniture needs replacing whether I want to do it or not. So, we'll be tackling those soon.

Writing this chapter has also inspired me to find a new dusting spray and possibly try to add some plants around the house. Hopefully, I can keep them alive! This is a real concern based on the current status of a couple of flower pots by the front door.

ENERGY USE

In this focus area, we will concentrate on general tips and techniques that can make small and large impacts on your overall energy use across all rooms in your home. We will look at opportunities to lessen your environmental impact and, ideally, save you some money.

The US Department of Energy estimates that the typical household can save 25% on utility bills by implementing energy efficiency measures (*Is Energy Efficiency Cost-Effective?* | *EnergySage*, n.d.). If your monthly energy bills are $200, you could save almost $700 annually. This would go a long way to providing funds for slightly more expensive eco-friendly cleaning products, food, or personal care items you will discover throughout this book.

HOME ENERGY AUDIT

A great first step in reducing your energy use and associated costs would be to consider a home energy audit. These assessments can be done on your own, by an independent company, or by your local energy company, which sometimes has low-cost options. The assessment will determine how much energy your home uses and where it is most inefficient. This knowledge can help you prioritize changes to be made to increase the efficiency of your home.

OPTIMIZING YOUR HEATING AND COOLING

When it comes to the overall heating and cooling of your home, there are several techniques that can save both energy and money. Below are just a few:

Programmable Thermostat: Installing a programmable thermostat ensures you optimize the temperature at different times of the day. For example, if you leave for work during the day, you can allow the house to get warmer in the summer and cooler in the winter while you aren't there. Then, the thermostat can get the house back to the temperature you want by the time you arrive home. You can also adjust for when you are sleeping or away on vacation. Studies have shown that each degree of change in thermostat settings equals 1% of energy use up or down (*How Much Can You Save By Adjusting Your Thermostat | Direct Energy Blog*, n.d.).

Smart Home Systems: These systems enable you to turn lights on and off and open and close window shades. All this can be done remotely if you leave the house and forget to turn off lights or keep the drapes closed in winter to keep the warmth in.

Service and Maintenance: Replacing your HVAC air filters regularly and doing routine maintenance keeps your system working at its best. The filters are sometimes hard to remember to replace. I've started putting a calendar note to change the filters at the recommended 3-month mark.

Windows and Doors: Old windows can account for 25-30% of a home's heat loss. Spending a weekend sealing off cracks in doors and windows with caulk and weather stripping could make a significant difference. When the time is right, you could also consider replacing old windows.

Window Treatments: When looking for blinds, cellular or honeycomb are more insulating than traditional slat configurations, and fabrics are better than metal or plastic. In addition to the blinds, buying thick curtains provides additional insulation. The key is to open the blinds when you want the sun's warmth and close them when it's dark or to keep the heat out.

Ceiling Fans: Ceiling fans are a great way to save on your HVAC. In the summer, run them counterclockwise to pull the hot air up; in the winter, run them clockwise to push the warm air down into the room. When looking for fans, look for the Energy Star label.

Insulation: Another weekend project to consider is adding insulation to the attic floor and basement ceiling. The recommendation for insulation thickness in an attic is 10-14 inches. However, this varies depending on where you live. Check your local energy company for recommendations in your area.

Programs and Rebates: Your local gas and electric companies likely have programs and suggestions for ways you can reduce your energy use and, as a result, your bills. Many have rebate programs for purchasing energy-efficient appliances, windows, and more. They may also have discounts on home audits and programmable thermostats. Before making energy efficiency purchases, check the websites to see if there are programs you can take advantage of. During the last check of my energy company website, I even found that they have an app I can use to track our energy use—I had no idea!

LIGHTING

On average, most homes use about 10% of their electricity on lighting. Below are three lighting tips that can make a positive impact on both the planet and your pocketbook.

Use Natural Light – The best way to save energy is by not turning the lights on in the first place. Open the shades in rooms during daylight hours to avoid turning the lights on.

Turn Lights Off – While this one seems obvious, forgetting is easy. There are two options: Practice turning the lights off until it becomes a habit or leverage technology like motion sensors and timers to turn the lights off on your behalf.

Replace Light Bulbs – Replacing the bulbs isn't something you should run out and do today. However, as lights burn out, having the right bulbs on hand for the replacement will make it more likely that you will start to transition away from what you've always used.

There are four types of bulbs used most often; Incandescent (the primary choice for homes 10-15 years ago), CFL (the squiggly looking ones), halogen (small filament), and LED (looks like incandescent, but is typically not see through). The recommendation is to replace incandescent and CFL bulbs with LED. When recycling halogen, CFL, and LED bulbs, search www.Earth911.org to find a drop-off location.

FAMILY ROOM CLEANING PRODUCTS

Family room cleaning covers the mainstream maintenance of your home, i.e., dusting, furniture, windows, and flooring. The challenge with cleaning products is that the ingredients in many mainstream brands are unhealthy for the people in your home or the planet. In addition, the packaging is often plastic and difficult to recycle. Product ideas in this section will include those with better ingredients, less packaging, and DIY solutions.

DUSTING AND FURNITURE POLISH

You have the dusting cloths and the furniture polish when dusting your home.

For cloths, microfiber naturally attracts dust and can be reused. A few brands to consider for general cleaning include Mr. Siga (www.mrsiga.com), Clean Green Gloves (www.amazon.com), and HDX Multi-Purpose (www.homedepot.com). For electronics, some brands to put on the list are MagicFiber (www.magicfiber.com), HTTX (www.amazon.com), Progo Ultra (www.amazon.com), and Amazon Basics Microfiber.

Light Green: If the cloths aren't enough on their own, below are some polishes and cleaners to consider. These have better ingredients but are still contained in more traditional packaging.

- **ECOS Furniture Polish + Cleaner – Orange** – This brand uses plant-based ingredients, including olive oil, to treat your wood. The product is listed as climate positive. www.ecos.com
- **Cleaning Studio Wood + Stone Natural Cleaner** – This is a multi-purpose cleaner that can be used to dust your wood furniture. www.walmart.com

DIY Green: The most straightforward dusting spray is created by mixing a few drops of lemon oil with ½ cup of warm water in a spray bottle. Shake to mix, spray onto a soft cloth and wipe. Then, wipe the surface with a dry, soft cloth.

WINDOWS

Like dusting, microfiber cloths are also recommended for cleaning windows. Two brands to consider are e-Cloth (www.us.e-cloth.com) and The Rag Company (www.theragcompany.com). For the window cleaners, some alternatives to consider are provided below:

Light Green: These options have better ingredients and traditional plastic packaging.

- **AspenClean Natural Glass Cleaner** – This all-natural cleaner is packaged in 100% recycled bottles. They also have microfiber cloths to go with their cleaners. www.aspenclean.com
- **Aunt Fannie's Glass and Window Vinegar Cleaner** – Non-toxic with a hint of lavender smell. www.auntfannies.com

Dark Green: These options have better ingredients and better packaging solutions.

- **TrulyFree Glass Cleaner** – This is a plant-based product. You purchase a spray bottle with the first purchase and then get refillable pouches to eliminate the plastic bottle waste. www.trulyfreehome.com

DIY Green: A simple window cleaner can be made at home using one part vinegar to four parts of water in a spray bottle. Just spray on and then wipe with microfiber towels.

HARDWOOD AND TILE FLOORS

As you look at the floor cleaner alternatives, ensure you read the details on how they are used. Some require a mop and bucket to clean, and others need you to "rinse" the floor after washing. Make sure the solution you choose fits your needs and lifestyle.

Light Green: These have better ingredients and plastic packaging.

- **Sensitive Home Wood Cleaner** – This cleaner has several certifications for healthy ingredients. www.sensitivehome.com
- **Aunt Fannies** – This mop and bucket solution is good on many floor surfaces and comes in a concentrate. www.auntfannies.com

Dark Green: These options have better ingredients and packaging.

- **Cleaning Studio Wood + Stone Natural Cleaner** – The same cleaner that was mentioned earlier for your furniture is also great for your floors. www.walmart.com
- **AspenClean Floor Cleaner** – This cleaner can be used on any flooring material. There is a spray bottle, and a concentrate is available for refills. www.aspenclean.com

DIY Green: Below are three DIY recipes based on floor type:

- **Wood**: Add ½ cup of white vinegar to a gallon of water. Mop the floor with this mixture and then use a clean, dry mop or cloth to wipe damp areas. Add a few drops of lemon or orange essential oil for a scented clean.

- **Tile**: Mix 2 cups warm water, ½ cup white vinegar, ¼ cup rubbing alcohol, a squirt of dish soap, and a few drops of lemon juice. Spray onto the floor and wipe with a mop.
- **Vinyl and Linoleum**: Mix 1 cup of vinegar and a few drops of baby oil in 1 gallon of warm water in a small bucket and mop.

VACUUM CLEANERS

For any home with carpeting, a vacuum cleaner is essential. There are many considerations in finding the right vacuum for your home—corded vs. cordless, bags vs. bagless, human-powered vs. machine powered. Technology is also changing frequently. At the time of publication, some of the more popular brands to consider that had a lighter environmental footprint included Miele, Shark, and iRobot.

CARPET CLEANERS AND STAIN REMOVERS

At some point, the inevitable will happen, and a stain ends up on the carpet. Many of the traditional cleaners on the market contain harsh chemicals. Below are a few alternatives to consider:

Light Green: These options have better ingredients and traditional plastic packaging.

- **Fit Organic Laundry & Carpet Stain Remover** – USDA Certified Organic. www.fitorganic.com
- **Grove Co. Carpet & Upholstery Stain Remover** – Certified B Corp. All natural. www.grove.co
- **Biokleen Bac-Out Stain + Odor Remover** – This stain remover has a blend of live enzyme cultures and is focused on tough stains and odors. www.biokleenhome.com

- **Only Natural Pet Stain & Odor Remover** – Designed with enzymes and organic cleaning agents to remove stains and odors from pet accidents, blood, and more. www.onlynaturalpet.com

DIY Green: Mix vinegar and water in a spray bottle for carpet stains. Spray on the stain and let it sit for several minutes. Clean with a brush or sponge using warm, soapy water. If your stain is extra troublesome, try mixing ¼ cup each of salt, borax, and vinegar. Rub the paste in and leave for a few hours. Then vacuum away.

ENTERTAINMENT

Entertaining in the family room covers televisions and gaming systems. While these devices might also be in other rooms of your home, this focus area will cover the details for any room where televisions and gaming systems reside.

When considering the Impact of these devices, the important elements include equipment choice, energy use throughout the product's life, and disposal. We will cover all three in this focus area. In addition, at the end of this section, we'll touch on some things to consider about streaming services and how they impact both your energy use and carbon footprint.

REPLACING OR PURCHASING EQUIPMENT

When replacing televisions and gaming systems, there are two considerations before shopping:

- Do I need this **now**? Could it wait a year?
- Do I need to purchase **new**? You may find that sometimes you want (or need) the latest model, but other times or purposes could go with used or refurbished.

After deciding the time is right to purchase and if used or refurbished is right for you, the next step is to select the product itself. Below are considerations for televisions and gaming systems:

Televisions: The two primary considerations for televisions are size and resolution. The smaller, lower-resolution televisions require less energy to use and are lighter on the environment. Plasma screen TVs are the least energy efficient, LCDs fall in the middle, and LED/OLED tend to be the most efficient.

Consider your space and the use of each television. For each purchase, lean on the smallest size and lowest resolution acceptable for that room.

Since television technology changes at a fast pace, doing research at the time of purchase is best. You can go to www.energystar.gov to look at the rating for the television you're considering. At the time of publication, brands I wasn't familiar with, like Sansui and Furrion, were topping the eco-friendly TV list.

Gaming Systems: Similar to televisions, gaming technology is moving rapidly, and I recommend looking online before purchasing. At the time of publication, the Nintendo Switch and Wii were lighter on the environment than the Xbox and Sony systems. They also had lower costs to purchase and operate over a lifetime.

The benefit of all modern gaming systems is that they have moved to downloadable games instead of buying game cartridges and disks. This saves a tremendous number of resources by eliminating the production, distribution, and disposal of the disks/cartridges and their associated packaging.

For those who prefer computer gaming, you can refer to thoughts and ideas from the office chapter about purchasing computer equipment.

USING AND CHARGING

Once you've selected entertainment devices that fit your home, use and charging habits become important. In addition to tips for televisions and gaming systems, we'll address batteries here, as they are important for TV remotes and gaming controllers.

Televisions: Sources online vary on how much energy a TV consumes in a year, depending on the television you buy, the energy costs in your area, and the device usage patterns in your home. Estimates range from $5/year to upwards of $50. No matter the actual cost, there are a few tips that can keep the impact on the planet and your pocketbook down:

- **Turn Off:** When you leave a room, turn the television off. Unless, of course, you will be right back, or others are watching!
- **No Standby**: TVs are left on standby for many hours a day in many homes. Instead of letting standby kick in, turn off the TV when not in use.
- **Extension Cords**: This might not work for everyone, but you can use a multi-plug extension cord to switch all the connected devices off when not in use.

Game Systems: Game systems should follow the best practices of televisions for turning off and not leveraging standby mentioned above. In addition, if you are going to watch Netflix or other streaming services, switch over to your television. Running streaming through your gaming system uses more energy than watching on your TV.

Batteries: Each year, Americans purchase and dispose of billions of batteries, contributing to 180,000 tons of hazardous waste (McFarland, 2022). When batteries are sent to the landfill, they are often crushed and release toxic chemicals like mercury, cobalt, and lead into our soil and drinking water. Below are three things you can consider to make your impact in this area lighter:

- **Use Rechargeable**: Rechargeable batteries cost a bit more initially and add a step to the process by needing the time to charge them. If you can plan for the time to recharge and you use a fair number of batteries, this could be the right choice for you. From a cost standpoint, it takes about two years to break even on the cost.
- **Consider Solar**: Solar chargers could be a good fit if you use rechargeable batteries. The advantage is that you can easily charge batteries even if you aren't at home, like hiking, camping, or at a kid's sporting event. There are solar chargers for both batteries (like AAA & AA) and products (like cell phones).
- **Dispose of Properly**: Most important in this category is to dispose of batteries properly. Many municipalities don't take batteries in weekly recycling. Instead, you need to store them until there is a hazardous waste day in your community or check www.Earth911.org to find a location near you for drop off.

Electronic Free-Night – To save energy and do something different, you could plan one night a week to be electronic free. Play board games together, sit outside enjoying a sunset and conversation, read a physical book, or have dinner on the patio with friends. There are many options, and this once-a-week activity away from the screens could end up being one of your favorites!

DISPOSING OF OLD EQUIPMENT

Electronic disposal is covered in detail in the office chapter. Here, I will provide a few tips to get you started. If you are always purchasing the newest technology in televisions or gaming systems, you could create a plan to sell your equipment when you upgrade. Likely, this would help you offset the cost of the new product.

If you aren't selling, the next best option is to give the items to family and friends or donate to a group that will get good use out of them in the coming years. The last resort would be to recycle. With all electronic recycling, there are two options; wait for a hazardous waste day in your community or search to find a local drop-off location at www.Earth911.org.

IMPACT OF STREAMING SERVICES

Streaming will also be discussed in more detail in the office chapter. The headline is that videos of any kind (streaming movies or a Zoom call) are more carbon-intensive than lighter content like text and photos. That said, there is some debate if this is worse for the environment than alternatives like going to the movie theater. I'm not going to weigh in on which is better, but rather make you more aware of your choices. So here are two options to keep in mind:

- **Listen Instead**: As you have streaming services on, consider if you are watching. Sometimes, we have TV shows on for "noise" in the background while doing other things. If this is the case, you could consider music (or a non-video show) as an alternative.
- **Smaller Screens**: If you are the only one watching the streaming show or movie, do you need to watch it on the largest screen in the house? Maybe a laptop, tablet, or phone would work just as well. These smaller screens can significantly reduce the environmental impact.

HOME IMPROVEMENTS

According to the State of Home Spending report, home improvement spending in 2020 averaged $8,305 per household (*State of Home Spending 2020: Year of the Home*, 2020). Home improvements can be a great way to freshen up our spaces. They can also make your home healthier for your family and have less environmental impact. This focus area will include considerations for painting, flooring, and remodeling.

PAINTING

Painting is a frequent and easy way to update a room. In fact, according to Fast Company, more than 750 million gallons of paint are purchased each year in the United States. In 2020, 34% of US households took on a home painting project (Segran, 2022).

The impact of paint on people and products comes from the paint itself and how we dispose of what is unused, including how we clean our brushes. Below are tips to keep in mind for your next painting project.

What to Purchase

Let's start with the paint itself. There are three things to look for in selecting a paint:

1. **Water-Based**: Selecting water-based is better for both people and the planet.
2. **VOC-Free or Zero-VOC**: VOC stands for volatile organic compounds, which are emitted into the air and can cause health problems. Avoiding them in your paints is recommended.
3. **Greenguard Certification**: This verifies a product has been tested for chemicals and VOC emissions. Greenguard Gold Certification is even better.

Many of the popular paint brands now carry water-based zero-VOC paints. These brands include Benjamin Moore Eco Spec, Sherwin Williams Harmony, and Behr Premium Plus. Some other lesser-known brands to consider include ECOS (www.ecospaint.net), Yolo Colorhouse (multiple stores like Home Depot), and AFM Safecoat (www.afmsafecoat.com). If you need stain, Earth Safe Finishes (www.earthsafefinishes.com) out of South Carolina has no-VOC stains, varnishes, and sealants.

Another company, UpPaint, is recycling the roughly 10% of paint purchased yearly that goes to waste. They collect, process, and resell the paint in limited colors. You can learn more at www.uppaint.com.

How to Clean Up

Cleaning up after painting can be more challenging than finding eco-friendly paint. While water-based paint can be cleaned off brushes and containers with water, you shouldn't wash them in the sink and send paint down the drain into the water system.

Instead, put water into a bucket or container and wash the paint off there. After you are finished, you can either allow the water to evaporate and place the residue in a baggie to take to the hazardous waste drop-off or pour the water through a coffee filter to separate the sediment from the water. Then, dispose of the filter and sediment in a baggie to take to the hazardous waste drop-off.

You can use white vinegar if water isn't getting the brushes clean. Just heat a jar of vinegar and let brushes soak for 30-60 minutes until they come clean.

Painting Tip – If your painting project lasts more than one day or painting session, you don't need to wash your brushes. Wrap them in plastic wrap or aluminum foil, and they will be ready for your next session. If it will be more than a day before you return to the project, place the brushes in the freezer. You'll just need to remember to get them out to thaw about ½ hour before you are ready to paint!

How to Dispose

If you use water-based or latex paint, cans can be thrown away in your regular garbage with the lid off. However, you can't throw away cans with liquid paint still in them. If there is too much to dry up just by leaving the can open to the air, you can solidify paint by adding kitty litter, newspaper strips, or sawdust.

For oil-based paints, you need to plan to take them to a Hazardous Waste event in your community or look up a drop-off location on www.Earth911.org.

FLOORING

When the time comes to replace flooring, the most popular options are carpet, hardwood, tile, and vinyl. Of all these types, vinyl is the first to take off your consideration list as it is made of PVC and is not recyclable or compostable. For the other flooring options, you want to avoid VOCs and formaldehyde emitted from many carpets and the stains and finishes used on wood floorings.

Several alternatives have a lower impact on the health of the planet and the people in your home. Below are options to consider:

Cork: Cork is becoming a more popular flooring option. Because the cork comes from the tree's bark and grows back within a few years, the material is considered very sustainable. In addition, some cork floors are produced using recycled wine bottle corks. Unlike other solid floor options, cork has some "give" that makes it comfortable to walk on and provides a layer of insulation. When looking for a cork floor, also be sure to consider the adhesive to install, and the sealant used to protect.

Bamboo: Bamboo comes up in many home products as an eco-friendly alternative because of the bamboo tree's fast growth and replenishment rate. The flooring has different grains, textures, and colors and can be refinished just like a traditional hardwood floor.

Linoleum: This flooring product used to be very popular but fell slightly out of style. While often grouped in a category with vinyl or laminate, linoleum is produced with entirely biodegradable materials like linseed oil, tree resin, limestone, and cork dust. The material is durable, and the options are becoming broader with more colors and designs available. A recent version of linoleum is called Marmoleum and can be an option to consider.

Tile: Tile is a good alternative when considering eco-friendly flooring. When selecting the tile, there are a lot of very interesting, recycled material choices on the market today, including recycled glass. Stone tiles are a natural material with many colors and textures available. When purchasing stone tile, consider the process of extracting the material and the weight, which will impact shipping.

Wood: When looking for a wood floor, choose wood that has the FSC (Forest Stewardship Council) label. This wood will be guaranteed to be cut from a sustainably managed forest. Two additional wood options are reclaimed and engineered hardwood. Reclaimed hardwood has been removed from other buildings during renovation or demolition. If shopping reclaimed, ensure the floors aren't painted with lead paint. Engineered hardwood has a solid veneer and a core of plywood or recycled materials. This looks like hardwood but doesn't use as much material from naturally sourced trees.

Carpet: If you decide to go with carpet, wool is a good choice as it is a natural, renewable resource and doesn't emit VOCs like synthetic carpets. If you look at synthetic carpets, a more environmentally friendly option is PET carpet, made from recycled plastic. The percentage of recycled content can vary, so look for those with a high percentage. Another consideration for carpeting is disposal. Today, billions of pounds of carpet end up in landfills each year. Look to donate your old carpet to a recycling center by searching www.carpetrecovery.com.

Rugs – Rugs can be a great addition around the house for many reasons. They can prolong the life of current flooring by covering up a flaw (carpet stain, crack in the tile, etc.). Rugs can also provide a layer of insulation to regulate heating and cooling better. In addition, they can add a colorful and unique personality to the room! Remember when shopping for rugs to look for sustainable materials.

REMODELING

There are many considerations for remodeling, depending on the project you are taking on. Because we won't be able to cover all rooms and options here, below are some tips to keep in mind as you make each decision in the overall project:

- **Question Replacement**: Before removing something, take some time to consider if there is a way to reuse and refresh what you already have. For example, can cabinets in a kitchen or bathroom be painted and knobs changed out to get a fresh look without the impact to planet and pocketbook that removing and replacing the cabinets would incur.

- **Know What You are Buying**: No matter what you look to purchase for your remodel, take the time to understand the materials used and the manufacturing process of the products you buy.

- **Look for Recycled**: When considering flooring, countertops, and tile, look for products with recycled materials.

- **Consider Upcycling**: Can you turn something that was once one thing into something else that would be interesting for your remodel? For example, a unique antique dresser could become a new vanity, or exterior home pillars could be cut down and become legs for a new kitchen island.

- **Dispose of Responsibly**: As you remove products and materials from your home, look to sell or properly recycle them vs. sending them to a landfill.

FURNISHINGS AND HOME DECOR

Furnishings and home décor are the final touches to provide personality to a room and make it feel like home. Like all other areas, there are ways to lessen your environmental impact. We will cover furniture, accessories, and plants in this focus area. For furniture and accessories, many brands are included to ensure you find some options that fit your personality and pocketbook.

FURNITURE

When shopping for furniture, a consideration, as with other home products, can be questioning the need to purchase new. Depending on the piece you are looking for, you might find a unique and perfect option in an online marketplace, at a resale shop, or even at a flea market. The thrill of the hunt can be enjoyable when you aren't on a tight timeline to make a purchase.

When buying new furniture, consider the use and look for pieces that will last over time. For wood pieces, check for the FSC Certified label. In all cases, consider the source of the materials and the manufacturing process. Below are some brands to consider as you start your search:

- **Vivaterra**: This brand has furniture and home products indoors and out. The name means "living earth" and highlights their purpose to operate in harmony with nature. www.vivaterra.com
- **Crate & Barrel**: This popular brand has focused on wood products certified by the Forest Stewardship Council (FSC). www.crateandbarrel.com
- **Joybird**: This brand has become more popular in recent years. They prioritize planting more trees than the wood they use to create their furniture. www.joybird.com
- **West Elm**: The brand known for modern design has been on Barron's 100 Most Sustainable US Companies list for the last five years. They also offer locally made products. www.westelm.com
- **Pottery Barn**: The brand has a Sustainability Sourced category that offers over 250 pieces of furniture in a wide range of styles. www.potterybarn.com
- **Etsy**: While not normally mentioned for furniture pieces, Etsy has a Reclaimed Furniture section with options for nearly every room in your home. www.etsy.com
- **The Joinery**: With Portland headquarters, this company focuses on sustainability and handcrafted hardwood furniture. www.thejoinery.com

- **Sabai**: If you aren't in a hurry for pieces, Sabai could be a good brand to consider. They create made-to-order pieces in the US. www.sabai.design

ACCESSORIES AND DECOR

When it comes to accessories and décor, there are hundreds of options out there to fit every style imaginable. As you look for accessories, consider the materials used and the production process—both carbon impacts and fair trade. Looking for local artists, shopping at art fairs, and on Etsy are great ways to find pieces that are lighter on the environment and fit your style and budget.

Below are brands that have products for many rooms in your home:

- **Shades of Green**: This brand has a variety of vases, candles, pillows, and baskets. All products are environmentally friendly and sustainably made. www.shadesofgreen.com
- **Citizenry**: The brand curates handcrafted items from across the world. Products are made with recycled, natural, or organic materials. www.the-citizenry.com
- **Made Trade**: This company is Carbon Neutral certified, which means that the carbon used to manufacture and deliver the products is completely offset. Products include wall décor, rugs, curtains, and more. www.madetrade.com
- **Ten Thousand Villages**: This site focuses on global artisans and has curated a large offering of products from personal accessories to home décor and more. www.tenthousandvillages.com
- **The Little Market**: This company supports artisan groups committed to sustainability. There are many white and neutral color options if that fits your style. www.thelittlemarket.com

- **Minna**: This brand partners with sustainable manufacturers and only uses natural dyes. The products include artwork, table décor, and even fabric by the yard. www.minna-goods.com
- **Obakki**: Obakki partners with artisans worldwide to offer sustainable and eco-friendly products. Accessories sold include candles, wall hangings, textiles, and more. www.obakki.com
- **Uncommon Goods**: This company offers unique curated items for your home. They are a Certified B Corp and offer home décor and gift-giving options. www.uncommongoods.com
- **Etsy**: I would be remiss not to add Etsy to the list. You can search for almost any home accessory and find many independent makers across the globe. www.etsy.com

PLANTS

Plants can be a great addition to all the rooms in your home. They not only provide great décor but can be very effective at improving air quality. They remove carbon dioxide and absorb toxins like benzene and formaldehyde. Plants are especially helpful if you remodel, paint, or install new flooring. To increase the toxin removal of your plants, you can remove lower leaves and expose more soil.

When adding plants to your home, you need roughly one plant every 10 square yards to clean the air. You could start with one room to see how it goes and then add plants to other rooms. In addition, if you have pets and small children, ensure the plants are safe for both in case they get into them. Below are ten plants to consider as you start the process of literally greening your home:

- **Spider Plant**: These plants are easy to care for and have great personalities. They love bright, indirect light and remove benzene and formaldehyde.

- **Snake Plant**: Very easy to grow. You can water heavily, and it survives in any location.
- **Aloe Vera**: Aloe is a succulent that is easy to grow and has the added benefit of being able to use it to treat minor cuts and burns. They also clean the air of benzene and formaldehyde.
- **Bamboo Palm**: A great houseplant that prefers part sun or shade. This plant removes benzene and formaldehyde.
- **Philodendron**: These plants are among the most popular houseplants and come in various sizes and colors. The best air cleaners are the heart leaf and elephant ear.
- **Gerbera Daisy**: This popular plant removes benzene from the air to add some color and personality to your home. Keep in mind they do best in temperatures above 75 degrees Fahrenheit.
- **Lily**: The lily comes in many varieties and are easy to care for. In particular, the Peace Lily and Flamingo Lily clear the air of formaldehyde, carbon monoxide, and ammonia.
- **Parlor Palm**: These are taller floor plants that are popular for their ability to adapt to low light. They are also good at removing benzene and trichloroethylene from the air.
- **Bromeliads**: These plants have bright flowers and clean up most pollutants from the air. They also have the benefit of working at night while you sleep. Indirect sunlight and low maintenance.
- **White Dendrobium Orchids**: This is the best orchid for cleaning the air of formaldehyde, chloroform, and acetone. Like the bromeliads, this plant does its magic at night. They are easy to care for by placing in strong light and watering by putting an ice cube in it once a week.

FAST FIVE IN THE FAMILY ROOM

Five steps you can take quickly to make an impact and celebrate some wins!

1. **Replace Light Bulbs** – Shifting from traditional to energy-efficient light bulbs is a small change that can make a big difference. As light bulbs burn out in your home, start to replace them one by one with CFL or LED lighting.

2. **Add Some Plants** – Plants not only add personality to a room but can also make the air inside a home better for the people who live there by removing toxins from the air we breathe. Find a few plants that seem interesting to you and give plant growing a try.

3. **Save Energy** – Become more conscious of your everyday energy use and take small steps to become more efficient. Turn off lights, televisions, and gaming systems when not in use. Make your HVAC more efficient by sealing windows and doors, leveraging window treatments to keep rooms warm/cool, and possibly even investing in a programmable thermostat.

4. **Shift Cleaning Products** – The mainstream brand cleaning products we use throughout our home often contain toxins that aren't healthy for the planet or the people in our homes. Start purchasing eco-friendly products by updating the brands you use for dusting, floors, and windows.

5. **Decorate Sustainably** – Thinking differently about the décor you bring into your home can have a positive impact. Look for sustainable materials and local artists. You can even consider bringing a little seasonal nature in to decorate—from pinecones to flowers, branches, and more—there is a lot of potential in decorating all natural.

THE KITCHEN

The kitchen is a complex room full of opportunities on your one shade greener journey. There are many things to consider, including energy use and what food to purchase. In addition, there are high levels of waste. That doesn't even consider the decisions to be made when you are not cooking and eating at home. Dining out and carry-out will be covered in the next chapter, the Dining Room.

The chapter will start with my story and then move into seven focus sections: Energy and Appliances, Kitchen Cleaning Products, Kitchen Waste, Dishes and Cookware, Disposable Kitchen Supplies, Planning and Grocery Shopping, and Food. Each focus area will dive deeper into the impacts and provide ideas to lessen your environmental impact.

MY ONE SHADE GREENER STORY

The kitchen is a room that I feel I never stop on my personal journey. When I began greening my home, I didn't cook much, as my husband did the bulk of the meal prep. We were both working outside the home, and the kids had school, sports, and other activities. We were busy, had meals on the go, and ordered carry-out 2-3 nights a week.

I made early changes, like switching to reusable grocery shopping bags, and after nearly fifteen years, I'm still using the same set of bags! I also started to be more aware of buying local and began a habit in the summer months of visiting the farmer's market for fruits and vegetables. The cleaning products I used in the kitchen also started to shift as I continued to make changes in cleaning products throughout all rooms in my home.

Fast forward to 2015ish, I started to learn more about cooking and took over this responsibility from my husband. He was now working different hours and not getting home until 7 or 8 pm (which was way past when myself and the kids wanted to eat). This change was the catalyst for many other shifts in the kitchen. I started weekly meal planning to ensure I only purchased what we needed and reduced food waste. I joined an online recipe service called Cook Smarts (www.cooksmarts.com) that provides four dinner recipes per week. Using this service helped teach me new cooking techniques and try foods our family hadn't had before. The recipes on the website can be automatically adjusted for the number of people, as well as options like paleo, gluten-free, and vegetarian.

Seven years in, I'm still subscribing to Cook Smarts each year. An additional benefit of this service has been advancing my journey toward healthier, non-processed foods. Now, I even make many of my salad dressings and sauces by hand instead of purchasing pre-made ones. I pay much more attention to the ingredients in what I buy and have gained an understanding of how companies are using terms like organic, farm-raised, and all-natural so that I can be smarter about food purchases.

Fast forward to today, and I'm still growing and making changes in the kitchen. Over the last year, I started to implement Meatless Mondays. Having some great recipes without meat has introduced me to a whole new world of meal alternatives. I no longer think that meat - beef, pork, chicken, seafood – is a "must" ingredient for dinner. So, one day a week is starting to merge into two days and sometimes more.

Finally, I've also realized the importance of organization and the tools I need in the kitchen. I continue to clear out equipment, dishes, and other items we don't use. Having a few things I often use right at my fingertips makes being in the kitchen more enjoyable.

UP NEXT IN MY HOME: Writing this chapter got me to dive deeper into composting, and I realized that options exist today that weren't there back in 2010. This is an area I want to try next. With a bit of research, I discovered that our municipality now has a weekly compost service, and I've signed up. I now have a 5-gallon bucket I fill and then leave on my front porch for pickup once a week. If our compost starts to outpace that size, I can just request another bucket. We'll see how the process goes.

ENERGY AND APPLIANCES

According to Consumers Energy, the kitchen is estimated to use approximately 15% of household energy in the United States (*Energy Efficient Cooking for The Holidays and Beyond | Consumers Energy*, n.d.). Most of the energy consumption comes from the refrigerator, with the dishwasher and cooktop/oven a distant second and third. This focus area looks at considerations when replacing appliances and how to make the appliances you own as energy efficient as possible.

REPLACING APPLIANCES

Depending on the age of your appliances, buying new may significantly improve efficiency. There are different considerations for each kitchen appliance. The sections below note areas to keep in mind.

Refrigerator: Look for the Energy Star shield. These products exceed energy efficiency criteria set by the US Environmental Protection Agency (EPA). You can visit www.energystar.gov to search for the make and model you are considering and see the rating.

In addition to the Energy Star rating, look for a large enough refrigerator for your needs, but not larger than necessary; the larger the refrigerator, the more energy it consumes. Top freezers consume less energy than bottom freezers or side-by-sides.

Dishwasher: Dishwashers are Energy Star rated, so you can check out the website for the brands you are considering. To achieve a base Energy Star rating, they must use less than 270 kWh/year and less than 3.5 gallons of water per cycle. The dishwashers rated as Energy Star Most Efficient use less than 240 kWh/year and less than 3.2 gallons of water per cycle.

Stovetop: The first decision with the stovetop is the type – gas, electric, or induction. The most energy efficient is induction. However, this is also the most expensive and can cost up to four times as much as a gas or electric unit. When narrowing down between gas and electric, there is a debate. For those on the side of gas, the energy cost of use will be less. For those on the side of the electric, the rationale is emissions and health. The gas stove emits carbon monoxide, nitrogen dioxide, and formaldehyde into the air you are breathing in your home. Stovetops do not have Energy Star ratings available.

Oven: Choices for ovens are gas, electric, and convection. The convection oven is the most efficient, using about 20% less energy because the food cooks quicker and at lower temperatures. However, like the induction stovetop, this alternative will be more expensive. When it comes to gas vs. electric, there was less of an environmental difference than we saw in the stovetop and more of a cooking preference; gas cooks food to be moister, and electric makes foods a bit crispier.

Microwave: This is another appliance that Energy Star doesn't rate. You can use www.ethicalconsumer.com to find options and ratings. However, this website is in the UK, and they have several different brands that we don't have available in the US.

Grill: While not technically inside the kitchen, I've included the grill here as an alternative cooking source – especially in warm weather. When considering a gas or charcoal grill, the gas grill is the most environmentally friendly for both energy efficiency and producing far fewer pollutants.

ENERGY USE

Even when you have purchased energy-efficient products, the way you use and care for them during their life in your home will have an impact on the energy efficiency and life span. Below are some overall cooking tips to save energy and some specific ideas around each appliance:

Overall Cooking: Batching your cooking is a great way to save energy. Cooking two nights of dinner at once can cut your energy use in half. Using the oven once to cook three or four dishes together saves even more. Also, the more meals prepped at once, the less cooking is needed each day.

Another overall tip is that ceramic or glass pans and dishes will hold heat better than metal. This means you can reduce cooking time or cook dishes at lower temperatures.

Refrigerator: Ensuring the settings of your refrigerator are at a proper temperature enables maximum efficiency. The fridge should be kept at 37 degrees Fahrenheit and the freezer at 0 degrees Fahrenheit. In addition, positioning the fridge 3 inches away from the back wall creates better airflow and efficiency.

When it comes to the maintenance of the refrigerator, there are two key areas. First, clean the condenser coils on the back or bottom of the fridge every 6-12 months. The second area is the door gaskets. You want to ensure the best seal possible when the doors are closed.

The final area to save energy is during use. Keeping the fridge organized, so you know right where things are located allows you to keep the doors closed and not let warm air in. Also, deciding what you will get out of the fridge or freezer BEFORE opening the door will prevent you from standing with the door open trying to decide what to eat. Aside from opening the doors, another consideration is to avoid putting hot food in the refrigerator. If you have leftovers, let them cool a bit (don't wait too long) so that the appliance needs to work less to lower the temperature.

Stovetop: The primary tip with the stovetop is to cover your pots and pans while cooking. This prevents the heat and energy from escaping and heats the food more quickly.

Oven: The primary tip for the oven while cooking is not to peek. Each time you open the oven, heat and energy are lost. Another idea for the oven is to consider if you could use an alternative, like the microwave or a toaster oven. The microwave uses 50% less energy and is one of the most energy-efficient cooking methods. The toaster oven has a smaller space to heat up and keep at a temperature.

Here's a fun, personal story: our oven stopped working (for an unknown reason) when our kids were around middle school age. We were busy, so we just bought a toaster oven instead of trying to figure out what was wrong with the main oven. The toaster oven worked great, and in the end, we used that countertop oven for 4-5 years before fixing the main oven!

A final consideration for the oven is cleaning. Two downsides to the self-cleaning feature are the energy used to heat to a high temperature and the smells and toxins released in the process. Consider not using that feature and cleaning by hand.

Dishwasher: When it comes to washing dishes, the dishwasher is more efficient than handwashing, primarily due to water use. To make the process even more efficient, start by not pre-rinsing the dishes. Scrape the food into the compost or trash and then place into the dishwasher. Wait until the dishwasher is full before running a load. Another tip to save energy is to turn off the drying feature. Let the steam from the washing naturally dry the dishes.

Grill: The first recommendation for the grill is to reduce pre-heat times, making sure you don't leave the grill running for too long. Gas grills are usually ready to cook in 5-10 minutes and charcoal in 15-20 minutes. When cooking meat, if you trim the fat before cooking, the meat will be healthier, and you will reduce flame flare-ups.

KITCHEN CLEANING PRODUCTS

Cleaning products in the kitchen are very important. You want to strike the right balance between keeping the surfaces that prepare food and dishes you eat off very clean while not cleaning with ingredients that could be harmful to your health.

When looking at the products in this focus area, I've mentioned ingredients to look out for and provided alternative brands to consider. The light green options have better ingredients but traditional or plastic packaging. The dark green options have addressed both ingredients and packaging. DIY is just that—alternatives you can make with ingredients you might have around your house already.

DISHWASHING DETERGENT

The ingredients to watch out for in dishwashing detergent are phosphates, artificial dyes, and fragrances. There are several different types of detergents – powder, liquid, and tabs. The options provided below have a mix of tablets and powder.

Light Green: These products have better ingredients and traditional plastic packaging.

- **Seventh Generation** – Detergent tablets in a plastic pouch. www.seventhgeneration.com
- **Love Home and Planet** – Detergent tablets. The company also offers a gel alternative, but the ingredients in the gel have more environmental concerns. www.lovehomeandplanet.com

Dark Green: These products have better ingredients and better packaging solutions.

- **Dropps** – Detergent tablets in a cardboard box that can easily be recycled. www.dropps.com
- **Earthley** – Powder detergent in a brown bag pouch. www.earthley.com
- **Blueland** – Detergent tablets. The first order comes with a tin for storage, and subsequent orders are sent in a brown paper pouch. www.blueland.com

DIY Green: The process of making your own dishwasher detergent is very easy, and with the addition of one ingredient, you can choose to make powder or tablets. In a bowl, mix 1 cup Borax, 1 cup washing soda, ¾ cup kosher salt, and four packets of unsweetened lemonade drink mix.

If you want to use powder, just store this mixture in an airtight container and use 1-2 tablespoons per load. This should last for about forty loads.

If you want tablets, add 1 cup of water to the mixture above. It will fizz for a minute or two, and then you put a scoop into ice cube trays. Press the mixture down to make the tablets dense. Then, wait until they dry and pop them out. Voila, you now have dishwasher tablets!

DISH SOAP

When considering dish soap, the alternatives to consider are liquid or bar soaps. The liquids tend to be rated light green, and the bars dark green due to the minimal packaging.

Light Green: These options have better ingredients and traditional plastic packaging.

- **Attitude** – The company has a refillable program where you purchase refill boxes and pour them into the original bottle. They also have special formulas for baby bottles. www.attitudeliving.com
- **AspenClean** – Made with natural ingredients and packaged in a 100% recycled bottle. www.aspenclean.com
- **9 Elements** – Made with natural ingredients and essential oils. www.nine-elements.com
- **Thieves Dish Soap** – Natural, plant-based ingredients free of sulfates. www.youngliving.com

Dark Green: These options have better ingredients and better packaging solutions.

- **Earthley Dish Soap Bar** – Rub a sponge or brush over the bar to suds it up. Little to no packaging. www.earthley.com
- **No Tox Life Dish Washing Block** – Like Earthley, you just rub the brush on the bar to create suds. This company also sells eco-friendly brushes with replacement heads made of bamboo and agave fiber bristles. www.notoxlife.com

DIY Green: Creating your own dish soap can be achieved with just a few simple ingredients. In a squirt bottle, combine ½ cup distilled water with 1T of kosher salt. In a bowl, combine ½ cup Dr. Bronner's Sal Suds with ½ cup white vinegar. Next, add the mixture from the bowl into the squirt bottle and shake. You can use this as is or add twenty drops of essential oils (lemon) for scent. Instead of the essential oil, you could add one tablespoon of a moisturizing oil like coconut or jojoba to be gentler on your hands.

HAND SOAP

When looking for eco-friendly hand soap in the kitchen, the primary consideration for many people is its antibacterial properties. Handling and cleaning up after food, we want to ensure our hands are clean and not spreading germs around the house. The ingredient in most anti-bacterial soaps that you should avoid is triclosan.

Light Green: These options have better ingredients and traditional plastic packaging.

- **Method** – These plant-based products leverage herbal extracts to fend off the smells of onion and garlic on your hands. www.methodhome.com

- **Blueland Foaming Hand Soap** – In the starter kit, you receive one lifetime bottle and three refill tablets. You fill the bottle with water, add the tablet, and in minutes you have soap. For future purchases, you just buy the tablet refills. While the packaging would make this one dark green, they do use sodium laurel sulfate. So, due to the ingredients, this one is categorized as light green. www.blueland.com

Dark Green: These options have better ingredients and better packaging solutions.

- **Bar Soap** – While many would prefer a pump solution in the kitchen, for those comfortable with bar soap, this is the greenest solution without all the packaging. A few brands to consider are:
  - **Pure-N-Simple** Peppermint Tea Tree (anti-bacterial) – www.purensimplesoap.com
  - **Makes 3 Organics** Unscented Super Shea – www.makes3organics.com
  - **Eco Roots** – www.ecoroots.us
- **CleanCult Hand Soap** – Uses a milk carton for refills. They also have laundry and other cleaning products in refillable containers. www.cleancult.com
- **Soapply Hand Soap** – Refillable hand soaps that come in glass bottles – www.soapply.com

DIY Green: The key difference between making your own hand soap and dish soap is shifting from the Sal Suds to Castile Soap. For this soap, find a pump soap dispenser you like and add the following: 1 cup Dr. Bronner's Castile Soap, 1 cup distilled water, and one tablespoon oil (coconut, sweet almond, or jojoba). In addition, you can add 20-25 drops of essential oils of your choice (like lavender) for scent.

For those interested in hand sanitizer for the kitchen, you need just two ingredients, aloe vera gel, and isopropyl (rubbing) alcohol. You create the amount you want by mixing two parts aloe vera and 1 part alcohol; for example, 1 cup aloe vera to ½ cup isopropyl alcohol. Store in an airtight squeeze bottle. In addition, you can add essential oils of your choice.

SWEDISH DISHCLOTHS – Linens are covered in more detail in the bedroom. However, a great mention in the kitchen is the Swedish dishcloth. These cloths are super absorbent and machine washable, so you can use them again and again. Two brands to consider are FEBU and SKOY (found on Amazon).

COUNTERTOP CLEANER

Countertops are likely the most frequently cleaned surface in your home. The material of the countertop may drive the decisions on products to use. If you are up for a DIY solution, I encourage you to explore that route here.

Light Green: These options have better ingredients and traditional plastic packaging.

- **Sensitive Home Marble and Granite Cleaner** – Eco-friendly and designed for marble and granite. www.sensativehome.com
- **Method, Mrs. Meyers, & Seventh Generation** – These mainstream brands are solid alternatives but rated a bit lower than the dark green options for the ingredients. They also offer concentrates. So, if you originally purchase the spray bottle, you can use the concentrate for many refills. www.methodhome.com, www.mrsmeyers.com, and www.seventhgeneration.com

Dark Green: These options have better ingredients and better packaging solutions.

- **AspenClean** – This brand comes in a plastic bottle, but you can purchase a concentrate for the refills that will make thirty-five more bottles. www.aspenclean.com
- **Cleaning Studio Wood + Stone Natural Cleaner** – To reduce the carbon footprint, this ships with 2oz of concentrate. You add water and shake when it arrives. Found at popular retailers.
- **Greenshield Organic (GO) Organic Multi-Surface Cleaner** – Ingredients are USDA-certified organic and non-toxic. The packaging is made from sustainable sugar cane and is 100% recyclable. www.greenshieldorganic.com

DIY Green: The simplest and very effective countertop cleaner is to mix equal parts white vinegar and water in a spray bottle. Just spray on the counters and wash clean.

For some, the only disadvantage is that they dislike the vinegar smell. There are two options to resolve this. Adding some essential oils in your preferred fragrance to the mix is the easiest. The second option is to put your leftover citrus peels with 1 cup of vinegar in a mason jar. At the end of the week, add this infused vinegar to a cup of water in your spray bottle.

STOVE AND OVEN CLEANERS

Stove and oven cleaners are a category where eco-friendly alternatives are hard to find. Popular products in the category are rated a "D" or "F" by the Environmental Working Group. What I found as an alternative are some products categorized as degreasers. Since one of the main challenges with the stovetop is grease, these seemed good to provide here.

Light Green: Cleaning Studio Soft Scrub – Can be used in the kitchen beyond the stove/oven for areas like the sink, pots, and pans. This is a tub of cleaner to be used with a sponge or cloth. The brand can be found at popular retailers.

Dark Green: Truly Free Heavy-Duty Degreaser – This product is packaged in a plastic bottle. However, you get the bottle free in your first order, and then all the refills are in a pouch that you mix with water in the bottle you have on hand. www.trulyfreehome.com

DIY Green: The type of stovetop you have and the issues you face (e.g., grease removal) are both important for finding the right DIY recipe. Most recipes include ingredients like baking soda, salt, vinegar, and lemon. Because the challenges are so unique, I suggest you do a quick online search for your type of cooktop and challenge rather than providing a recommendation here.

STAINLESS STEEL – There were not a lot of eco-friendly options for stainless steel cleaners available as I researched this book. However, the DIY solutions suggested putting either white vinegar or olive oil on a cloth and rubbing it on the surface. This was too simple; I had to try it. The solution works GREAT!

I personally preferred white vinegar because the oil needed more rubbing in. If DIY is not for you, I found two Light Green Solutions: Breathe (www.breathecleaning.com) Stainless Steel Polish and Eco-Me Stainless Steel Polish (www.eco-me.com).

KITCHEN WASTE

When it comes to waste at home, the waste generated in the kitchen is the primary challenge. There is obviously the waste of food scraps or food that expires before eating. However, there is also the challenge of food packaging – cardboard boxes, plastic containers, glass jars, and bottles.

With all of these, the strategies are similar: Bring less into your home, reuse, recycle, and compost. We'll cover food, organic scraps, and packaging materials in this focus area, providing ideas and inspiration to lighten your impact. First, let's talk about two terms you will likely hear when it comes to waste, compostable and biodegradable.

COMPOSTABLE AND BIODEGRADABLE

I have been confused by the use of these two terms. I'll try to summarize what I've learned. Something is biodegradable if it can break down into smaller parts. This may take a long time, but the product will break down. According to "Measuring Biodegradability" from the Science Learning Hub, biodegradation can take anywhere from a few days (vegetable scraps) to 500 or more years (plastic bag) (*Measuring Biodegradability — Science Learning Hub*, n.d.).

Compostable means that materials will biodegrade under human conditions, like a compost pile in your backyard or community composting facilities. Composting causes biodegradation to occur faster because humans optimize conditions like air and moisture.

Much of the confusion and challenge comes in when these terms are used for plastics, often called bioplastics. Biodegradable plastics are plant-based, but they are still plastics. They can be composted, but only at an industrial facility, not in your backyard compost. In general, staying away from plastics, including biodegradable ones, is the greener choice.

FOOD SCRAPS

According to the EPA (Environmental Protection Agency), every American throws away 1.3 pounds of food scraps every day! (*Preventing*

Wasted Food At Home | US EPA, 2013). This results in 108 billion pounds of waste every year (*Food Waste in America | Feeding America*, n.d.).

When it comes to food scraps at home, the ideal solution is to produce less waste. In a 2018 EPA study, food waste accounted for 24% of the total Municipal Solid Waste (*Food Waste and Its Links to Greenhouse Gases and Climate Change | USDA*, n.d.). Fresh food is the main challenge here as it will go bad quickly. A few strategies to combat this include:

- **Shop Twice** – Pick up fresh foods (fruit, vegetables, meat) twice a week instead of once.
- **Plan** – Intentionally determine what fresh foods will be eaten daily and only purchase what you need.
- **Individual vs. Packaged**: Look for the right amount of fresh food, so you don't end up with leftovers. For example, can you purchase green beans loose so you get just the right amount for one meal vs. purchasing a bag with a set amount included?
- **Plan Portions**: Ensure that meals have just enough food to prevent leftovers. Unless you intentionally plan to eat what is left, like packing the leftovers in your lunch the next day. My grandmother was a master at this!
- **Recipe Ideas**: When you have random food left that you need to use and aren't sure what to do with it, check out www.MyFridgeFood.com or www.Supercook.com. You enter what you have on hand and the sites give you possible recipes.
- **How Long Will It Last?** – There is a resource— www.eatbydate.com—which lists how long you can keep things in the refrigerator or freezer. Strive to use before they go bad.

COMPOSTING

While you can improve on producing fewer food scraps, it would be impossible to remove the scraps entirely. The next best solution is to compost and avoid sending waste to landfills.

Composting at Home: There are various options and techniques for composting at home. These range from outdoor piles to indoor machines. Between those two extremes, there are alternatives inside and outside the home. There are a lot of choices to be made when determining the right composting solution for your home, including location, the appearance of the unit, the type of composting solution (i.e., worms or not), and the price you are willing to pay.

Composting Drop-Off: More businesses and communities are starting to establish compost facilities to take food scraps. You collect your compost materials and then drop them off at the local location. Some have suggested freezing your scraps in a bag until you go to drop them off. This will ensure there is no smell in your home.

Scheduled Pickup: Another alternative in your area might be a scheduled service. Our community just started offering weekly pickups. The company provides buckets with sealed lids to collect the scraps in. I was surprised to see all the items you could put into the bucket. I expected it would include fruits, vegetables, eggshells, and coffee grounds. What I didn't expect were items like meat and bones, napkins, pizza box bottoms (the ones with the grease on them), and more. This alternative likely comes with a fee. For our location, the charge is $16/month at the time of publishing this book.

PACKAGING WASTE: REDUCING AND RECYCLING

According to the EPA, paper/paperboard, glass, and plastics combined accounted for 39% of the total Municipal Solid Waste (*National Overview:*

Facts and Figures on Materials, Wastes and Recycling | US EPA, 2017). Much of this waste comes from food packaging in the kitchen.

When it comes to the packaging, the best plan is to bring less into the house to begin with. A few strategies to help reduce or improve packaging include:

- **Fruits and Vegetables**: Including more fresh fruits and vegetables in your diet is not only good for your health but will also have less packaging. When purchasing fresh, resist the urge to buy already cut-up vegetables which often come in a plastic container or bag.
- **Buy in Bulk**: Bulk products will typically have less packaging than their small-serving counterparts.
- **Glass Over Plastic**: Glass recycling is less complex than plastic. If a product has glass and plastic options (e.g., spaghetti sauce), consider choosing a brand in a glass bottle. And, if there happens to be a metal can option, this is even better.

To recycle easily in the kitchen, find a spot near the garbage can to place a recycle bin. This way, recycling becomes second nature, and no one needs to run to the garage all the time to put items in the large, weekly bin. I had a recycling bin added to a cupboard next to the sink about five years ago, and I can't express what a convenient difference it has made in how our kitchen recycling functions.

PACKAGING WASTE: INNOVATIVE REUSE

Sometimes, you can find a great way to reuse items that might otherwise go into the garbage or recycling. Below are just a few ideas for inspiration. If you want to dive deeper, a quick search online for things you are recycling can provide almost limitless options.

- **Parmesan Cheese Tops**: These fit a mason jar perfectly! Put a drink in the jar, use straw in the holes, and/or keep your drink covered when you are outside for the day. If you have young children, you could fill a jar with Cheerios or snacks and shake them out while out and about.
- **Milk Jug**: These can easily be repurposed to become watering cans.
- **Rice/pasta Water**: Pour it into a milk jug; it is great for providing nutrients to your garden.
- **Plastic Cereal Bags**: Recycle the box and reuse the bag as waxed paper.
- **Glass Jars**: Keep jars from things like pasta sauce and use them for storage (flour/sugar/pencils).
- **Bacon Fat**: Keep and use to replace cooking oil.
- **Wine Bottles**: Self-water plants by filling bottles with water and burying them upside down.
- **Soup Cans**: Tie a bit of raffia around them and fill them with pens and pencils on desks.
- **Plastic Containers with Lids**: Use to freeze soup or leftover portions.

DISHES AND COOKWARE

There are A LOT of supplies in the kitchen, and there would be no way this book could cover all the options and alternatives. So, as you need a new item for the kitchen, do a quick search online with "eco-friendly" in front of the item. This should provide you with facts and options in the category. In this focus area, I'll provide some high-level guidelines for dishes, cookware, pots, and pans.

DISHWARE

When considering dinnerware (plates, bowls, cups, etc.), some alternative materials include ceramic, bamboo, stoneware, and recycled glass. The materials recommended to avoid are plastic and melamine. While plastic dishware has come a long way, and most is now BPA-free, choosing a non-plastic alternative for day-to-day use is still recommended. The same is true for melamine. Both have material challenges and, unlike other options, also cause recycling challenges.

Secondhand: If you aren't in a hurry to purchase, I've had a lot of fun over the years picking up all kinds of dishes (e.g., coffee mugs, stemware, glasses, serving platters, plates, and bowls) at yard sales and secondhand shops. These items often have no visible wear, come at a great price, and can add some fun to your mainstream dishes. If live sales aren't for you, Etsy, eBay, and Facebook Marketplace are great sources for secondhand while someone else has already done the initial searching for you.

Brands to Consider: Besides the best materials for your health and the environment, you can look for brands with sustainable manufacturing processes. A few to consider include:

- **Our Place or Costa Nova**: Both are made of recycled ceramics, and Our Place has many audits in place to ensure the best manufacturing process for the workers and the environment. www.fromourplace.com and www.costanova.pt (also found at popular stores)
- **East Fork:** If you don't mind spending a bit more, this is great pottery made in North Carolina. www.eastfork.com
- **Blue Marche and Natural Home:** These brands use melamine-free bamboo. Bamboo is the best alternative to plastic for a material that

won't break and is good for children. www.bluemarche.com and www.naturalhomebrands.com

POTS, PANS, AND COOKWARE

When considering new pots and pans, nonstick coatings are the most challenging material for both people and planet. Many would say the best alternative is to go back to what our grandparents used—the cast iron pan. This may not be the right alternative for your home, but it is worth considering. Below are a few non-stick brands that have a lighter impact:

- **GreenPan Lima Hard Anodized Healthy Ceramic Nonstick**: These pans are nonstick with a coating free of materials that cause toxic fumes. www.greenpan.us
- **Ozeri Green Earth Cookware** – This cookware comes in many shapes and sizes. They are also nonstick options. However, they cannot be placed in the oven. www.ozeri.com
- **Corningware** – This is a solid choice for cooking, serving, and storing. www.corningware.com
- **Gotham Steel Nonstick Bakeware** – They sell cookie sheets, muffin pans, and more. www.gothamsteel.com
- **Aluminum Wire Racks** – Place them on top of the cookie sheets or place them directly in the oven. These also have the added benefit of making some foods crispier.

OTHER COOKING SUPPLIES

There are so many supplies in the kitchen that it would be impossible to discuss all of them in this chapter. Below are two guidelines to keep in mind when shopping for your next salad tongs, cheese grater, or spatula.

Consider Secondhand: Again, this is a good category to shop secondhand for the unique supplies that others purchased and never used. I'm thinking of items like a melon baller, cheese grater, and tongs. When you need a new product, you might even consider asking relatives or friends if they have the item and don't use it. They might be happy to give it to you and empty up the space in their kitchen.

Avoid Plastic: This continues to be a theme. Look for items without plastic whenever possible. Look for wood, metal, bamboo, and silicone.

DISPOSABLE KITCHEN SUPPLIES

Another challenge in the kitchen is the waste created by some popular cooking, storage, and cleaning solutions, including aluminum foil, paper towels, and waxed paper. The sections below will provide some options to consider to reduce the waste produced when cooking, storing, and cleaning up.

COOKING

Aluminum foil and parchment paper are popular products to use for cooking as they can handle the temperature of the oven or grill. An easy alternative to consider is a pizza stone. If this isn't an option, you could consider a silicone mat. You may wonder if silicone is a plastic; it is not. Most believe the material is safer for food than plastic, with less risk of leaching. Some brands to consider are below:

- **Silpat Premium** – Eco-friendly and designed for marble and granite. www.silpat.com
- **OXO Good Grips Silicone Pastry Mat** – If you bake frequently, this mat has conversions, substitutions, and circular crust sizes printed right on the mat. www.oxo.com

- **Kitzini Silicone Mats** – Come in packs of 1-4 and are available from popular retailers.
- **GQC BBQ Grill Mat** – These are made of Teflon and can withstand the grill's heat. They come in a pack of six and are also dishwasher-safe (available from many popular retailers).

STORING AND SAVING FOOD

When storing and saving food, we most often reach for aluminum foil, plastic wrap, and Ziploc bags. Below are a few brands to consider for removing these disposable products.

- **Stasher** – Reusable food storage bags that are oven, microwave, and dishwasher safe. They come in many sizes depending on your use. www.stasherbag.com
- **Wrappas** – Reusable food storage wraps in cute prints. www.wrappa.com.au
- **Etee Organic Reusable Food Wraps** – Made of beeswax, they are reusable and biodegradable. www.shopetee.com
- **Wegreeco Reusable Bowl Covers** – These cloth covers fit snugly around the bowl and protect food for leftovers or taking something to a picnic/party. www.wegreeco.com
- **Food Huggers Lids** - Stretch to go over bowls you already own. They also have products that help save/protect half of products like onions, lemons, and avocados. www.foodhuggers.com

CLEANING UP

Paper towels and napkins are the most widely used products for cleaning up in the kitchen. The challenge is that they can't be recycled because of the food waste that is on them. Most of the popular paper towel options are bleached, which also makes them unable to be composted.

Below are several types of products to consider from light green options like chlorine-free paper towels to dark green options that replace the disposables with dishcloths and cloth napkins.

Light Green: These paper towels have removed chlorine, enabling the products to be composted.

- **Seventh Generation** – 100% recycled and chlorine free. www.seventhgeneration.com
- **Ever Spring** – 100% recycled and chlorine-free (available from popular retailers).
- **Reel** – Chlorine free. www.reelpaper.com

Medium Green: These products can be reused but have a shorter life than dark green alternatives.

- **Rakot75 Cloth Towel** – These towels are made of bamboo and have a long lifetime. I've used them for two years and have only gone through ½ the roll. www.rakot75.com
- **Bambooee** – A paper towel/dishcloth hybrid, which is reusable up to 100 times and machine washable. www.bambooee.com
- **Grove Tree-Free Reusable Paper Towels** – 100% bamboo that you can use for up to a week. They also have compostable kitchen wipes. www.grove.co

Dark Green: Able to be reused many times.

- **Mioeco Reusable Unpaper Towels** – Bleach-free, washable, and made of organic cotton. www.mioeco.com
- **Marley's Monsters Rolled Unpaper Towels** – Cotton cloths that cling together and sit around a roll that provides the convenience of a paper towel roll. www.marleysmonsters.com

- **J Cloths** – Once you see them, you will likely recognize them as the blue cloths that have been around for years. For me, my memories of them are from the garage, not the kitchen, but they can be used anywhere and are super absorbent and machine washable. www.jcloth.com

> **TRASH BAGS** – Many more brands are moving to biodegradable and compostable trash bags. These keep traditional plastic out of landfills, and since the bags break down quicker, they get the trash itself to break down quicker as well. Three brands to consider are Reli (www.shopreli.com), Green Paper Products (www.greenpaperproducts.com), and Primode (popular retailers). In addition to reducing your volume of trash, shifting to one of these options could be a great fit for your home.

PLANNING AND GROCERY SHOPPING

Everything in the kitchen starts with planning and grocery shopping. The sections below will dive into ideas and inspiration to be more conscious while planning and shopping for the food you will buy.

DESIGNING YOUR PLANNING PROCESS

A healthier plan for your kitchen's food and products starts with planning. Going into the grocery focused on what is needed will help you have the right ingredients on hand and not end up with foods that spoil before you have time to use them.

The first step is to plan the meals. Some, like myself, go for detailed planning for dinners. I like to have a recipe on hand for each evening that is determined ahead of time so that I don't need to decide each day what to make. Others prefer a more general approach like "chicken for Tuesday" and "leftovers on Thursday." That provides the flexibility to create a meal with the main ingredients based on what you are in the mood for at the time.

WHERE TO SHOP

The general rule of where to shop is at a location that requires the food to travel the least distance to get to you. Typical produce travels 1500 miles from where it's grown to your table. So, buying local when possible is the best option. Depending on where you live, farmers' markets are great places to shop for fruit and vegetables in season. The food will be fresher, and the experience will be an enjoyable alternative to the grocery store.

Beyond the farmers' markets, consider locations where you can buy staples in bulk. This typically reduces the packaging that you need to find a way to recycle. The items to avoid in bulk are fresh fruits and vegetables, meats, and dairy, which will likely go bad before you can use them up.

REUSABLE BAGS

This is an area I'm passionate about. Each year, Americans throw away 100 billion polyethylene plastic bags, and only 1-3% get recycled! (*Tax the Plastic*, n.d.). While there are now locations where you can recycle the bags, I believe the best solution is to remove them all together. In addition to removing the plastic waste, other advantages I've discovered in the 10+ years I've been bringing my own bags include:

- **Fewer bags** – More groceries fit in reusable bags than plastic, which equals fewer bags to carry.

- **Handles/Straps** – My bags have long handles that let me carry them on my shoulder like a tote. This helps me make fewer trips from the car to the kitchen when unloading groceries.
- **Durability** – The bags are thick and hearty. I don't worry about heavy items ripping the bag.
- **Insulated** – Several of my bags are insulated to keep cold/frozen food from getting warm.

While there is an initial investment in the bags, you will get use for years to come. Many of the bags I'm still using are the ones I purchased nearly fifteen years ago.

When shopping for bags, look for a couple that are insulated, made of sturdy material, and have long handles so you can hold them over your shoulder. In addition, there are vegetable bags to consider. These are small mesh bags that replace the plastic bags in the produce department. For fresh bread, there are also cloth bread bags that can be found online. I did a search of all bags and feel confident that you can get started for as little as $20 and add to your collection over time.

FOOD

According to NewScientist.com, food production contributes around 37% of global greenhouse gas emissions (Charles, 2021). In addition, where and how food is grown impacts the environment. In fact, entire books and blogs are devoted to education and information in this category. I hope the tips in this section will get you started on your journey, and you can dive deeper into the most interesting and relevant areas of your lifestyle.

A rule of thumb regarding food choices is that the lower the food is on the food chain, the smaller the carbon footprint. This means fruits, vegetables, seeds/nuts, and grains are better than meat and dairy. In addition, making food from natural ingredients is healthier than processed and frozen food. Moving beyond those general guidelines, this focus area will cover a variety of topics, including how to extend the life of food, sorting through all the confusing labels, and considering DIY alternatives.

Slow Food Movement – To dive deeper into food, I recommend checking out Slow Food. They are a global, grassroots organization working to make sure everyone has access to food that is good (quality, flavorful, and healthy), clean (produced in a way that doesn't harm the environment), and fair (accessible prices for customers and fair pay for producers). www.slowfood.com

WHERE TO RAISE AWARENESS

Before diving in, I had to do a bit of sorting to determine what to cover. Many articles have been published on foods with the most and least impact on the planet. Some of the greatest offenders are meat, cheese, farmed seafood, chocolate, coffee, palm oil, and cane sugar. I've summarized the food section into these categories:

- **Fruits and Vegetables** – What to consider
- **Seeds, Nuts, and Grains** – What to look for
- **Meat** – Includes beef, lamb, chicken, turkey, pork, and seafood
- **Dairy** – Milk, cheese, and butter
- **Challenging Staples** – Chocolate, coffee, palm oil, & cane sugar
- **The Pantry** – Processed food and DIY alternatives
- **Beverages** – Coffee, tea, soft drinks, beer, wine, and cocktails

We'll start with the groups to eat more of (fruits/vegetables and seeds/nuts/grains), and then we will head into the categories that require more diligence to begin eating one shade greener.

FRUITS AND VEGETABLES - TYPES

Overall, fruits and vegetables are a category with a light environmental impact. The main challenge in this category is to buy the right amount and not allow fresh produce to go bad before you can eat it. A second area to be aware of are the farming practices where your fruits and vegetables are grown. While most fruits and vegetables are good choices, below are several that are especially light on the environment:

Legumes: Doing this research, I now know the difference between a legume and a bean! Legume is the broad category; within it, there are beans and pulses. The pulses are legume seeds that grow in pods—think peas, lentils, and chickpeas. Legumes have many benefits for the planet and the people in your home. They have a very low carbon footprint, require little water to grow, and clean the soil to make it easier to grow other crops. For people, beans and pulses are filled with fiber, protein, and other nutrients. Another benefit is that they are inexpensive and light on our pocketbook.

Leafy Greens: Leafy greens are both healthy and easy to grow quickly. They are versatile to be used in a wide variety of recipes, both hot and cold, and contain many nutrients. From an environmental standpoint, they require minimal resources to produce large quantities.

Mushrooms: Mushrooms are often a great substitute for meat because of their texture and flavor. They are also beneficial for the environment as they grow in places where many other foods would not. With over 2000 edible varieties, the opportunity for recipe ideas is extensive.

Algae: While not a common part of many diets, algae are growing in popularity and are very good for our health and the planet. For us, algae provide protein, Vitamin C, essential fatty acids, antioxidants, and iodine. A Berkeley publication indicates that algae produce 70% of all the Earth's oxygen (*Oxygen Levels - Understanding Global Change*, n.d.). Another benefit is it can be grown throughout the year without the use of pesticides or fertilizers. When purchasing, you can look for nori, seaweed, or spirulina (powder).

FRUITS AND VEGETABLES - CONSIDERATIONS

When purchasing any fruits and vegetables, below are a few considerations.

Buy Local and In Season: When purchasing fresh produce, the best alternative is to buy what is grown locally during that season. Taking advantage of the seasonal foods in your area will keep variety in your food choices and lessen the environmental impact. When purchasing non-seasonal fruit, I was pleased to find that bananas, oranges, and apples are all fruits that have lower impacts because of their longer shelf lives, which enables them to be shipped more efficiently.

Organic: Produce is organic if it's certified that the soil it is grown in has had no synthetic fertilizers and pesticides applied three years before harvest. The Environmental Working Group has created a list called "the Dirty Dozen." These twelve fruits and vegetables would be the ones they consider most important to purchase organic. The list includes strawberries, spinach, kale, nectarines, apples, grapes, bell/hot peppers, cherries, peaches, pears, celery, and tomatoes.

Extending the Life of Produce: There are many tips online to extend the life of your produce. Below are just a few ideas to get you started. If you have something getting close to the end of life, do a quick search to see if there are ideas available to stretch it a bit longer or recipes to use it up.

- **All Produce**: Wash when you are ready to use, not when you get home from the grocery store.
- **All Produce**: Turn veggie scraps and meat bones into homemade soup stock.
- **Soft lettuce** – Soak in water overnight to retain crispness.
- **Asparagus** – Trim the bottoms and store upright in an inch or two of water.
- **Tomatoes** – Store stem side up.
- **Berries** – Dip in a solution of one part vinegar and three parts water and then dry them. This helps fight off bacteria.

SEEDS, NUTS, AND GRAINS

After fruits and vegetables, seeds, nuts, and grains are the next healthiest choice for foods that have a lighter environmental impact.

Nuts and Seeds: Overall, nuts and seeds have a low carbon footprint and are a great source of protein. However, when choosing between nuts and seeds, water is a consideration. Tree nuts are among the most water-intensive crops. Below, different types of nuts are categorized based on how water-intensive they are to grow:

- **Light Green**: The lightest green (or most water-intensive) options are pistachios and almonds.
- **Medium Green**: Nuts slightly less water-intensive include walnuts, hazelnuts, and cashews.
- **Dark Green**: The best alternatives are seeds like sunflower and pumpkin.

Grains: Whole grains are a good part of your diet. They typically require the least amount of water to grow, less than fruits, vegetables, nuts, and seeds. The most popular are whole wheat and rye. Some grains also high in protein include cornmeal, quinoa, wild rice, and oatmeal.

As you start to add more grains to your diet, there are all kinds that you can consider in addition to those listed above. Just a few include farro, bulgur, and sorghum.

MEAT

Meat is the most impactful and controversial part of our diet. A University of Leads research study found that meat eaters produce 59% more greenhouse gas emissions than vegetarians due to methane gas from the animals, water/land impact, processing, and transportation (Kaja, 2021).

In countries like the United States, our diets center around meat as the primary element of the meal, especially at dinner. While I'm not here to suggest you become a vegetarian (this is a personal choice), I would encourage you to consider making some changes to your meat intake. Below are some ideas to consider around the meats you bring into your home:

Eat Less: The easiest way to reduce your impact is to eat less meat. I know this might seem daunting and not desirable. However, you might consider giving Meatless Mondays a try. I recommend purchasing a good vegetarian cookbook (I really like "Everyday Vegan") so that the meals you try are unique and flavorful. Once you try it one day a week, you may find you want more meat-free meals.

Choose Wisely: Regarding "meat," not all types are created equal. The little-known meat with the most impact is lamb, even more than beef. That said, beef is a much more common dinner choice, and it has a much higher carbon footprint than the other options and should be used sparingly. Chicken and turkey are the best meat choices, followed by seafood (covered in the next section) and pork. How the animals are raised is also a key consideration and will be discussed later in "the labels."

Reduce Waste: When you do purchase meat, do everything you can to use it up before it expires. An easy option is to put the meat in the freezer. Beef should last four months, ham up to six months, and pork and poultry will last a year. When eggs are nearing expiration, you could consider hard boiling them, extending their life by a week.

The Labels: There are so many labels used I won't be able to cover them all. The Environmental Working Group has a helpful site that you can reference at www.ewg.org/research/labeldecoder. The best label to look for is the USDA Certified Organic. This means the animals eat only organically grown feed and aren't treated with hormones or antibiotics. Animals must also have access to the outdoors.

The additional labels provide some information, but most importantly, they likely indicate they are missing something that prevents them from being USDA organic. Here is the meaning of a few:

- **Grass Fed** – Animals have access to grass & hay year-round.
- **Free Range** – Animals are allowed to move about the pasture freely.
- **No Antibiotics or Hormones** – Straightforward, these aren't used in raising the animals.
- **Cage Free** – Animals aren't raised in cages, but they may be raised indoors.
- **Natural** – No artificial ingredients have been added.
- **rBGH or GMO-Free** – No growth hormones were used.

Consider purchasing your meat directly from farmers in your area where you understand the care and treatment of the animals.

Seafood: Considerations when shopping for seafood include where the seafood was caught, the fishing practices used, and if the seafood was farm-raised. Look for seafood caught close to home.

When it comes to fishing practices, you want to avoid seafood caught with nets. There are several different types of net fishing, but none eliminate the problem that they catch a lot of unintended ocean life that is disturbing the natural ecosystem. In addition, the nets are often lost or discarded and play a big role in the ocean's plastic challenge.

The concept of farm-raised is not cut and dry. There are different types of farm-raised and the conditions for both the environment and employees can be challenging. Below are some recommendations for the most popular types of seafood in the United States:

- **Shrimp** – Most sold in the US are farm-raised overseas. Look for wild-caught or US farm-raised.
- **Salmon** – There are many issues surrounding salmon fresh and farm-raised globally. Like the shrimp, look for wild-caught Alaskan salmon.
- **Tuna** – Look for pole and line caught and choose either albacore or skipjack over yellowfin.
- **Shellfish** (Oysters/Clams/Mussels) – Unlike shrimp and other fish, farm-raised shellfish is a great choice. Because they are filter feeders, they can help improve the water quality in the areas where they are farmed.

When purchasing seafood, a great resource is www.seafood-watch.org/recommendations. This website has ratings for seafood from around the world. Type in what you want to purchase, and it will provide what to look for.

Meat Alternatives: More and more alternatives to meat are coming onto the market. Some to consider include tofu, tempeh, black beans, portobello mushrooms, and chickpea. Three additional alternatives I found in my research were seitan (slices well for sandwiches), jackfruit (texture like pulled pork), and soyrizo (like chorizo).

DAIRY

When it comes to dairy, the challenges are the same as those in the meat section, i.e., methane gas from the animals, water, and processing/production. The animals' care and quality are also an important part of the equation.

Milk: Plant-based milks are becoming more popular and prevalent to purchase. The alternatives include oat, almond, soy, and rice. With milk being a staple in most homes, try purchasing a plant-based milk and see what you and your family think. You might start to blend animal and plant-based milks for different uses in the kitchen. You don't have to go 100% plant-based. Just look for some ways to possibly cut your animal-based milk consumption by a percentage that feels right to you.

Cheese: Like milk, cheeses are made from plant-based alternatives. Determine the cheese you want to use and search for "xxx plant-based cheese alternative" or "vegan xxx." There will be options for brands you can purchase and, in some cases, recipes for making the cheese at home. I was surprised at the simplicity of the DIY cheeses—some require ground nuts, and others are nut free.

Butter: Butter also has vegan brands available and can be made at home. You can find options by searching "vegan" or "plant-based." A few brands to consider include Miyoko (www.miyokos.com), Flora (www.flora.com), and WayFare (www.wayfarefoods.com).

CHALLENGING STAPLES

There are considerations for all your staples. However, four items significantly impact the environment – chocolate, coffee, palm oil, and cane sugar. All are impacting the world's rainforests through deforestation, soil erosion, and water pollution. These are key ecosystems to both absorb CO_2 from the air and maintain the world's water cycle. Below is a bit of information on each of these key food products:

Palm Oil: Palm oil should be avoided whenever possible. Rainforests are being burned to clear the path for production, and wildlife is being killed along the way. While you might think, "I don't use palm oil," you will learn that it is in a LOT of products you purchase. The World Wildlife Foundation indicates that 50% of the products in the grocery store, from food to hygiene, include palm oil (8 *Things to Know about Palm Oil | WWF*, n.d.). A few products to watch when shopping include ice cream, cookies, margarine, chocolate, and pizza dough.

Chocolate: In addition to the rainforest impact, there are often poor labor conditions when farming cacao trees. When buying chocolate, look for fair trade, focus on dark chocolate, and check the ingredients to avoid a lot of additives. There are a lot of specialty brands available. However, many do come at an increased cost. Limiting the amount of chocolate you eat will make it worth the splurge on special occasions.

Coffee: When purchasing coffee, look for Rainforest Alliance certification, fair trade, and organic. Also, purchasing from a local roaster in your area may provide additional information on the beans. Another important consideration with coffee is the recent trend toward disposable coffee pods. These have the added environmental challenge of recycling and, in many cases, are more expensive. While they may be a convenient choice, the quality, and taste of a great, responsibly grown coffee bean can't be beat.

Cane Sugar: While cane sugar doesn't impact the rainforests, it does impact tropical islands and coastal areas. The environmental challenges are like the others – soil erosion, water quality, and emissions/solid waste from production. This is the toughest to avoid, as many of the processed foods we purchase include cane sugar. Avoiding sugar drinks and desserts, as well as reading labels on items like spaghetti sauce, are a great way to both eat healthier and protect the environment. When cooking at home, there are many great alternatives to get sweetness into your dishes, including honey, maple syrup, and applesauce, just to name a few.

Additional Staples: For the rest of your staples, here are some considerations:

- **Flour**: Flour has a relatively low carbon impact. When shopping, look for organic (no fertilizers) and non-GMO (genetically modified). While all-purpose flours are the most popular, you may want to try some alternatives that are considered to have more nutrients, like whole wheat, almond, and coconut.
- **Spices**: The concerns with spices center around the working conditions of farms worldwide. Two labels to look for are fair trade (favorable worker conditions) and USDA organic (limited pesticides and non-GMO).
- **Oil**: Currently, there don't seem to be any great solutions for oil. While olive and avocado have historically had less impact, there are increasing environmental impacts with recent demand. Vegetable, coconut, and sunflower oils can be good alternatives. However, with any oil purchase, look for organic. And, as mentioned above, avoid palm oil.

PANTRY

When it comes to the pantry, I'm referring to the products that are not staples, like sugar, spices, and oils. This leaves a lot of food typically packaged in cans, boxes, glass, and plastics. Below are considerations for the pantry to extend the life of pantry foods and some ideas to possibly dip your toe in the water of making your own pantry staples:

Extending the Life of Pantry Items: Searching online for just about any pantry item will give tips for extending the life of these items. Here are just a few that bubbled to the top:

- **Bread** – Over 240 million slices of bread are thrown away each year (Igini, 2022). Consider freezing if you are close to the expiration date. Alternatively, make croutons by cutting them into cubes, adding some olive oil and seasoning, and then baking at 350 for 15-20 minutes.
- **Tortilla Chips** – If the chips are a bit stale, toss them in the oven for 10 minutes at 350.
- **Cookies** – As cookies are getting stale, put them in a plastic bag with a piece of bread overnight.

Try DIY: The healthier route for most of these is to make the products at home. While the convenience of pre-packaged goods is an integral part of our lives these days, consider if there are some products you could shift to something homemade. There are many benefits, including better flavor, the ability to select the ingredients, reduced packaging waste, and saving money. For many items, you will be surprised how quickly you can make them.

You could incorporate weekly bread or cookie baking as a fun, family weekend activity. You could start making your own condiments as some personal time just to relax and unwind. The recipes will keep your mind off all the other nagging to-dos in your life. Looking online for the product you want to make will provide lots of recipe options to choose from to find the one that is right for you. Here are just a few to consider:

- **Catsup** – You use organic tomato paste as a base, and the process takes 3 min or less.
- **Mayo** – Using egg, mustard, vinegar, and oil, the recipe takes less than 5 min. You can then add items to this base to make specialty sauces; examples include dill, garlic, or sriracha.
- **Salad Dressing** – Any type of dressing you can imagine has multiple recipes online. I've been making fresh dressing with dinner for about five years now. It takes no time with the making of the meal, and I love the variety we can have.
- **Bread** – While bread can be a bit more complex than the condiments above, many recipes still do not take much time. If you make the process part of your weekly routine, you'll get very efficient and likely start trying new techniques and types of bread.

While not staples, considering making your own products that are typically bought in cans or jars would be equally light on the planet and your pocketbook. This would include soups, pasta sauces, and canned vegetables.

BEVERAGES

Beverage choices can positively and negatively impact people's health, the planet, and pocketbooks. Below are some considerations for different beverages and brands to put on your list:

Water: The healthiest drink is often water. Water keeps you hydrated and doesn't have artificial ingredients. Filtering your water is a good idea and many refrigerators today have filtration right in the system. Another option would be a filtration pitcher that you keep filled with water chilling. I've also seen a lot of ideas lately for unique water infusions.

Coffee: Coffee was mentioned in the "concerning staples" section. Yet, it's worth repeating here with the other beverages. When purchasing coffee, look for Rainforest Alliance certification, fair trade, and organic. Buying beans or ground would be preferred over disposable pods.

Tea: When shopping for tea, using loose tea instead of tea bags will reduce waste. Labels to look for include Certified Organic and fair trade. A few brands to consider include Numi (www.numitea.com), Hobbs (www.hobbstea.com), T Project (www.tprojectshop.com), and Arbor Teas (www.arborteas.com).

Soft Drinks: There are a lot of health and packaging challenges with soft drinks. While healthier alternatives are available in Europe, it is more difficult to find options in the US. The Zevia brand (most retailers) is one that has become more popular and available in the US. However, all these brands don't provide any less impact on the environment than traditional alternatives.

Energy Drinks: Most energy drinks contain a lot of sugar and caffeine. Natural energy drinks give a boost of natural caffeine through vitamins, minerals, and antioxidants. There are a lot of natural energy drinks brands that you can explore, like MatchaBar Hustle Energy (www.matchabar.co), Runa (www.runa.com), and Zoa (www.zoaenergy.com). Like soft drinks, these may be healthier but won't provide a lighter impact on the planet.

Beer/Wine/Liquor: In general, when choosing between alcohol options, beer and wine have a bit lighter impact on the planet than liquors. Considerations to keep in mind when purchasing alcohol include how the plants are grown and harvested, the distilling/brewing process, and the company's environmental practices. Supporting local brewers is always a great choice as you can understand how the product is made and the shipping impact is removed. Below are some brands to consider:

- **Beer**: New Belgium, Sierra Nevada, and Great Lakes Brewing
- **Wine**: Benziger, Ferrari-Carano, Silver Oak, Far Niente, and Bonterra Organic
- **Liquor**: Purity Vodka, Vivir Tequilla, Don Q Rum, Elephant Gin, and FAIR drinks

Mocktails: The mocktail industry continues to grow and provides a lot of organic, natural recipes with many flavors without the downsides of an alcohol alternative.

FAST FIVE IN THE KITCHEN

Five steps you can take quickly to make an impact and begin to celebrate some wins!

1. **Rethink the Role of Meat** – Meat significantly impacts your carbon footprint. And not all meat is created equal. Consider your meat choices and try at least one meat-free day per week. When eating meat, include more chicken/turkey/seafood and less lamb/beef/pork.
2. **Consciously Consider Labels** – The ingredients and practices used in producing the foods we buy impact the health of both people and the planet. Understand where your foods come from and make conscious choices in categories like coffee, seafood, and palm oil.
3. **Reduce Waste** – The kitchen is a primary source of waste in our homes for the food that goes unused, the packaging the food arrives in, and single-use items like plastic shopping bags. To combat the

waste, consider intentionally planning meals, ensuring you use up what you buy, recycling packaging, buying reusable shopping bags, and trying a compost bin.

4. **Audit Your Pantry** – Set goals to fill your pantry with less processed foods and consider trying to make some staples (like bread, condiments, and sauces) from scratch. The result will be healthier for both the people and the planet.

5. **Shift Cleaning Products** – The kitchen is the place we prepare food. You want the surfaces to be clean, but you also don't want toxins moving from those surfaces into the food you consume. Evaluate your current products and determine if there are areas to make a change.

THE DINING ROOM

The dining room is an extension of the kitchen, where you eat the food you've prepared and entertain guests on the weekends and special occasions. There aren't appliances or technology to consider. We will use this chapter to look at entertaining, carry-out, and meals or snacks that members of your house eat while out and about at work, school, sporting events, and more.

The chapter will start with my story and then move into three focus sections: Dining Outside the Home, Carry-out, and Entertaining. Each focus area will dive deeper into the impacts and provide ideas to lessen your environmental impact.

MY ONE SHADE GREENER STORY

I started becoming aware of my habits in this area at the very beginning of my personal journey. The first changes I made were in the entertaining category, so I'll start my story there. I shifted all single-use plates, cups, and cutlery to reusable, dishwasher-safe products. During that time, our children were young, and our neighbors all had children the same age. Many weekend evenings were spent at one of our houses having dinner, letting the kids play, and generally just hanging out. Typically, there were anywhere between 15 and 30 people (adults and children) in the mix. So, I purchased enough products to cover 30 people. While this was a small investment initially, I've more than made up the cost over the 15 years of use. I also enjoyed the benefit of knowing we were adding less waste to landfills.

My choice of materials at the time was BPA-free plastic, so the items could be used indoors or outdoors depending on the season, and we wouldn't worry about anything breaking. While this was a good choice at the time, there are other alternatives available today that I might have considered instead; we'll discuss those later in the chapter.

Another change I made in 2016 was to purchase cloth tablecloths for the fold-up tables we use when entertaining. That year, our oldest was graduating from high school, and the timing was right to make the purchase. These cloth tablecloths fit the tables perfectly and hang to the ground. I don't have to tape them down or worry about the wind blowing them off as I did with the plastic ones. They are also easy to care for; just toss them in the laundry after the party. I purchased them in black, which works for any occasion, and I don't need to worry about stains. I wish I had made the swap sooner. I could have avoided purchasing plastic table covers for many birthday parties and other events over the years!

In addition to entertaining changes, in 2015, I began reducing waste when I was eating and drinking outside the home. Those changes included taking a mug to the coffee shop to eliminate my daily disposable cup, purchasing reusable glass containers to replace paper lunch bags, and packing my lunch most days to avoid the waste of purchasing carry-out while at work. I also purchased water glasses for my office and a water bottle for when I was on the go. I've kept all these habits and have prevented a lot of disposables from ending up in landfills.

Through the years, our family's biggest dining room challenge has been carry-out. We have always eaten out 1-2 days a week (more when the kids were in middle and high school), but one of those was typically live at the restaurant. COVID changed all that. We obviously stopped going out, and we increased carry-out to 2-3 nights a week. I have tried to start looking for and returning to restaurants with compostable and/or recyclable containers and requesting no cutlery or condiment packages. That said, this is an area that our household needs to focus on and get back on track for reducing waste.

> **UP NEXT IN MY HOME**: As I mentioned above, carry-out is an area of focus moving forward. I want to get back to dining out and reduce the number of times we pick something up weekly. Another area on my list, but not a high priority yet, is replacing our entertaining dinnerware. We've gotten nearly 15 years of use out of the BPA-free plastic, and I'm ready to try one of the new material options.

DINING OUTSIDE THE HOME

Most of us dine outside the home more than we realize. Coffee picked up on the way to work, grabbing a bottle of water or another beverage at the gas station or drive-through, and lunches packed for work or school. In addition to these day-to-day activities, we also have sporting events, picnics at the park, field trips, road trips, and other meals on the road. This focus area will dive into these situations and provide alternatives and tips.

BEVERAGES OUTSIDE THE HOME

Grabbing a coffee, water, or other beverage while out and about is very convenient. However, each purchase comes with cups, straws, aluminum cans, glass, and plastic bottles that need to be disposed of. The statistics on these items are often published, and the headlines cover the billions of each product used and the low recycling percentage. In fact, many disposable paper cups can't even be recycled because they have a layer of plastic film to hold the liquid so that the cup doesn't leak. Let's look at several of the most popular drinks on the go and consider alternatives.

Coffee: The best solution here is to bring your own mug. Most coffee shops will now fill your mug instead of using their disposable option—some even give you a discount for bringing your own. Once you have used the mug fifteen times, you have surpassed the sustainability of a disposable cup. Considering that you might purchase a coffee on the way to work every day and you work 48 of the 52 weeks each year, that is 240 coffee cups a year you can personally keep out of a landfill. You will also automatically have your mug with you if you drink another cup at work. To take this one step further, you could consider brewing your coffee at home and taking it with you. This would protect the planet and provide savings for your pocketbook.

Water: Similar to coffee, the best solution is to get a great water bottle and take it with you when you are away from home. Unlike coffee, where people typically pick up just one cup a day, water is often consumed all day long. An individual could drink five or more bottles of water per day, exponentially increasing the waste numbers shown for coffee above.

Fast Food Beverages: Driving through the nearest fast-food location or stopping inside the gas station for a fountain drink has the complexity of the coffee cup with the added challenge of a straw. This one isn't as cut and dry as the coffee and water solutions. I would still encourage you to find a reusable container and straw. However, you will need to ask at the various locations to see if they will allow your reusable container to be used. This practice isn't as commonplace yet as it is in coffee shops.

Bottles and Cans: For all the other on-the-go beverages, the first choice should be to avoid them or use a reusable container. That said, I was surprised to find which types of containers had a more or less overall impact on the environment. The first choice is simple—aluminum cans. They are easily collected in all municipalities, and aluminum can be recycled again and again. The second choice is a surprising one—plastic. While the number of times it can be recycled is limited, the impact is less than the third choice of glass. The thing to remember with plastic is to recycle it. Today, only 15% are recycled (*The Plastic Waste Problem Explained*, n.d.)

Just Try It – Taking your own beverage container can seem daunting at first. This month, just give it a try. Make a challenge to take a coffee mug and/or water bottle along with you when you are away from home. Set a goal of using a coffee mug or water bottle every day all month long. I imagine by the end of the month, you will realize this change is easy and doesn't have a negative impact on your routines.

Containers to Consider: There are many choices out there for reusable drink containers. A few of the popular brands are below:

- **Hydro Flask**: This brand has stainless steel coffee mugs and water bottles. www.hydroflask.com
- **Klean Kanteen**: There are choices for many different types of mugs and bottles. This brand also has containers for packing lunches and snacks on the go. www.kleankanteen.com
- **Yeti**: Again, multiple choices for different uses. They have mugs with handles and lids with straws for those who like those features. www.yeti.com

- **Keep Cup**: Cups for coffee, water, or soda. Their look resembles the disposable they replace. www.keepcup.com/us
- **Circular & Co Travel Coffee Mug**: This one is interesting because it takes non-recyclable paper coffee cups and turns them into reusable mugs. Each mug is made from six discarded cups. www.circularandco.com
- **Straws**: Searching for plastic straw alternatives provides several material options. From stainless steel to glass to bamboo and other materials, here are a few to consider:
  o **Final**: These straws are metal and disassemble to fit in a tiny keychain holder. www.final.com
  o **OXO Stainless Steel Straw**: Come in packs of four with a cleaning brush. www.oxo.com
  o **Jungle Straws**: Made of bamboo and come in a two-pack. www.junglestraws.com
  o **Strawesome**: Glass straws with unique designs make a statement. www.strawesome.com

PACKING LUNCHES FOR WORK AND SCHOOL

Packing lunch for work or school has three main benefits: healthier, less expensive, and lighter on the planet. That said, the challenge is the convenience of purchasing lunch on the go. Packaging a lunch can be quick and easy with a little planning. Like eating at home, fruits and vegetables are better choices than processed foods. In this section, we'll focus less on what you decide to pack to eat and more on the packaging to make your lunches one shade greener.

Single-Use Packaging: While it's easy to buy pre-packaged chips, cookies, yogurt, and more to drop into a lunch, this is not the best approach for your pocketbook and the planet. These single-use packages are more expensive and create more waste that isn't easily recycled.

Ziploc and Paper Bags: The greener alternative to single-use packaging is to buy foods in bulk and put them in Ziploc bags that you reuse. Once they can no longer be reused, drop them off at your local recycling location. While this is a bit better, the dark green solution is to replace paper and Ziploc bags with reusable containers covered below.

Sustainable Lunch Containers: When selecting containers for food in your lunch, much has been written about not using plastic containers. Not only are they difficult to recycle, but the plastics can leech into your food during use. Newer plastics have been designed BPA-free and with other formulas that reduce the concern. However, I tend to focus on products and companies that use plastic alternatives. Here are some to consider:

- **PlanetBox**: Stainless Steel bento box containers and other products. www.planetbox.com
- **Stasher**: Silicone-based resealable "bags" to replace Ziploc bags. www.stasherbag.com
- **Fluf**: Lined organic cotton snack and lunch bags that can be put in the laundry. www.fluf.ca/us
- **Etsy**: Lots of unique alternative products are on Etsy for any category. www.etsy.com
- **Glass Containers**: While I don't have a specific brand, glass containers with snap lids are also a good option. They go against my mention of "no plastic," but the plastic lids don't typically touch the food. These work well both for lunches and storing leftovers at home.

CARRY-OUT

When weeknights are busy, the convenience of carry-out and fast food has become a regular part of our lives. With COVID-19, we shifted from eating in restaurants to picking up carry-out or getting delivery. This has increased two of the main challenges with carry-out:

1. The waste created from the takeout containers, cutlery, and condiments
2. The emissions from picking up the food or having it delivered to you.

The other consideration we will not address in this focus area is the food. Many carry-out options have highly processed foods, high calories, and ingredients that aren't as healthy as home cooking. Being conscious of your choices in this category can positively or negatively impact the health of the people in your home.

Focusing on the packaging, carry-out is a difficult category because there aren't many options to improve the situation. While we aren't going to eliminate carry-out from our lives anytime soon, below are some things to keep in mind the next time you order out:

Carry-out Less: The obvious solution to reduce carry-out waste is to order out less. Consider how many times you get carry-out meals each week. Could you cut this down by one meal per week? That will be 52 fewer meals of packaging waste heading to landfills. This doesn't necessarily mean you must cook another meal at home. You could just shift the carry-out meal to a dine in the restaurant meal—same food minus the packaging waste. That said, eating 52 meals made at home vs. carry-out would also positively impact your pocketbook.

Say No to Extra Stuff: If you are eating at home, consider typing in the "special request" box while ordering that you don't want plastic utensils and little packs of condiments included with your meal. When you go in to pick up the food if they start to put these in a bag, mention you don't need them—eliminating another piece of waste.

Choose Your Restaurants: Over time, you can become more aware of your favorite restaurants' packaging. You can consider ordering more frequently from those that have more sustainable packaging. If the restaurant is privately owned, you could also make suggestions to the owner on options that might have a lighter impact.

Recycling: No matter how sustainable a restaurant is with its packaging, you will still have materials that you need to process. Below are tips on the most common types of packaging and how to dispose of them:

- **Pizza Boxes** – Boxes that have no oil on them can be placed in your curbside recycling. Those areas with oil can be picked up by professional municipality composting.
- **Paper Bags** – A much better choice over plastic. These can be recycled curbside if they are oil-free. If they have food oil on them, rip that section off, put it in the trash, and recycle the rest.
- **Paper Sandwich Wrappers** – If they are free of food and grease, they can be recycled.
- **Styrofoam Containers** – While these containers have a lighter impact on the environment in production, they cannot be recycled in any form, making them a choice to avoid if possible.
- **Aluminum Containers** – These are the ones where the bottom is aluminum, and the top is a paperboard. Both can usually be placed in your curbside recycling if no oil is on the top.
- **Cardboard Containers** – These are recyclable if they don't have a plastic coating and are free from food waste and grease.

- **Chinese Containers** – The ones with the little metal handle aren't recyclable.
- **Plastic Containers with Lids** – Some, but not all, of these containers can be recycled. You need to check the pieces for the number 1-7 recycling mark and then determine if those are accepted in your municipality. These are also good for washing and keeping around the house. When you have guests over, you can send them home with leftovers, with no dish to return.
- **Plastic Utensils** – Not recyclable.
- **Plastic Bags** – Only recyclable at special drop-off locations.

ENTERTAINING

One of the most challenging times to lessen your impact on the planet is when you have a party and entertain at home. Our default is often to bring paper plates, cups, and cutlery. We also purchase party supplies like plastic tablecloths, streamers, and various decorations. These products are often used only once and headed off to a landfill. Consider the ideas in this section for your next party or dinner in with friends.

PLATES AND BOWLS

You will need to find the best mix of choices for people, planet, and pocketbook based on your entertaining situations. Here are some questions to consider before diving in:

- How many people do you need to purchase sets for (maximum)?
- Do the dishes need to be microwaveable? Dishwasher safe?
- Do they need to be unbreakable based on adult/child mix and indoor/outdoor entertaining?
- How concerned are you with the occasional use of BPA-free or melamine products?

With the answers to these questions in mind, the sections below describe alternative products and brands to explore in your search for the right solution for your home:

Ceramic, Porcelain, and Glass: Using dishware like what is recommended for your everyday use is definitely an option here. The key consideration is breakage. If you have a lot of children at events or many of your entertaining situations are outdoors, this is likely not the right recommendation for you. If this is an option for you are a few alternatives to consider:

- **Additional Sets**: You could purchase additional sets of your everyday dinnerware to cover the number of guests you typically entertain.
- **Lower Quality**: You could buy a larger set of dishes that aren't quite the same quality as your day-to-day sets, so they come at a lower price point.
- **Secondhand**: This is a great option as you can hunt garage sales and resale shops for interesting finds. You may end up with eclectic and mismatched items, but that could just add to the whimsy of your events.

Bamboo: If you are looking for an alternative that won't break, bamboo is a good option. These dishes are made without pesticides and will be safe and non-toxic. Brands to consider include Bamboozle (www.bamboozlehome.com), Zungleboo (www.zunglestore.com), and Ekobo (www.by-ekobo.com).

BPA-Free Plastic and/or Melamine: While I suggested in the kitchen chapter to avoid plastic or melamine products, entertaining is one exception where I believe these materials are a solid alternative to balance the impact on people, planet, and pocketbook.

If you are only eating on these occasionally and not every day, the risk of the toxins would be minimal. However, there are articles written by people who indicate that they would never eat off these plates. Please do your research and determine what you are comfortable with. Keeping the products for many years of entertaining would have a much smaller impact on the planet.

The added advantage is that BPA-free plastic and melamine products are great for both indoor and outdoor events without the risk of dinnerware breaking. When you search for options, make sure you are paying attention to dishwasher and microwave safe if you want to be able to heat things up on them and not hand wash them after the event.

Stainless Steel: As I was researching non-breakable alternatives to plastic and melamine, I came across stainless steel as an option. While you can't put stainless steel in the microwave, you can put it in the dishwasher. Heat up foods in another container; this could be a great option for your home.

Compostable Products: If purchasing a permanent set of dishes isn't right for you, there are more compostable product options on the market today. A few brands to consider include Stack Man, Ecovita, Gezond, and Perfectware. These are available at mainstream retailers.

In addition, there are compostable plates made of bamboo and palm leaves with a higher price point that look much more upscale. This could be the right choice for a special event.

CUPS

Like plates and bowls, you can consider glass, BPA-free plastic, and melamine. There are also a lot of stainless-steel alternatives, including specialty glasses like wine and martini. Some stainless-steel options come with silicone sleeves so you aren't directly holding the cup, which could be hot or cold from the drink inside.

When looking for disposable cup alternatives, cups are trickier than plates because many prefer a plastic cup. Solo has a sub-brand called Bare that is made of 20% recycled plastic and can be recycled. While this could be an alternative, non-disposable cups are the greener choice.

CUTLERY

Buying larger quantities of your everyday cutlery or buying a less expensive set just for entertaining would be the best option. If reusable won't work in your home, compostable options are available. Some brands to consider are Biofase (www.biofase.eu), GreenWorks (www.greenworks.com/my), and Ecovita (www.ecovita.co).

SERVING DISHES AND PLATTERS

For the "extra" items you might want when entertaining (serving dishes and platters as an example), I heard an interesting story. Someone purchased these items at a local Goodwill store just before the party, used them for the event, and then took them back to the store as a donation. I thought this was a unique alternative to renting dishes and had the benefit that the items didn't need to be stored in their home. If this option doesn't feel right for you, stick with the same materials suggested throughout this section, like glassware, ceramic, BPA-free plastic, melamine, and stainless steel.

TABLE COVERINGS

I mentioned in my personal story the advantages I discovered by purchasing cloth table coverings. If you have a set of tables you always use when entertaining, I recommend you consider this option. After using them just a few times, you will start saving money by not purchasing the plastic covers over and over again, which is good for both the planet and your pocketbook.

You can go beyond the table coverings and look for table runners, placemats, and napkins to really pull together a great dinner party look. When searching for table linens, look for organic cotton, linen, hemp, palm fiber, grasses, and bamboo. Also, consider purchasing secondhand.

EVENT AND HOLIDAY DECOR

There are endless options available when it comes to décor for the holidays and entertaining. In fact, books are written on these topics. Below are a few tips to keep in mind:

- **Leverage Nature**: Find materials in season (flowers, pinecones, grasses, fall leaves, etc.) and decorate with these products from nature. Place them in bowls and vases around the house for a very seasonal, natural, yet festive feel.
- **Chalkboards**: Using chalkboards to note a birthday or other special event enables you to use the same décor again and again as the events change over time.
- **Repurpose**: Shop your home for containers and decorations that can be transformed into centerpieces or party decorations.
- **Shop Secondhand**: This is another area where purchasing used might be the perfect way to find some decorations for your event that are barely used.

FAST FIVE IN THE DINING ROOM

Five steps you can take quickly to make an impact and begin to celebrate some wins!

1. **Reusable Coffee Mug and Water Bottle** – If you purchase coffee outside the home and/or frequently drink from disposable water bottles, buy a great travel coffee mug and water bottle. This will have a huge impact on your personal contribution to eliminating disposable cup waste.

2. **Conscious Carry-out** – Consider the foods you are purchasing for carry-out and pay attention to the containers and products those restaurants use for packaging to reduce overall waste.

3. **Greener Entertaining** – Instead of paper plates, cups, and plastic cutlery, consider purchasing reusable items, cutting future purchase costs.

4. **Packaging Lunch on the Go** – Explore what you currently use to pack lunches (paper and plastic bags) and consider switching those for reusable alternatives.

5. **Holiday Décor** – As you consider decorating for the holidays or just having guests over for dinner, look for natural products or items you already have around the house. You could also consider purchasing secondhand for an event and then donating them back after the party.

THE OFFICE

The home office took on a whole new meaning worldwide when COVID-19 hit in March 2020. Adults were working from home, children came home from college, and students from kindergarten up shifted to online learning. Two years later, many knowledge workers are still working out of their homes, and colleges continue to offer more online classes.

The "office" areas in your home may or may not be a physical room. This could be a desk in the kitchen, a space in the bedrooms, or even a repurposed dining room table.

The chapter will start with my story and then move into five focus sections: Office Technology – Devices and Charging, Office Technology – Use, Office Technology – Recycling, Minimizing Mail, and Office Supplies. Each focus area will dive deeper into the impacts and provide ideas to lessen your environmental impact.

MY ONE SHADE GREENER STORY

The office areas in my home have undergone many changes and iterations over the years. Back in 2010, I was working a few days a week at home with a dedicated office, my kids had workspaces in their bedrooms, and my husband worked outside our home. By 2015, we were all working or going to school outside the home every day. Then with COVID-19, everything shifted dramatically. Both my husband and I worked 100% from home, and my youngest shifted to taking his college classes from his bedroom. Today, my husband and I work from home 2-3 days a week, and our son is back at college taking classes live. All these shifts created adjustments to the office spaces in our home.

Thinking about the advancements in technology that have happened at such a pace over the years since I've been on this journey, it's no wonder I feel like we have had challenges in the office. Back in 2010, when we started thinking about a greener lifestyle, laptops were just getting to be more mainstream, cell phones weren't yet "smart," social media (Facebook) was fairly new, and we had no idea of the challenges and opportunities that would come so quickly. As a result of this rapid pace combined with the rapid pace of life when the kids were in middle school and high school, we have purchased many technology items, from desktops to laptops, cell phones, tablets, and more.

With technology flowing into the house, the challenge we faced was that it was not flowing out at an equal pace! I was overwhelmed by the task of data removal and struggled with both sunk costs and memories the devices held (especially the mobile phones). The result was a growing pile of electronics in a corner of the basement, gathering dust. For the last couple of years, I have been slowly plugging away at clearing them and then recycling them. Many are so out of date there is no opportunity to sell them or donate them. My approach has been to take anything that is ready (data removed) to the hazardous waste drop-off day in our municipality or returning it to a big box electronics store that accepts old devices. For the phones, we have done a better job recently of returning them to our carrier when we get a new phone so that they can be refurbished and used by someone else in a second life.

In addition to computers and phones, I have an eReader. Later in the chapter, we'll discuss the breaking point for purchasing an eReader vs. physical books. Believe me, I read A LOT (3-4 books a month), so the math makes sense for me. I will still occasionally purchase a physical book, but most are purchased electronically. I prefer having the book on my reader and phone so that I have something to read if I find myself somewhere waiting with extra time on my hands. The eReader is a device that I won't upgrade until it stops working because it does everything I need currently, and I don't need more features.

As I started to write this chapter, I thought I was in good shape on the technology use front. I am focused on efficient shutdown and charging habits. I have an established and regular shutdown routine at night to ensure computers aren't running while we sleep. I TRY to charge devices during the day to be more efficient. However, I haven't landed on a routine, so I end up with something uncharged and flashing red all the time! What I learned as I wrote the chapter is the impact other uses create. We'll discuss that in the "up next" box below.

In our home, much of the office has gone digital. Yet, we still have a cabinet of traditional supplies and a need for them on a reasonably frequent basis. When the kids were in middle school, I consolidated all office supplies into one location as they had previously been spread across the kitchen, office, and bedrooms. This shift lets me keep better track of what we have and when we need something vs. the extras just being in a spot we forgot to look.

For the supplies themselves, I've been purchasing recycled paper and other green office supplies for years. I have become fond of papers where you can see the fibers; I feel they have a cool personality that is perfect for me.

I also enjoy searching for new notebooks with recycled paper and upcycled or low impact covers. From cork to recycled magazines, there are interesting finds if you start to look around. I've tried a lot of different pens and pencils and always look for new brands and eco-friendly alternatives when we need replacements.

UP NEXT FOR MY HOME: Now that the kids are grown and on their own, I am learning more about the impact of technology on the environment. While I have implemented some of the recommended changes, writing this chapter has inspired another wave of the journey.

I didn't realize the impact that our personal computer habits have on the environment. Areas like email, meetings, file storage, the content you post, and even the social media channels you choose to follow. With all the advancement, I feel I missed a wave of things to consider. I'm now making more intentional decisions using technology.

OFFICE TECHNOLOGY – DEVICES AND CHARGING

Technology. Most have a love/hate relationship. We love what it adds to our lives; convenience, connection, information, and more. We hate other things like time disappearing while seeming to have accomplished nothing, the feeling that you need to be "always on," and sometimes the pressure we feel from watching others' lives through social media. The key is finding the balance between the benefits and potential pitfalls.

In 2019, the average household had 11 connected devices. Today, that number has more than doubled to 25 (*Report: Connected Devices Have More Than Doubled Since 2019 - Telecompetitor,* n.d.). Each of these devices has an impact from manufacturing to daily use and recycling. The challenges are increasing because technology is constantly improving, and it is very tempting to upgrade computers, printers, cell phones, eReaders, and other office devices.

This focus area will dive into the devices in your home office and provide ideas and inspiration for reducing the impact of those you choose to purchase and how to keep those devices charged to maximize energy efficiency.

REPLACING EQUIPMENT

When it's time to replace office electronics, two considerations before you start shopping are below:

1. Do I need this **now**? Could it wait a year?
2. Do I need to purchase **new**? You may find that you want the latest model laptop, but your tablet could be used or refurbished. Many manufacturers today offer refurbished products, which are as good as new and healthier for the planet and your pocketbook.

Because technology changes so quickly, I'm not recommending specific brands. You should search for eco-friendly alternatives when in the market for a new device. While shopping, you can leverage the following three resources:

- **Epeat** (www.epeat.net): This website gives products a bronze, silver, or gold rating.

- **Ethical Consumer** (www.ethicalconsumer.org): This website has a technology section that provides things to consider and ratings of popular brands.
- **Bloggers**: Many are providing thoughts on the most eco-friendly office products.

Below are some additional considerations for each device to keep in mind as you shop:

- **Computers** – Laptops require less energy and fewer parts than desktops. So, if you are comfortable with either option, go with the laptop.
- **Printers** – When looking for a new printer, search for one that is "eco-solvent." The solvent inks are biodegradable and healthier for those in your home as they don't emit VOCs (volatile organic compounds). Also, look for refillable ink cartridges to eliminate cartridge waste.
- **Keyboards and "Mice"** – If you do searches online for eco-friendly keyboards and mice, you will find some interesting options that replace plastic cases with bamboo or other eco-friendly choices. Not only are they better for the planet, but they also look cool.
- **Cell Phones** – With cell phones launching new features regularly, this is a category where many people would be fine with a used or refurbished device. Often, the set of features most people need are on phones a couple of generations behind.

E-READER VS. PRINT BOOKS

There is much debate about the environmental impact of physical books vs. eReaders. Both industries have negative effects on the environment. However, a choice must be made for those who love to read. From my research, there was a wide swing in the number of books you need to read—from 25 to 100—to reach the breakeven point of an eReader.

If an eReader is the right choice for you, considering used or refurbished could be an alternative. People buy tablets and then find they don't use them and resell them quickly. This is also a technology area where new features aren't necessary, and a product several years old is very similar to the current model. This route will be better for the planet and lighter on your pocketbook.

Many people out there may easily get to either of those numbers, but just like the "feel" of holding a real book in their hands when they read. Below are some eco-friendly tips for readers:

- **Use the library!** – The library provides a great way to read anything you want while not having the expense of a new book, the environmental impact, and the challenge of getting rid of it in some way when you are finished reading it.
- **Purchase Used** – Estate sales, used bookstores, and online sites could be a great alternative to buying a new book. Even Amazon has a used book purchase option. This is a great option for those who want physical books and don't want to give them back.
- **Device Multi-Tasking** – Consider the devices you already have before purchasing an eReader. The reading apps can be downloaded on computers, tablets, and phones. You may find you have the right solution in your home already.
- **Audiobooks** – This option has an impact based on the size of files and storage, yet this is much lighter on the planet than either the physical book or eReader. Another advantage of audiobooks is that they give your eyes a rest from screens and/or print. You can listen while taking a walk or driving. If you haven't tried audiobooks, you should give them a "read."

Fun Repurpose Idea – Do you have a lot of old books lying around? What about old textbooks that will be difficult to sell or donate? If you have some, I highly recommend a quick search online of "wall art from used books" or "art from used books." You will be amazed at the beautiful pieces you can create with simple folding techniques!

REDUCING ELECTRICITY USE

With all the electronics in our offices, energy use is a key area of consideration. Take a minute to think about everything turned "on" in your office (lights, computers, monitors, etc.). Below are some tips and ideas for adjusting your device habits to save energy:

Shut Down at Night – There are a lot of people who don't shut down their computer at night. This is causing unnecessary energy draw. To make it effortless, you can use settings to have the computer shut down automatically every evening.

Unplug Your Laptop – When in use, leave laptops unplugged and use the battery. Using your laptop with the charger plugged in results in twice as much energy consumption.

Go Without the Monitor – If you use an external monitor with your laptop when you work and are going to use the computer for less than 20 minutes, don't turn on the monitor.

Unplug Charging Cords – Unplug chargers when they aren't in use, as they will continue to draw power even when they aren't charging a device.

Charging Your Cell Phone or Tablet – Charging your cell phone or tablet during the day (vs. overnight) will reduce the time it's on the charger fully charged and wasting energy. In addition, putting the device in airplane mode during charging will speed up the process.

Disconnect the Cell Phone – When not using Wi-Fi, GPS, and/or Bluetooth, turn the features off to preserve battery life.

Minimize Open Programs/Apps – Programs, apps, and windows that are open but not in use consume battery power working in the background. This uses energy and can cause your device to run slower.

Change Screen Settings – There are two energy savers relating to your device's screen. First, turning down the brightness of your screen will use less power. Second, reduce the time before the screen saver comes on when the device isn't in use. Both can be adjusted in your settings.

PRINTING MORE EFFICIENTLY

While all your devices consume electricity, the printer has the additional consumption of ink and paper to consider. Ink cartridges, in particular, tend to be both expensive and challenging to recycle. The tips below can set you on the path to making your printing one shade greener:

- **Avoid Printing** – Do you need to print? This is the best question to ask to reduce the volume.
- **Use Sustainable Ink** – Search for a vegetable or soy-based ink that can be used in your printer.
- **Recycle Cartridges** – For those who don't have refillable cartridges, find where they can be returned and recycled on Earth911. These are important to return as 97% of a toner cartridge is recyclable.
- **Use Recycled Paper** – When purchasing paper refills, look for paper made of recycled material.

- **Print Double-Sided** – When printing a draft, consider printing the first version double-sided instead of single-sided.
- **Consider Greyscale** – Printing in black and white is more efficient than color. Whenever possible, put the settings on black and white to avoid printing in color.
- **Change Fonts** – Another way to save ink is through font selection. Of the traditional fonts, Century Gothic is the most efficient. Times New Roman, Garamond, and Courier are also good alternatives. If you want to try fonts explicitly designed to lessen their impact, you can check out Ryman Fonts and EcoFonts.

OFFICE TECHNOLOGY – USE

In addition to the devices' impact, the cloud now has a greater carbon footprint than the airline industry! In fact, a single data center can consume the same amount of electricity as 50,000 homes (The MIT Press Reader, 2022). While larger brands, like Google and Amazon, are offsetting their carbon impacts, many smaller data centers are not.

While reducing time spent online definitely helps reduce your impact, we also need to consider what we are storing, sending, receiving, and posting. The rest of this focus area will provide tips and ideas to keep your cloud and data center impact to a minimum.

KICK OFF A "DIGITAL CLEANING" HABIT

Consider starting a habit (weekly or monthly) to reduce your cloud storage. You can look at what you have stored in the cloud and consider several questions:

- Do you need the files? If not, delete them.

- Do you have a lot of file "versions" saved of the same document? If so, can you delete some?
- Do you use the files regularly? If not, can you move them to an external drive?

This can also be an opportunity to organize files. Knowing where things are quickly can have the added benefit of peace of mind. As Gretchen Rubin says, "Outer order leads to inner calm."

KEEP EMAIL CLEAN

We can all often feel like we are drowning in email. This content is also flooding large portions of the cloud. While one email's carbon footprint is small, they do make an impact when compounded. In fact, according to Science Focus, sending sixty-five emails is the carbon equivalent of driving a car one mile (Villazon, 2018). Changing email habits can also go a long way to providing peace of mind and feeling more in control.

Take action on one or all of the ideas below to reduce your email volume and the impact on the cloud.

- **Reduce Email Accounts** – Do you have multiple emails? Maybe you started years ago with Yahoo and then migrated to Gmail, or you had a childhood address that needed to be upgraded when job searching. If so, consider going in and deleting an account you no longer use.
- **Clean up your Box** – Delete emails you no longer need, clear out your sent file, and delete the items you have sent to your trash (they stay there until you formally remove them!). If you don't empty the trash regularly, set a habit of doing it once a week, maybe on your physical trash day.
- **Unsubscribe** – We can quickly find ourselves on all kinds of email lists, from store coupons to newsletters and more. As those emails

pop into your inbox, ask yourself, "Do I want to continue receiving these?" If no, go to the bottom of the email and click "unsubscribe."

- **Sending Emails** – When you send emails, there are a few things to consider that can reduce the impact. Reducing the file size of an attachment or not attaching something at all will significantly reduce the email size. Avoid copying a lot of people on a note, and when you are replying, don't "reply all" unless required.

- **Consider Your Email Provider** – You can visit www.ethicalconsumer.org/ to look at the rating of your current email provider and compare it to other providers available. There are several lesser-known providers with very high ratings. While this is an option for your home email, you could also talk to the technology team at your company to advocate for an efficient provider for your work email as well.

EVALUATE YOUR MEETINGS

While working from home saves the negative planet impact of the commute, all-day video calls have their own impacts on the planet and the people spending the day looking at a screen.

There is a website that can give you an idea of your meeting impact at www.utilitybidder.co.uk/business-electricity/zoom-emissions/. You enter your types of meetings—1on1 vs. group, the average number of hours each week you spend in this type of meeting, and the resolution of your computer screen. The site then calculates your electricity and carbon use, giving you an equivalent in "equal to xx miles driven."

Think about your video meetings and ask the following questions:

- Is there an opportunity to handle any of them via email or phone instead of a video meeting?

- Can you reduce the time of a meeting?
- Do you need all attendees, or can the invite be more targeted?
- If you have standing meetings, can the time between them be increased?

On video calls, strive for efficiency to get through the topics and end the session early. Also, consider when it is appropriate to have cameras on vs. off. By turning your camera off, it is estimated that you can reduce the environmental impact by more than 95%. However, I don't think this is the solution for all meetings. In a world where many aren't going to physically live meetings as frequently, it is good to have moments when we do "see" others we are working with. The video call is a great connector if we use it thoughtfully and intentionally.

RAISE AWARENESS OF ONLINE CHOICES

As we move through our day-to-day activities online, we make choices regarding internet searches, purchases, and social media. Below are some tips and little-known facts about your online use. Consider shifting approaches in the areas below to reduce your impact as you surf the web.

Your Favorite Sites – A great place to start is understanding the environmental implications of your current social media use. There is a very simple calculater to determine your annual social media impact at www.comparethemarket.com.au/energy/features/social-carbon-footprint-calculator. You enter the average amount of time you spend each day on various social media platforms. Then, the system calculates the number of grams of CO_2 you use on an annual basis. The results are provided in grams. Keep in mind that driving a car one mile uses roughly 400 grams of CO_2 (*Document Display | NEPIS | US EPA*, n.d.).

Your Content – The content you engage with for viewing and sharing also impacts your carbon footprint. Streaming video has the greatest impact, followed by photos, then emojis, and finally text. When sharing, consider if the photo adds to the text and if the video accomplishes something that text and/or a photo can't. When scrolling consciously, spending less time on video-based platforms will also have a lighter impact.

Your Notifications – The notifications on your phone and desktop from email, social media, meeting reminders, and more are also adding to your carbon footprint. Consider turning these notifications off. This will not only reduce your carbon impact, but you may also find yourself feeling less stressed.

Your Connections – Using your phone on your mobile network requires at least twice as much carbon as using Wi-Fi. So, whenever possible, connect to social media, email, and web surfing while at a location with Wi-Fi. As you make this trade-off, ensure the Wi-Fi you use is secure.

Your Web Searches – The search engine you use also has an impact. Replacing your current search engine with Ecosia - www.ecosia.com - donates a tree for every forty-five searches you make.

Your Website – Another consideration for those who have a website for their business or personal use is the carbon load of that website and associated marketing. The load of your current site can be determined by visiting www.websitecarbon.com. You type in your URL, and the site calculates how you compare to other websites. From there, you can make changes that could lessen your impact.

REDUCE TIME SPENT WITH TECHNOLOGY

Statista completed a study in March of 2022, which indicated that the average person in the United States spends two hours and twenty-seven minutes daily on social media sites (*Global Daily Social Media Usage 2022 | Statista*, n.d.). For those with office jobs, a 2018 study indicated that office workers spend 6.5 hours of every workday in front of a screen (*Study: Average Worker Spends 1,700 Hours In Front Of Computer Screen - CBS New York*, 2018). Combine that with social media and personal use, and over half our waking hours are engaging with technology.

My last piece of technology use advice is to encourage you to take a break. Spend a day or two being conscious of when you are on a device and ask the question, "Could I be doing something else instead?" Reducing your time on devices will help the planet, but, more importantly, it can provide you with some peace and quiet to "just be." Relax and enjoy the day!

OFFICE TECHNOLOGY - RECYCLING

As we have discussed, office technology is being upgraded at a fast pace, and this is causing used equipment to pile up. Adding to the challenge, only 17.4% of e-waste generated annually is recycled (Admin, 2022). This is compounded by the personal complexity of recycling.

Because we typically pay a great deal for the devices we own, we sometimes struggle with the sunk cost we've put in and want to sell them to get money back. If you don't sell the device right away, the product will become obsolete, and then it goes into the pile of e-waste in the basement (at least, that's where mine ended up).

The other challenge is the data. All the data and information we have stored on the device needs to be backed up and then wiped clean from the device before selling or recycling. This takes time and is the second reason piles in the basement keep getting larger. The longer electronics sit in that pile, the fewer options you have for either repurposing the device or selling it to get some cash back.

The rest of this focus area will provide some tips and advice for preparing, selling, and recycling your old equipment. If you have a big pile of old electronics somewhere in your home, you can start slowly creating plans for the devices and getting them out of the house. At the same time, when newer devices reach the end of life, deal with them immediately and don't add them to the existing backlog.

PREPARING DEVICES

Getting your equipment ready for sale or recycling starts with removing all the data and wiping the device clean of information. While the task can seem daunting, once you dive in, you will find it goes faster than you think. Start by transferring all the content to an external hard drive. For extra security, you can consider having two duplicate backup drives.

After the information has been transferred, the next step is to wipe the content off the device. You will need to look up online how to do this on your specific device. There are a lot of sites and instructions, and it usually just takes a few clicks to make it happen. Once the information is removed, you are ready to sell or recycle.

SELLING DEVICES

Depending on the age of your equipment, resale is always an option. You can look at selling back to the manufacturer, posting in an online marketplace (eBay/Facebook), or looking for a buyback company.

For cell phones, check with www.gorecell.com. This company will recycle the phone parts and give you some cash, depending on the age and condition of the device.

If you choose to list in an online marketplace, take quite a few good photos and write a compelling description. I see a lot of postings that have one photo, the name of the device for sale, and a price. With this, I usually keep looking. I want to see several photos from different angles, an image with the device on so I see that it works, and one with all the cords and accessories that are included.

In the description, I want to know the size and dimensions, when it was purchased, how much it was used, and more. Any details you can provide help the buyer decide to choose your product. Presenting the product professionally will raise you up on the consideration list compared to those who give the bare minimum information.

RECYCLING DEVICES

In the US, it is illegal in some states to throw away electronics, so knowing how to recycle is important. Many communities have a few days a year for hazardous waste collection. Electronics are usually on the list of items accepted on these days. Check your municipality website to find dates and put the next one on your calendar. This deadline might be just the incentive you need to pull the data off the devices and get the pile out of your house. Other options exist for dropping off electronics throughout the year at electronic stores and recycling facilities. Look at www.earth911.org to find locations in your area.

MINIMIZING MAIL

A great place to start on the non-technology side of your office is reducing the amount of paper, magazines, and catalogs coming into the house. Statistics show that every person in the US receives 560 pieces of junk mail in a year (Velasco, 2009), and during that time, 100M trees are used to produce these pieces (D'Arcy, 2020). In addition, if we spend just 3 minutes each weekday processing junk mail, that is 13 hours each year just processing junk mail! Below are some tips and ideas for reducing paper flow in your home.

REDUCE INCOMING CATALOGUES AND JUNK MAIL

Many mailboxes overflow with magazines and catalogs that aren't read or used. Here are some ways to reduce the volume:

- **Magazines** – If you subscribe to magazines, consider shifting the subscription to digital. Or, if you find you aren't reading them, cancel the subscription to save money and paper.
- **Catalogs** – A great website to selectively remove your name from catalog lists is www.CatalogueChoice.org. This site allows you to select which catalogs you want to unsubscribe from, and then they handle the cancellations for you. The service is free, but you can donate to help fund the program if you choose.
- **Remove Your Name from Lists** – A more general site to remove your name from broader direct mail lists is www.dmachoice.org. This site also provides options to register the deceased, register as a caregiver, and remove your phone number from call lists.

SHIFT TRANSACTIONS ONLINE

After reducing the catalogs and magazines from your physical mail, the next step is to take some time and move any bills or other paperwork you continue to get in the mail over to digital, both the bill paying and paperless statements (like bank and investment statements). Many stats have been published on the positive environmental impact of making these moves. In addition to helping the planet, converting to paying just five bills online each month will save you $36/year in postage alone!

To start the process of converting any remaining bills or statements to paperless. Each time a bill or statement arrives in the mail, take 5 minutes to convert that bill or statement to online. Before you know it, the process will be complete.

OFFICE SUPPLIES

As we move into office products and supplies, the biggest area that comes to mind is paper. However, there are many other products to consider; pens and pencils, staplers, and post-it notes, to name a few.

CONSOLIDATE SUPPLIES

In my story, at the start of the chapter, I mentioned consolidating my office supplies into one location instead of having some in different parts of the house, like the office, kitchen, bedrooms, and more. Office supplies are a category where many households tend to over-purchase because the supplies are spread out in many different parts of the house.

If your office supplies aren't in one spot, I recommend this as a great first step. With all your supplies in one place, you can better understand when things are running out and have the time to look for a greener alternative. Defining a home base for your office supplies will let you track the inventory over time. And, as a bonus, you may be better able to find a new pen when you need it! Now, let's dive into office supplies.

PAPER

There are a LOT of facts available on the impact of paper on the environment. I believe the most important fact is that the pulp and paper industry is the world's fourth-largest industrial consumer of energy. (*Pulp and Paper*, n.d.). In addition, paper production uses more water to produce a ton of product than any other industry. These two facts don't even consider the 900M trees that paper/pulp mills cut down yearly.

Spend some time thinking about how paper is used around your home and determine if there are ways to reduce use overall. In addition to reducing the amount of paper used, consider more environmentally friendly paper when ready to buy more supplies. There are a lot of recycled paper options out there to consider. Some look just like regular paper, while others have the recycled content more visible. I really like the personality of those that show the fibers.

NOTEBOOKS AND PLANNERS

When looking for notebooks and planners, eco-friendly options are growing rapidly. Recycled paper content is a key ingredient to look for when you are shopping. Regardless of the type of notebook you prefer (traditional, spiral bound, composition), you will find a variety to choose from.

I've often wondered about recycling notebooks that are spiral-bound and/or have a fabric cover. You should separate the spiral from the paper for the spiral bound, as both pieces can be recycled. For fabric covers, there is mixed information on what to do. You can definitely pull out the paper and recycle that. For the cover, you will need to check with your municipality.

As you start to look for notebooks and planners, below are a few companies to consider:

- **EcoJot** – www.ecojot.com – Notebooks, planners, and stationery made with 100% recycled paper in a sustainable paper mill. Also, a portion of your purchase is donated to a global cause (different ones based on the product you select).

- **Paperage** – www.paperage.co – This company has a traditional-looking journal in various colors, all made from 100% recycled paper. They also have a pen and marker sets. Both are made with water-based ink but still in plastic shells.
- **Greenfield Paper** – www.greenfieldpaper.com – This company has notebooks made of hemp combined with recycled paper. They also have stationery and products made of seed paper that can be planted after use.

POST IT NOTES

Post It Notes are often an office staple. There are some mixed reviews online about the recyclability of the notes. In the end, you could check your local municipality to be sure, but most believe they are recyclable. When shopping for notes the next time, Post It now offers a product called "Greener Notes." These are made with a water-based adhesive and recycled paper. If you were looking to try some alternatives to Post It Notes, here are a few to consider. All can be purchased at popular retailers like Walmart and Amazon:

- **Slicky Notes** – These notes don't use an adhesive and cling to the wall with static. You can move them around by pressing with your finger. They are 100% recyclable and non-toxic.
- **McSquares** – These are reusable, sticky whiteboard notes in different shapes and sizes. They are produced sustainably and can be used for five years.
- **Virtual Sticky Notes** – An alternative to physical notes will be to use virtual ones on the computer. Microsoft has a product to post notes on your desktop. In addition, virtual brainstorming software (like Miro) enables virtual participants to post notes on a virtual wall.

PENCILS

There are two challenges with pencils, wood, and lead. Over the last 20 years, many alternatives have been introduced. Graphite is now used instead of lead, and innovative solutions like recycled newspaper are being used to replace the wood. There are lots of brands and choices on the market. Here are three to get you started:

- **Sprout Pencils** – These can be planted after use and will grow a variety of plants. www.sproutworld.com
- **Treesmart Recycled Newspaper** – As the name suggests, these are made of recycled newspapers. www.treesmart.com
- **Ecotree Recycled Rainbow Paper** – Besides being sustainable, these have a fun design. They can be found at popular retailers like Amazon and Walmart.

PENS

According to Earth911, Americans throw away 1.6 billion disposable pens every year (Earth911, 2020). These pens end up in landfills and are often made of harmful plastics. Like pencils, many alternatives have been developed in the last decade. Below are a few brands that can be purchased on Amazon to consider putting on your list:

- **Agile Eco-Friendly Pens** – These are 100% recyclable, and the price point is good.
- **Conscience Concepts Cork & Recycled Wheat Straw** – Nice design and 100% recyclable.
- **Bamboo Retractable Pens** – A little more expensive but have a nice design.

HIGHLIGHTERS AND MARKERS

There are also interesting alternatives to highlighters, like moving from the traditional marker to a highlighting pencil. They come in a variety of colors and are suggested to be a better option for left-handers because they don't smear like a traditional highlighter. Two brands to consider from retailers like Amazon include Eco Highlighter Pencils and Stubby Pencil Studios.

Markers are a different challenge. This category is difficult to find eco-friendly alternatives. Searches don't produce alternatives to the plastic casing. The best are those with recycled plastic and water-based ink. The Office Depot brand (sold at other stores) has a low-odor marker made with recycled materials for whiteboard markers.

OTHER SUPPLIES

There are many other supplies occupying space in our office. I know this chapter can't cover all of them. Below, I've collected a list of a few that may be in your office with some tips about what to look for when shopping for a green alternative:

- **Binders and Folders** – The most prevalent issue with binders is their plastic cover. When looking for alternatives, search the term "naked binders" for some plastic-free options.
- **Staplers** – If you don't typically staple more than 6-8 sheets of paper together, consider a "stapleless stapler." If you search online, you will see many sizes and options available. While the staplers are made of plastic, they make recycling paper easier as there is no need to remove the staple.

- **Scissors** – When buying new scissors, look for handles made of recycled plastic. While there aren't more eco-friendly options that I could find, at least we aren't adding new plastic to the mix.
- **Paperclips** – Acco offers a paperclip made from 100% recycled steel wire. One thing to avoid in this category is the paper clips that are covered with rubbery plastic. The decorative colors might look good, but they can't be recycled. These can be found at Office Depot and other retailers.

SCHOOL SUPPLIES

Other specialized supplies are on the list for those with children in the home. Many articles have been written online with many products and tips for eco-friendly school supplies. I recommend doing some quick searches if you want to dive deeper. A few companies and things to keep in mind are below:

- **Crayons** – The biggest challenge with crayons is that they are made with paraffin wax which is petroleum based. This makes recycling them a challenge. When shopping for crayons, avoid those with paraffin and look for alternatives like beeswax and soy. A couple of brands to get you started are Prang (soy-based) www.prang.com and Honeysticks (beeswax) www.honeysticks.com.
- **Glue** – This is a tougher category, and there aren't a lot of alternatives available. The main challenges with glue are that it is made with a petroleum-based ingredient, and the packaging is plastic for liquid glue and glue sticks. Three brands to consider are Elmer's Earth Friendly glue, Coccoina, and plant-based Onyx Green. All can be found on Amazon.
- **Notebooks** – Look for recycled paper. One company to consider is Roaring Spring Paper Products (www.rspaperproducts.com/). Their

website has notebook and folder products for school like the three and five-subject notebooks that many older children use for school. While you can't purchase on the site, you can search for the products you want and then look for them at your favorite retailer.

- **Backpacks** – This is a very fun category to find something both eco-friendly and stylish. By searching "upcycled backpacks," you will find backpacks made of all kinds of materials, from old billboards to truck tarps, seatbelts, and more. With the variety available, you can find a design with a perfect, unique style. Start with general searches or a website like Etsy.

- **Lunch Boxes** – The key when it comes to lunches is to look for containers that will be used all year long. This includes the lunch box itself as well as the containers inside that hold all the food. Replacing the paper bags and Ziploc bags is the goal. More on this topic was covered in the Dining Room chapter.

FAST FIVE IN THE OFFICE

Five steps you can take quickly to make an impact and begin to celebrate some wins!

1. **Reduce Mail** – Remove your name from mailing lists using cataloguechoice.org and dmachoice.org. Also, shift your monthly bills and statements online.

2. **Recycle Electronics** – These old devices are likely taking up space (in your home and nagging in your mind). Take a day or two and remove the content. Then, leverage Earth911 to find a drop-off in your area. They will be out of your space and provide you with peace of mind.

3. **Electronic Shut Down and Charging Routines** – Create a routine at the end of each day for shutting down your computer overnight. In addition, charge devices during the day and unplug the charger from the wall when charging is complete.

4. **Online Habits** – Reduce the amount of time spent online and on social media. Connect to Wi-Fi if you are on your phone. Finally, be conscious of what you are posting; stick to text or a photo, if possible, as video wastes more resources.

5. **Writing Utensils** – As you run out of pencils, pens, markers, crayons, and highlighters, search online for replacements that don't contain plastic, lead, and other harmful materials.

THE BEDROOM

A s we look at the bedroom, we will cover all the places people sleep in your home. The family room chapter covered making basic updates to the rooms, including painting, furniture, window treatments, and décor.

In this chapter, we will start with my story and then explore three additional focus areas: Mattresses, Linens, and Aroma. Each focus area will dive deeper into the category and provide ideas on reducing your environmental impact.

MY ONE SHADE GREENER STORY

My bedroom story is a relatively easy one; the master bedroom has pretty much been the same for the last 20 years. The furniture is a classic design that has stayed in style over the years, and the paint color and décor have been something I enjoyed spending time in. You will see below that I'm ready for a refresh, but overall, the room has had a very light impact.

The other bedrooms in our home have been similar. I purchased good furniture for the kids' nurseries with the intention that all but the crib would last them through their childhood. For each of them, we bought a twin bed when they were around three, updated the décor (paint/linens/desk/accessories) when they went into middle school, and gave their rooms another refresh mid-way through high school. The last refresh included moving to larger beds, new mattresses, and updating some dressers.

While the comforters in the kids' bedrooms changed as they grew up, the bedding in the master stayed the same. We also bought very few new bath linens. What we had worked just fine, and we use them until they wear out. I struggle to spend money on new bath linens. When I do, I'm always looking for a deal. Next round, I need to look more at the brand, materials, and manufacturing process.

The last area of the bedroom is the "aroma" category. Out of my whole family, I'm probably the least likely to burn a candle or use a diffuser. I have bought candles as décor, but sometimes I feel I'm wasting money if I burn them. I'm starting to have more interest in this area, though. There are many more eco-friendly options than traditional candles, and I'm intrigued by the use of scent to promote sleep, encourage focus, or provide energy.

UP NEXT IN MY HOME – I'm getting ready for an update to the bedroom, which has been the same for nearly 20 years. I plan to freshen the color from deep purple to something lighter and brighter. I've already decided to keep the furniture. However, as mentioned in the family room chapter, I painted the drawer with a darker metallic color to update the look.

I need a new mattress. I've been looking at the Avocado brand, but I'm struggling with its impact on my pocketbook. Likely, I'll also do a bit of thrift store shopping to see if I can find some cool, new-to-me accessories and wall hangings for the room that will change the feel

This chapter also got me thinking about aromatherapy. I want to learn more and start to try working with essential oils to incorporate more scents into my everyday life.

MATTRESSES

Mattresses have many challenges related to their impact on the planet. The materials used to produce popular brands contain petroleum and volatile organic compounds (VOCs). The manufacturing process and transportation are also carbon heavy. And there is not yet a good recycling infrastructure in all states. This means many old mattresses are thrown in landfills, causing additional problems.

PURCHASING

When purchasing a new mattress, try to avoid polyurethane foams and fire retardants. Instead, look for materials like organic cotton, wool, and natural latex, which have a lighter impact.

There are third-party certifications for mattresses, including Greenguard and Oeko-Tex. For natural latex, look for the Global Organic Latex Standard Certification. Cotton should be 100% organic. Another Certification to consider is MadeSafe, which ensures harmful chemicals aren't used in production. You can find many products for the home evaluated on their website at www.MadeSafe.org.

As you look for eco-friendly mattresses, below are some brands to add to your list:

- **Avocado**: This brand is rated high for healthy ingredients and comfort. The materials include organic cotton, wool, and natural latex. The mattresses are handmade in the US and have many certifications. www.avacadogreenmattress.com

- **Plushbeds**: These mattresses are also made in the US and carry several certifications. They are made of organic cotton, wool, latex, and FSC-certified wood frames. www.plushbeds.com
- **My Green Mattress:** This brand has Greenguard Gold certification and is manufactured in the US. The mattresses are made of organic cotton, organic wool, and OEKO-TEX-certified latex.
- **Awara**: These mattresses are certified organic latex, cotton, and natural wool. They have several certifications and are also considered good for "hot sleepers." www.mygreenmattress.com
- **Brentwood Home Organic Mattresses**: These mattresses are made of organic latex and cotton, coconut husks, wool, and CertiPUR memory foam. They are Greenguard Gold certified. www.brentwoodhome.com
- **Saatva**: This brand is manufactured in the US and uses plant-based materials, natural latex, organic cotton, and wool. www.saatva.com

DIY Mattress??!! – During my research, I came across an interesting company that provides materials for making your own mattress. You purchase the kit, which includes cloth tubes, then use buckwheat hulls to fill the tubes. You can also make lavender hull pillows and shredded cork-filled bean bags. The company is out of New York, and I found the products to be an interesting alternative to consider. You can find all the details on their website at www.openyoureyesbedding.com.

RECYCLING

While the materials in mattresses can be easily recycled, there isn't a good infrastructure to recycle them. This means, according to Earth911, that we throw away 15 to 20 million mattresses each year (Mazzoni, 2018)!

The Mattress Recycling Program has made headway in four participating states in the US. Those states include California, Connecticut, Rhode Island, and Oregon. This company will take old mattresses, disassemble them, and recycle them accordingly.

For those not in the four states listed, you'll need to do a bit more research to ensure your old mattresses are recycled. The first and easiest option is to talk to the company you purchase the new mattresses from and see if they will recycle the old mattress. You need to be sure to ask if they are recycling, not just disposing of the mattress. The second option is a quick search of www.Earth911.org to see if there is somewhere near you that recycles. However, with this option, you'll have to have a way to get the bulky piece from your bedroom to the location. If neither option is available, you can find companies who will take and recycle the mattress for a fee.

LINENS

Linens are found all over the house in every bedroom, bathroom, and even the kitchen. There are environmental considerations when purchasing, habits to consider during use to extend their life, and impacts when it's time to dispose of or recycle. This section will cover all three areas to ensure you find the right products that balance the impact on people, planet, and your pocketbook.

Because the linens are spread throughout the house, we can sometimes forget what we already own. You could consolidate what you own in one place to take inventory before going out to purchase something new. Taking stock ensures you don't have a new set or two tucked in a place you had forgotten.

PURCHASING

Linens in your home serve many different roles; sheets in the master bedroom vs. sheets for a toddler, a pillow for yourself and someone else who likes different firmness, towels in the guest bedroom vs. the master, hand towels in the kitchen, and hand towels in a half bath. For each of the roles, there are different considerations like "needs to be really soft," "must have good absorption," and "king size." Once you know the requirements, you can dive into the brands and materials to find the right eco-friendly alternatives for your situation.

WHAT TO LOOK FOR

When purchasing linens, there are several materials to choose from. Below is a short description of the most popular:

- **Organic Cotton**: Cotton is the most known and popular alternative. The fabric is easy to find, less expensive, and easy to take care of. When shopping, ensure you look for the 100% organic label to ensure pesticides weren't used. One negative with cotton is the high water levels needed in the production process.
- **Bamboo**: This material is softer than cotton, doesn't trap heat and moisture (which keeps dust and allergens away), and is very durable.
- **Natural Linen**: This material looks beautiful and is stronger than cotton. However, like your favorite pair of linen pants, they will wrinkle. If the wrinkled look isn't for you, another alternative could be a better choice. Look for 100% natural fibers.

- **Natural Hemp**: Hemp products can look like linen and feel a bit softer. Like natural linen, the material is stronger than cotton, with hemp being up to eight times stronger. This material is also more prone to wrinkles than cotton.
- **Soy**: Soybean fiber is a good alternative for sensitive skin. The antibacterial and hypoallergenic material will help prevent irritants like dust and bacteria.
- **Eucalyptus**: Eucalyptus fiber is an alternative that is soft, resistant to dust and mold, and naturally cooling.
- **Tencel**: Tencel is the brand name for the raw material lyocell. This material is made from natural wood fibers from eucalyptus, birch, or beech trees. Tencel is an alternative to silk and has the benefits of being antibacterial and moisture-wicking. Products made of Tencel are completely recyclable and have a more minor production impact than other materials.

When considering any of these materials, always ensure that no chemicals, insecticides, or pesticides were used during production. Some third-party certifications to keep your eye out for are the Global Organic Textile Standard, OEKO-TEX, and Better Cotton Initiative.

Pillows and Comforters – You will also want to consider the fill material and the top fabric when purchasing pillows and comforters. There are a variety of options available. The brands to consider in the next section have eco-friendly pillow and comforter alternatives.

BRANDS TO CONSIDER

When purchasing linens, consider how long you plan to use the item before recycling and buying again. This might help with considering what you are willing to pay. For example, a set of sheets that are $200 seems much more reasonable when you think you will own them for five years and use them daily. That breaks down to just $0.11 per day, which is not bad for something you will enjoy every day.

Below are some eco-friendly brands to consider as you start your search. Several of these brands not only have bedroom and bathroom products but also carry décor and other products that could be used throughout your home.

- **West Elm:** This mainstream brand offers several eco-friendly material options, including organic cotton, linen, Tencel, and hemp. Many items carry certifications. www.westelm.com
- **Made Trade**: They have many material options available and note attributes about each brand they sell, like vegan, fair trade, and women owned. www.madetrade.com
- **Boll & Branch**: They carry mattresses, bedding, and bathroom items. The products are fair trade certified and sent in recycled packaging. www.bollandbranch.com
- **American Blossom Linens:** Products are made in the US with 100% organic cotton grown in Texas. They carry bedding (including crib sheets), towels, and other products. www.americanblossomlinens.com
- **Pact:** This brand carries several options of bedding and towels and has clothing lines. Products are made of organic cotton, and they implement carbon offsets for their products. www.wearpact.com
- **Parachute**: This brand features premium sheets, towels, rugs, throws, pillows, and more. The company is 100% carbon neutral, and most products are handmade by artisans. www.parachutehome.com
- **Under the Canopy**: This brand carries bedroom and bathroom products. They are fair trade certified and use eco-friendly dyes in their textiles. www.underthecanopy.com

- **Shades of Green**: This brand features bedding made of linen. They also offer a lot of products outside the bed and bath. However, price points are higher. www.shadesofgreen.com
- **Coyuchi**: They have a wide range of organic bedroom and bathroom products in many styles that will fit almost any home. www.coyuchi.com
- **Cozy Earth**: This brand carries bedding, bath products, and clothing. The products are made of bamboo. These sheet sets are more expensive. However, they are noted for being 2-3 degrees cooler, moisture-wicking, and having many certifications. www.cozyearth.com

CARING FOR BEDDING AND TOWELS

If you purchase eco-friendly products that cost more than the mainstream alternatives, you can ensure you extend their life with careful care. The recommendation is to wash the linens once a week. This schedule removes the oils and dirt that accumulate from our bodies which is more harmful to the fibers of the products than the laundry products.

Sheets: When washing bed linens, they should be in a load of their own to avoid washing them with other materials that could accelerate wear. They can be washed using tips from the laundry room chapter, i.e., in cold water with eco-friendly detergents and dryer sheet alternatives.

Pillows: To extend the life of pillows, ensure you use pillow covers in addition to pillowcases. Wash the pillowcase every week, the pillow cover once a month, and the pillow itself twice a year. Down pillows typically last longer (5-10 years) than other materials (2-3 years). I also read that you can put your pillow out in the sun if it's lost some of its "fluff," and that will bring it back and extend its life.

Comforters and Duvets: If you have a duvet or comforter with an insert, it's recommended to wash the outer layer once a month. The insert can be washed less frequently—about twice a year.

Towels: Towels are like sheets. Wash with other towels (or your sheets) and no other clothing that could damage the material. Using just one towel for the whole week is also not recommended. The most recommended frequency is using the towel 3-4 times between washing.

RECYCLING

The EPA has been tracking the manufacturing and disposal of towels, sheets, and pillowcases since 1990. In the most recent year of data (2018), the EPA estimated that 1.5M tons were produced and just 15.8% were recycled. These rates are double the levels of 1990 (*Textiles: Material-Specific Data | US EPA*, 2017).

When disposing of linens, you could try to sell or give away those with little use. However, most of us likely use our linens until they wear out. You could use old linens as rags in the garage or cut them into squares for dusting around the house.

Another great alternative is to consider donating them to a local animal shelter. The shelters can repurpose the pieces for both cleaning and animal bedding. A challenge in this category is that there aren't recycling alternatives. So, use your linens until you need new ones, then try to repurpose the materials or donate them to animal shelters whenever possible.

CANDLES AND AROMA

When adding a fresh scent to your home, candles and air freshener sprays are the go-to alternatives for most. This focus area will provide tips on what to look for when purchasing your next candle or spray. In addition, we'll look at some less popular and even DIY alternatives that achieve the same result of a fresh-smelling home. With all the choices, I'm sure you can find the right fit for your personality, pocketbook, and the planet.

If your home is anything like mine, products to provide a fresh scent are EVERYWHERE! There are at least a couple of candles, possibly a diffuser, some oils, and more in every room of the house. Pulling these items into one location can help you understand what you already have and know when it's time to purchase new ones. I started moving mine to one place and then sorting by "season" (e.g., cinnamon in fall) so that we know the choices as we enter each time of the year and don't overbuy.

CANDLES

Candles add a wonderful ambiance to a room, like the flickering glow and the beautiful scent; plus, they are an easy and inexpensive addition to your home. It's hard to imagine that burning candles might have negative effects. Yet, the ingredients used to create the candle can produce soot and fumes that negatively impact both the people in your home and the planet. Below are considerations to look for as you shop:

- **Soy**: Soy candles are slow burning, and you can consider how the soybeans were produced (pesticide free if possible). Also, look for cotton or wood wicks.
- **Beeswax**: As with any product, the more you learn about the manufacturing process, the better. Good quality beeswax candles will have a darker amber coloring.
- **Scent**: Look for essential oils and natural, not manufactured fragrances.

- **Packaging**: Candles in jars lead to jars you need to dispose of. Take that into consideration and possibly consider free-standing candles. However, these will need to be watched more closely when burning.

Light Green: These are made with more eco-friendly ingredients and come in traditional packaging.

- **Mrs. Meyers Clean Day Soy Candles** – This mainstream brand can be found easily at many large retailers. They are packaged in glass jars, but the ingredients are better than mainstream candles, and the price point is good. www.mrsmeyers.com
- **Ever Spring** – This brand can also be found at major retailers like Target, Walmart, and Amazon. The 100% soy candles are USDA biobased certified and use essential oils for their scent.
- **Swan Creek Candle Company** – While not at the big box stores, I wanted to feature a brand from the town I grew up in, Swanton, Ohio. This brand uses locally grown soybeans to create their soy wax candles and ships them in recycled packaging. www.swancreekcandle.com.
- **P.F. Candle Company** – This company is another smaller brand that started as an Etsy shop out of California and has grown over time. Their candles are made from 100% soy wax produced in the US and are vegan, cruelty-free, and phthalate-free. www.pfcandleco.com

Dark Green: These are made with more eco-friendly ingredients and have eco-friendly packaging.

- **Slow North** – Soy candles with cotton wicks and essential oils for the scent. While they are still in a glass container, the lids are made with sustainable cork. www.slownorth.com

- **Grow Fragrance** – This company has reusable candle vessels. You purchase the vessel with your first order, and then you can buy candle inserts in recyclable aluminum containers. This eliminates waste and saves money over time. www.growfragrance.com
- **Ranger Station** – These soy-based essential oil candles are contained in high-quality whiskey glasses. They also include a cocktail recipe with each candle. www.rangerstation.co

DIY Green: The web is full of DIY candle options. You can buy individual ingredients, kits and even attend classes to learn how to make your own. If this is a hobby of interest, I suggest diving in and finding the right next step for you!

ROOM SPRAYS

An alternative to candles is a room spray. Natural sprays use essential oils rather than synthetic perfumes, formaldehyde, and VOCs. These can be used for freshening a room or targeted for a particular purpose; examples include lavender sprays for sleep or peppermint to increase focus.

Light Green: Room sprays with better ingredients and traditional packaging.

- **Grow Fragrance** – Mentioned above in candles, Grow has air sprays that are 100% plant-based and toxin-free. Here, they are listed as light green because they don't have alternatives to the spray bottles (no large refill options). www.growfragrance.com
- **Mrs. Meyers Clean Day Room Freshener** – These products are made with essential oils and plant-based ingredients. www.mrsmeyers.com
- **Ever Spring** – Non-toxic with a hint of lavender smell. Found at Amazon, Target, and Walmart.

Dark Green: Better ingredients and eco-friendly packaging.

- **Refillism** – This brand has vanilla and lavender sprays made of plant-based ingredients. You purchase a spray bottle and then use refillable pouches. The pouches can then be sent back to the manufacturer for recycling. www.refillism.com
- **Grove** – A recyclable glass bottle is provided in the first purchase, then you buy refill concentrate (just add water). www.grove.co

DIY Green: Room sprays are easily created with just a few ingredients. You use water and your choice of essential oil. Then, you need an additive like alcohol, witch hazel, or sea salt to get the water and oil to combine appropriately. Place the mixture in a spray bottle, and you are ready to go!

Here is a sample recipe to get you started. Use a 4oz glass spray bottle, add 4 tablespoons of water, 1 tablespoon of Witch Hazel or Vodka, 10 drops of vanilla, and 10 drops of lavender essential oil. Shake to mix and then spray around the room.

ESSENTIAL OIL DIFFUSERS

Essential oil diffusers have become a popular alternative to candles in recent years. You purchase a diffuser and select the right oils for your situation and mood. When purchasing a diffuser, keep in mind the size of the room and the material of the diffuser; look for eco-friendly alternatives to plastic. Two options to consider are the Vitruvi Stone Diffuser (www.vitruvi.com) and the Happy Place Lava Rock Diffuser (www.happyplacestore.com). Etsy (www.etsy.com) is another great shopping spot for alternatives like ceramic or terra cotta.

Always research the company you purchase essential oils from and look in detail at the ingredients. You want to make sure you buy essential oils, not fragrance ones. The brand should list the plant the oil comes from, and it should have additional ingredients. Three brands to consider include Plant Therapy (www.planttherapy.com), Mountain Rose (www.mountainroseherbs.com), and Thrive Market (www.thrivemarket.com).

DIY Green: If you have the time and interest, you can make your own essential oils. There are options for purchasing a still (relatively expensive) and other options using a crockpot in your kitchen.

REED DIFFUSERS

Reed Diffusers are like a candle without the flame. Considerations to ensure your selections are environmentally friendly include the reeds (look for bamboo or rattan), the oil (shop like the essential oil diffusers above), and the container (look for glass). There are many great options available on Etsy. You can shop around for fragrances and containers that are right for you.

DIY Green: A low-cost alternative is to create your own reed diffusers. Packs of 100 reeds can be purchased for under $10 on Amazon and will last a long time. You could look around the house or a nearby thrift shop for small vases or jars to hold the reeds. Then, you add a mixture of carrier oil, essential oils, and an additive like alcohol to mix the oils and get the mixture to move up the reeds.

A simple recipe to get you started is to mix ¼ cup of sweet almond oil, 1 tablespoon of Vodka, and 20-25 drops of essential oils in any scent combination you prefer. Mix and add the reeds. You can flip the reeds each day or two to freshen the scent. The mixture should last a month or two.

POTPOURRI

Potpourri is another alternative to add fragrance to a room. If you purchase potpourri, I recommend looking for local makers or a shop on Etsy that sells organic potpourri.

DIY Green: There are many ways to bring the scent of the outdoors into your home. Ideas include:

- **Bowl of Dried Ingredients** –Fill a bowl with items like pinecones, dried flowers, cinnamon, dried fruit, and more.
- **Cinnamon** – Boil cinnamon in water or add to apples in a crock pot for a wonderful fall smell.
- **Pomanders** – Create by pressing cloves into an orange. This is often done during holidays.

FAST FIVE IN THE BEDROOM

Five steps you can take quickly to make an impact and begin to celebrate some wins!

1. **Change Linen Washing Habits** – To extend the life of your linens, wash them once a week with other linens, use cold water, and follow washing tips/products from the laundry room chapter.

2. **Donate** – Collect all your towels, sheets, and blankets that you no longer use. For those that still have good life in them, donate to a non-profit in your area. If they are too worn for their intended use, donate them to an animal shelter for use as cleaning towels or animal bedding.

3. **Shift Your "Aroma" Products** – Scan the options in this chapter to replace traditional paraffin candles and find an interesting alternative. Purchase one and give it a try!

4. **Find Brands for the Future** – Since mattresses and linens aren't something you purchase often and tend to cost a bit more, spend time looking at the brands in this chapter and find a few that resonate with you. Then, you'll have a list at your fingertips when the purchase need arises.

5. **Consolidate Products to One Location** – To better understand what you already own and not accidentally over-purchase, consolidate aroma products and linens (towels and bedding) into one location. This can be a one-time activity or designate an area you keep as the "central hub."

THE CLOSET

While, technically, closets are an extension of another room, they are an important part of our home and hold clothes, shoes, coats, and accessories we wear every day. With all the complexity and opportunities to lessen your environmental impact, I decided that this "room" needed to have a chapter all its own. We'll talk about the entire lifecycle of clothing and accessories, from what to bring into your home to when it comes time to move pieces out.

The chapter will start with my story and then move into six focus sections: Shift Your Perspective, Capsule Wardrobes, Exploring Your Style, Connecting with the Secondhand Community, Recycling, and Purchasing New. Each focus area will dive deeper into the impacts and provide ideas to lessen your environmental impact.

MY ONE SHADE GREENER STORY

The closet may be the Achilles heel of my aspirations for a greener home, specifically the clothes. I've tried and tried different strategies over the years that I'll describe below, but it is clear to me that this is an area I will always need to revisit and keep trying to find the right solutions as I continue my journey to lessen my footprint. Not only would this be lighter on the planet, but also my pocketbook and my peace of mind.

Ever since I can remember, clothes have been important to me. I like shopping to find the perfect piece for an event or every day. I especially like finding unique items that express my personality and are pieces you don't see every day. I mix and match what I have to avoid wearing "the same thing" more than once a month. In fact, if I'm totally transparent, I've even used different methods to track my outfit each day so I don't end up in a monthly meeting wearing the same thing as last month! I realize this is a bit over the top, but I think it illustrates how I have enjoyed and focused on what to wear over the years. Today, I have moved away from tracking, but I still enjoy having a wardrobe I love.

When shopping for new items, I try to discover eco-friendly brands. I know I have an opportunity to learn more about the brand alternatives and widen my consideration set. I also love searching for unique pieces from independent makers at art fairs and on Etsy. Occasionally, I'll purchase secondhand. However, I'm much less likely to purchase secondhand clothes than I am to buy secondhand furniture and home décor.

Regarding shoes, jewelry, bags, and other accessories, I'm much better than with the clothes themselves. I'm an under buyer of shoes and bags. I don't love to shop for them as many others do, and I will tend to keep the ones I love until they wear out.

With jewelry, I look for unique pieces that make a statement. Typically, I purchase a piece or two from art fairs each year, which keeps my collection growing without much impact. In addition, about ten years ago, I started making upcycled jewelry from wine and beer bottles, using labels, glass, corks, and bottle tops to create unique designs. This remains a fun hobby; if I don't have the right accessory, I make my own!

MY CAPSULE WARDROBE ASPIRATION

In the last five years, I have experimented with capsule wardrobes. Much of what you read suggests that a capsule is thirty pieces of clothing or less. I was almost there during the height of COVID lockdowns. I realized working with a smaller choice set was far easier when I wasn't leaving the house.

I'm now settling into a lighter impact where I'm doing "expanded" capsules by season. I define a few colors that are my base year-round and then shop my closet to fill the capsule before purchasing something new. This helps curate my clothes into just the pieces I love and want to wear. I still have room for improvement. However, I do feel I'm slowly making progress.

RECYCLING, DONATING OR SELLING

While I have started reducing the size of my closet, I struggle to address getting unused clothes out of the house. They are like the electronics—in bags in the basement that need to be sold or donated. I struggle with "sunk costs" and feel my unwanted items are worth more than the market will pay, so they sit and, ironically, continue to lose value. I know there is a problem, but I just haven't found the system to solve it yet.

OTHER CLOSETS

While I've focused the story above on my own closet, many of the issues described spread to the other bedrooms and closets in my home. In particular, I remember an overwhelming time back in about 2015. I still had bins of baby clothes in my basement, and the kids were both in high school! As they were growing up, there was so much going on I didn't feel I could deal with getting rid of the clothes and so I stuffed them in bins and put them in the basement—out of sight, out of mind. That year, I

FINALLY held a garage sale and sold most of what we had. Then, I donated what was left. This process made me wish I had done better dealing with the outgrown items along the way. This would have provided peace of mind that I didn't have a pile of unused clutter in our space and the clothes were being used and enjoyed by other children elsewhere.

UP NEXT IN MY HOME – When it comes to my closet, what's next is always the same: Keep making progress and trying new techniques to pare down and curate more. As I move into the next season, I will follow some of the tips in this chapter and try the forty base pieces plus capsule. I haven't tried that one before, and I think it might work better. I also aspire to focus on the bags of clothes in the basement and get those cleared out of the space, giving me peace of mind and some literal space to use for another purpose. Writing this chapter has reminded me that the pieces continue to lose value each day as they sit there. I'm also planning to host a clothing swap with friends and co-workers. This would be a fun social event and allow us to clean and freshen our closets.

SHIFT YOUR PERSPECTIVE

Over the last two decades, fast fashion has grown around the globe, and closets in our homes have increased in size. Along with these shifts, the impact of fashion on the environment has also steadily increased. Ironically, more clothes at less expensive prices still haven't solved the fundamental challenge many of us face daily when we question, "What should I wear?" In fact, studies have shown that most of us wear 20% of our clothes 80% of the time (Lowe, 2018).

I can't decide if I'm approaching the closet a little differently than the other rooms because it needs a different approach or because I've struggled with this room and want to provide even more ideas to help you get started on a path toward a greener closet. Either way, this first focus area is dedicated to mindset shifts foundational to moving away from fast fashion to a more curated, higher quality, and less "full" closet. I hope you find the tips here helpful as you begin your journey.

BUY LESS

The easiest way to be greener in your closet, like all the other rooms of the home, is to buy less. Purchasing less creates more space in your closet, peace of mind from fewer daily choices, a lighter impact on the planet, and more money in your pocketbook.

According to Statista, Americans purchased thirty-two pieces of clothing per capita in 2021 (Smith, n.d.). From the same source, the 2020 data indicated that the individual spend on those pieces of clothing was just over $600 (down from $800 in 2019). So, that means an average family of four brings nearly 150 items into the home for $2400 each year; that is just the average! That means some families/individuals are spending and bringing in even more.

The life stage does come into play here. For example, if you have young children growing out of clothes rapidly. However, I think this provides a good metric for adults. Do you know how many pieces of clothing, shoes, and accessories you purchase each year? Are you above or below the $600 per person each year? We are all at different stages of our journey, so don't use this number as "good" or "bad"; just use it as a reference when creating your personal plan. Maybe you set a goal of buying 10% less (whatever 10% might be) next year and then another 10% after that. Eventually, you will get to a level that feels right for you.

QUESTION YOUR PURCHASES

When shopping, a strategy for buying less is to question all the items. Make sure you aren't purchasing just another version of something you own, like another pair of black pants or jeans. It would be far better to have one or two pairs of black pants you absolutely love than to have five or six that are just OK.

Another piece of advice comes from Livia Firth, who began a campaign called #30Wears. Her philosophy is that every time you buy something new, you should ask, "Will I wear this at least thirty times?" If the answer is no, you shouldn't buy the item.

A special event might be the exception to this rule. In these situations, you might want to consider renting an outfit. There are a variety of companies like Rent the Runway that offer a wide selection at reasonable rental prices

QUALITY OVER QUANTITY – SAME BUDGET, BETTER/FEWER PIECES

A sometimes-difficult shift to make is to start spending more on individual pieces of clothing. The fast fashion industry has trained us to look for pieces as inexpensive as $20 or $30. As you move to an eco-friendlier wardrobe, you can try not to increase the amount of money you spend but buy fewer higher-quality items. You will start to really think about the pieces you are buying to ensure that they fit well, and you will get a lot of wear out of them.

We have been trained over the years to want "more." I'm still personally working on the shift in mindset from "more" to "better." I'm getting there, but it has taken time. You will also start to think differently about investing in pieces. Spend the money on what you wear every day vs. things purchased just for a special occasion. As mentioned in the last section, consider renting some things which may enable you to save money that can be invested in something like a great pair of jeans you'll wear weekly.

Over time, your high-quality, curated pieces will build up, and you will have that wardrobe that feels perfect for you. I'm on the journey and will keep that as my inspiration to continue.

TAKE GOOD CARE OF YOUR CLOTHES

When you purchase less and have more pieces you love, taking good care of them is critical. In the laundry room chapter, there is a lot of information on products and techniques that will be gentler on your clothing. In addition, there are two pieces of advice worth mentioning here.

First, find a great tailor. If you have clothes you love, make sure they fit you perfectly. This will make you want to keep them even longer. The other advantage of having a tailor at the ready is knowing who to go to when there is an issue—pants need hemming, a seam rips, or something else.

Second, keep two products in or near your closet, a steamer, and a lint remover/fabric shaver. The steamer would be preferred as an efficient and gentler alternative to an iron. The lint remover/fabric shaver can get the pill off clothing and prolong the life of knits. Below are some brands to consider for fabric shavers or lint removers.

Light Green: Gleener Ultimate Fuzz Remover Fabric Shaver & Lint Remover. This option doesn't use throw-away sticky tape. While this product is made of plastic which isn't ideal, it has three interchangeable edges to de-pill fabrics of all types. No batteries are needed, and this tool can be used again and again. www.gleener.com

Dark Green: These options don't use throw-away sticky tape **AND** are made without plastic.

- **Grove Two-Sided Lint Brush**: This brush has a fabric side to remove lint and dust, while the other side has rubber bristles to pick up larger lint and hair. The brush is reusable and made from recycled plastic and bamboo. www.grove.co
- **Ruri Lint Remover**: This reusable lint remover has a copper head and beech wood handle. Purchase at major retailers like Amazon, Target, and Walmart.
- **Redecker Lint Brush**: This lint brush is made with sustainably harvested beechwood and sustainably sourced rubber for the bristles. www.redecker.de

CAPSULE WARDROBES

Capsule wardrobes are often mentioned when discussing minimalism and eco-friendly living. They are used by people who love clothes and shopping and those who would rather do just about anything than go shopping and dealing with their closet.

While there is a lot of conversation around capsules, there is no aligned formula on what a capsule is. Some rules say the capsule has just ten pieces, while others could allow up to 100. If 100 seems like a lot to you, I recommend you take a reading break, head to your closet, and start counting all the clothing, shoes, purses, and accessories you have. When you reach 100, what percent of your closet have you counted? For many, you're likely under 25%.

THINKING ABOUT HOW TO APPROACH

I think the best way to go with capsules is to try something and then learn and adjust as you move forward. I'm still finding my way. However, I have learned some things that work for me. I think about capsules by season. Here in Michigan, the clothing you wear in January is VERY different than in August. I "flip" my closet four times, i.e., December through February, March through May, June through August, and September through November. Clothing that is off-season is kept in baskets on the shelves grouped by type, like tops, bottoms, shoes, etc. I was keeping the baskets by seasons but realized I should group them by category type to have the right pieces for transitions.

Nearly EVERY season, I try new things—different quantities to work from, organizing the closet differently—by function (work, exercise, day at home, etc.), type (tops, pants, etc.), or color (base and accent). Some things stick, and others don't. Over time, you will find approaches that work well for you.

It could be interesting for those with young children at home to try a capsule for them. We have discussed how they grow out of clothes so quickly. You might be able to come up with a capsule plan that is a "formula" each time a new size needs to be purchased. This might make you feel ahead of the game on the clothing front instead of constantly chasing something they need.

A STARTING POINT

With all my research, one blog post stuck and seems like a reasonable and attainable start to a capsule wardrobe. The post is ironically on a food blog site, not a wardrobe site! The blogger is Lindsay from www.PinchOfYum.com. If you search for her post titled "How to Start a Capsule Wardrobe," you can read all the details and even get a downloadable guide. You may also find a new source of inspiration for recipes in the kitchen!

Her philosophy is that you start with a base wardrobe of 50 pieces that won't change throughout the year (even with weather changes for seasons). She suggests these pieces come from five categories: workout, lounge, layering, outerwear, and formal. You would select ten items in each category to achieve your base.

From there, she adds a quarterly capsule that consists of nine tops, five pants, and five shoes. These items will create combinations of outfits for the season. You can go to her post to learn more about how her process works and details on how to pull it together.

ADDITIONAL CONSIDERATIONS

While I like the idea of a "base" in the starting point above, I'm not sure the mix/number of quarterly pieces she uses is the right mix for everyone. Some other tips that I've read (and many that I've tried) are summarized below:

- **Use Neutrals as a Foundation**: Selecting two or three neutrals for foundational pieces each season can ensure you have easily mixed and matched items. Colors to consider are black, white, blue, gray, and camel.

- **Narrow your Accent Colors**: Adding one or two accent colors to your neutrals will liven up the looks but keep the capsule editable and easier to mix and match. You could find a couple of "signature colors" that are always your accents or have different accents for each season.

- **Make YOUR Rules**: This capsule wardrobe is yours. You should determine the number and types of pieces that are right for you. If you have friends or family members making their own capsule, share ideas, but don't compare solutions.

- **Don't be Afraid**: Some are reluctant to start a capsule because it feels complicated and intimidating. Keep the end in mind; the goal is to have a closet full of just those things you love, making it easy each day to answer the question, "What should I wear?" Start. If the solution isn't right, adjust and try again.

- **Create a Challenge**: Consider a challenge for a season to jump-start the process. Set your rules. For example, 50 base pieces with 30 additional, no shopping until the season ends, and no pulling from what wasn't selected. At the end, assess what worked, what didn't, and how you want to adjust.

CAPSULE INSPIRATION – In 2009, I came across The Uniform Project. That year, Sheena Matheiken pledged to wear and reinvent the same little black dress for a whole year. She wanted to explore sustainability and the versatility of a fashion staple. The rule was that she had to wear the dress every day (she had seven of them made) and accessorize only with secondhand purchases or donations from her friends' closets. I looked forward to her post every day that year, curious about what outfit she would create next. Everything was so fashionable, and I was inspired to see what you could do leveraging what you own or buy secondhand. The website with all the outfits is still live. For a bit of inspiration, I would encourage you to visit the site at www.theuniformproject.com

CONNECT WITH THE SECONDHAND COMMUNITY

Before we move into brands to consider when buying new clothes, I want to start with the more sustainable choice, purchasing secondhand. Understanding the secondhand options is good for purchasing and a great alternative for selling the items you no longer need or wear.

When considering secondhand, there are several categories: Garage or Estate sales, Thrift or Secondhand Stores, and Online Communities. Online communities have several different formats to consider. The rest of this focus area will provide a brief overview of these alternatives.

GARAGE OR ESTATE SALES

Clothes aren't always a part of garage/estate sales, but when they are, you can often find some great pieces that the owner is looking to get rid of quickly. Garage sales can be a great place to find kids' clothes as they go through growth spurts. Especially for younger children, they won't know or even care where their clothes were purchased.

If you are looking for items for yourself, consider what you wear to shop. If you have on a tank top, leggings, and socks, you can try on items over your clothes to see if the fit is right.

Your Turn – In addition to shopping at garage sales, you could have one of your own to sell some items you or your family members no longer need.

THRIFT OR SECONDHAND STORES

If you know your style, shopping at thrift, vintage, and secondhand stores can produce great finds at great prices. There are the mainstream options like Goodwill and the Salvation Army. However, you can also search your local market for interesting secondhand boutiques in the community.

The fun part of shopping secondhand is that every piece is unique. You can shop in the same store twice in one week and see completely different products. Secondhand stores could be the right match for those who love the thrill of the hunt for the perfect item for their closet.

Your Turn – Secondhand shops sell items and are a great resource for removing things you no longer need. You can donate to businesses like Goodwill or consign your items at a resale shop. Consignment gives you a percentage of the sale price. I've not found the amounts to be much, but it is an alternative to donation.

HOST A SWAP PARTY – Related to the secondhand community, you could host a swap party among your friends. Invite a group to bring up to 30 items from their closet they no longer need/wear. Each person puts a tag on their items that includes their name, price of the piece, and Venmo address (this makes the payments to one another smooth). You can also have people bring snacks and drinks and make an event out of shopping for something "new to you."

ONLINE – LOCAL

Buying and selling online doesn't have to mean shipping is required. Sites like Facebook Marketplace and Craigslist allow you to shop and sell locally. The benefits include trying things on (or at least looking at them live) before buying and not dealing with the hassle and environmental impact of shipping. While I haven't purchased clothing on one of these sites, I have purchased home goods with great success.

Another online local option is freecycle groups. These are network sites where people post things they no longer want, and all you need to do is pick them up. In my community, there is a "Buy Nothing" Facebook group. Search buy nothing with your community's name and see if a group is in your area.

Your Turn – Selling or giving away unused items in local online groups is extremely easy. You take a photo, write a description, add the price, post, and wait for replies. Items are picked up at your home or a public location, and payments are cash or Venmo. No shipping hassle is required.

ONLINE MARKETPLACES

Online marketplaces can be great for finding unique pieces that are often gently worn or not worn at all. There are several websites to consider. Below is an overview of the options:

- **Etsy**: Etsy is best known for handmade items. However, there is a large community of vintage sellers on the site. Search the site for "vintage _____" to find clothing and accessories. www.etsy.com
- **eBay**: eBay has all kinds of items available. Just search for what you are looking for and see what unique items pop up. www.ebay.com
- **Poshmark**: This online marketplace features fashion, home goods, and electronics. The primary focus is on women's clothing. www.poshmark.com
- **Zulily**: While this site has a bit of everything from clothing to home goods, the original purpose was a secondhand store for children's clothes. This is a site to consider if you want secondhand items for your kids. You can shop by article and size. www.zulily.com
- **Vestiare Collective**: This global online store features luxury and premium brands. This one is newer to me than those listed above,

but it looks interesting and worth considering.
www.vestiarecollective.com

Your Turn – Online marketplaces can expose your items to a much larger audience than local options. The marketplace communities enable you to sell the items at the prices you set, and the marketplace takes a fee for items sold. You will be responsible for shipping.

ONLINE CONSIGNMENT

Online consignment stores look like online marketplaces; if you are purchasing, you won't see a difference. The approach between consignment and marketplace is different if you plan to sell items. Below is an overview of some online consigners to consider:

- **ThredUp**: This online consignment shop focuses on women's fashion, including a maternity section. They also have children's clothes. www.thredup.com
- **Swap**: This is an online thrift and consignment store that offers used baby, children's, maternity, men's, and women's apparel. www.swap.com
- **Swap Society**: This site lets you send your items in and get SwapCoins. Then, you can purchase items on the site with your SwapCoins. This is a bit like consignment but leverages a cryptocurrency for transactions. www.swapsociety.co

Your Turn – Online consignment takes some of the burdens from selling in an online marketplace; there is no photographing or posting. And the shipping is just to one location. However, your opportunity to set the price and maximize your income is reduced. You trade off money for convenience.

DONATION AND RECYCLING

Before getting to the section on purchasing new, we'll cover the other two ways to get rid of items you no longer want or need; donate or recycle. The first and most desired option in this section is to take any clothes you decide not to sell secondhand and donate everything in good shape. One cause for gently used women's workwear is Dress for Success. This global program takes donations and supports women on the journey to financial independence. Additional options in most areas include the Salvation Army and Goodwill.

Nike has a program to send back the shoes if you have athletic shoes of any brand that could either be reused or refurbished. You can find more details on their website.

I hope that by the time you reach this section, you have very little that needs to be recycled. Most of the pieces would have been sold secondhand or donated to a great cause. Yet, we all know that some pieces you love right to the end are too worn to donate. For those, here are a few options to consider:

- **Rags**: You could cut clothing up and use them as rags around the house and garage.
- **Drop Off**: Search www.Earth911.org in your area to find drop-off locations.
- **Compost**: I was surprised to find this alternative! If the clothes are made of natural materials (like cotton), you can cut them into small squares and put them in the compost pile.
- **Zappos for Good**: This program recycles jeans with more than 90% cotton and any shoes in any condition. Instructions on the site are straightforward, and you can mail them in via a label you print in your Zappos or Amazon account and then drop them off at UPS.

This program also has a donation component for items in better condition. www.zappos.com

PURCHASING NEW

Purchasing new clothes has several considerations involved. The materials want to be natural, organic, and not petroleum based. Manufacturing can be fraught with unfair working conditions, so you want to look for fair wages and good working conditions. Finally, consider other factors like dyes used, packaging materials, and shipping.

CONSOLIDATE AND TAKE INVENTORY

Before venturing out to search for needed items, you might want to consolidate what you have and take inventory. Our closets and drawers can become spaces where items are "lost," and we forget about things we already own.

For example, pull out all your shirts and sort them by season. You can then ask questions like; why do I have so many winter tops and just a few for summer? Do I need to buy some tops for this summer and/or get rid of some sweaters I don't wear? In addition to clothes that may all be in one closet, items like coats, shoes, and boots can tend to be spread around the house and tucked into multiple closets.

RATING RESOURCE – GOOD ON YOU

As the introduction chapter mentions, the Good on You website (www.goodonyou.eco) and associated app are great resources when shopping. This site provides a five-point overall scale from Poor to Great that is achieved by a combination of scores in three areas:

- **Planet**: The brand's environmental policies ensure you see through any greenwashing. They consider materials, business models, commitment to circularity, and textile waste practices.
- **People**: This dimension assesses the brand's impact on workers across the supply chain.
- **Animals**: This aspect considers animal welfare policies and how well, when applicable, they trace their animal products.

In addition, they note where the brands are headquartered and provide costs from one $ to four $$$$.

MATERIALS TO CONSIDER OR AVOID

As with anything you are purchasing, make sure you look at the labels so you know the materials you are buying. When shopping for clothing, there are two primary fabrics to avoid. First are traditional synthetic fabrics, including nylon, polyester, and spandex. These materials are very energy intensive to produce and don't completely break down, leaving toxins in our water. The second to avoid is conventionally grown cotton which requires a lot of pesticides and water. Instead, look for these:

- **Organically Produced Hemp and Linen**: They are grown with little water and no petrochemicals.
- **Bamboo**: Bamboo linen is best, as other forms use chemicals in production.
- **Organic or Recycled Cotton**: Organic uses less water and no pesticides vs. traditional. If you can get recycled, this would be best.
- **Eco-Friendly Synthetics**: Tencel is made from dissolved wood pulp and is an alternative to cotton. Pinatex is made from pineapple leaf fibers and used as a replacement for leather.

- **Recycled Synthetics**: Materials that you might see recycled into a new piece of clothing are recycled polyester, nylon, spandex, lyocell, and biobased plastics.
- **Peace Silk** – If you look for silk, this process lets silkworms live their entire lives.

The remainder of this focus area looks at different categories of products in your closets, including clothes, shoes, outerwear, purses, jewelry, and more. Brands to consider next time you are in the market are provided for each.

BRANDS TO CONSIDER – CLOTHING

As we investigate clothing brands, I've included a couple of mainstream brands and added more of the little-known ones that you might want to add to your list. I also included the current (at the time of publication) ratings of these brands from www.GoodOnYou.eco.

The brands included have a rating of either Good or Great, the top two ratings. In addition, all brands included are $$ or $$$. I didn't find many $, and the $$$$ prices felt out of reach for most.

Mainstream Brands – Those you have heard of and relatively easy-to-find locations in the US:

- **Patagonia**: Patagonia is focused on the materials used, safe and fair production, and transparently shares information across its supply chain. Every product lists the materials used, and they have an extensive area on their website that details all these areas. They have products for the whole family, rated Good and $$. www.patagonia.com
- **Eileen Fisher**: The Eileen Fisher women's brand is a B Corp focused on protecting the planet and people since the beginning. They look

at first life (sustainable production), second life (resell at www.EileenFisherRenew.com), and third life (waste no more accessories). The company is rated Good and $$$. www.eileenfisher.com

- **Gap/Banana Republic/Old Navy/Athleta:** I did a lot of searches on the Good On You website of more mainstream brands to find some to include here. I include the Gap family of brands as an exception to the Good/Great rating, as they have products for every member of the family and every price point. They are rated as "It's a Start" (the middle rating). As I'm sure you would expect, the price ratings varied across the four brands, with Old Navy at $, Gap at $$, and the other two at $$$. www.gap.com, www.oldnavy.com, www.bananarepublic.com, www.athleta.com

Lesser-Known Brands – These are brands that you may not have heard of but that I discovered and think should be on your consideration list.

- **Two Days Off**: This women's brand focuses on deadstock (manufactured but unused) fabric and virgin linen textiles. They prioritize natural fiber textiles, including linen, cotton, wool, and hemp, because they have a lighter environmental impact. Shipping is plastic-free, and the packaging is reusable and recyclable. Rated Great and $$. www.twodaysoff.com
- **Vetta**: For women looking to create a capsule wardrobe, this brand would be one to look at. They have curated nine capsules with themes like "Getaway" and "Utility." There is even a style quiz to determine which is your match. They use sustainable materials and production. The website goes into the details of each product. Rated Good and $$. www.vettacapsule.com
- **Reformation**: This women's brand is based in LA and makes all its products from low-impact materials, deadstock fabrics, and

repurposed vintage clothing. They put out limited collections each week to only make what is needed. Rated Good and $$.
www.thereformation.com

- **Pact**: This brand has products for every family member, from babies to adults. They are focused on GOTS-certified organic cotton products. They use organic because no toxic chemicals are used, and production uses over 80% less water than non-organic. They have products for the whole family and items for bed and bath. Rated Good and $$. www.wearpact.com

- **For Days**: This brand has clothing for men and women. Their products are 100% recyclable and designed for a closed-loop cycle; what you return to them can go into future products. They manufacture locally and offset all their shipping. Rated Good and $$. www.fordays.com

- **Frankie Collective**: This Canadian brand focuses on innovating streetwear for women. They salvage vintage garments destined for landfills and create reworked looks. They also have their manufacturing scraps recycled by Fabcycle. Rated Great and $$. www.frankiecollective.com

- **Outerknown**: This brand is committed to protecting the environment and supporting fair labor. I like how they say, "We haven't figured it all out, but we continue to learn every day." They have a large product line for men and women. Each product lists the materials used. In addition, they have a pre-loved area on their site where customers can buy and sell Outerknown products to one another. Rated Good and $$. www.outerknown.com

- **Threads 4 Thought**: This US company has activewear and everyday basics for both men and women. Rated Good and $$. www.threads4thought.com

- **Mate the Label**: This brand is focused on women (even some maternity styles) and made sustainably in Los Angeles. They operate on their Mate Eight principles – Clean, Essential, Organic, Ethical, Women-Centered, Plastic-Free, Circular, and Local. Each product lists the materials used, and they have a recycling program. Rated Great and $$$. www.matethelabel.com

- **Cotopaxi**: Outdoor clothing company that features clothing for men and women and outdoor gear like backpacks, hats, and coolers. Rated Good and $$. www.cotopaxi.com
- **LA Made Clothing**: This is a women's clothing brand. As the name indicates, they are manufactured in Los Angeles, providing workers with a clean environment, fair wages, and benefits. They purchase the materials for their comfortable pieces locally and are focused on sustainability. Rated Good and $$. www.lamadeclothing.com

Hangers – Did you know that 3.5 billion wire hangers get dumped in landfills every year (Greene, 2020)? The most popular wire hanger alternative is plastic, which is not better for the environment! As your hangers wear out, consider replacing them with materials like bamboo, corn, or wheat alternatives. Some hanger brands to put on your list include B Green (www.bgreenhangers-store.myshopify.com), Simply Green (available on Amazon – www.amazon.com), and Ditto (www.ditto-hangers.myshopify.com).

BRANDS TO CONSIDER – UNDERGARMENTS AND SWIMWEAR

Regarding undergarments and swimwear, I found four brands rated well by Good On You with a wide range of products and pricing. If one of these doesn't quite fit your style, you might also search on Etsy for some smaller makers.

- **Parade**: This brand has a wide product line and strives to make all products from reclaimed, recycled, responsible, renewable, or regenerative materials. Their website provides a rating for each product based on three dimensions: climate, social, and circularity. Good and $. www.yourparade.com
- **Girlfriend Collective**: This brand is focused on undergarments, swimwear, and athleisure. Products are made from recycled materials, and the breakdown of materials is listed on each product page. Their packaging is 100% recycled and recyclable. They also have a small men's athleisure shop. Rated Good and $$$. www.girlfriend.com
- **Boody**: Boody is an Australian company using sustainable bamboo fabrics. Their bamboo is organic and grown without pesticides. They focus on undergarments, loungewear, and athleisure for the whole family. Rated Good and $$. www.boody.com
- **All Sisters:** This is a swimwear brand located in Spain; they ship to the US. They use recycled fabrics to create modern-looking swimwear at reasonable prices. Products are manufactured in socially responsible workplaces. Rated Great and $$. www.allsisters.com

BRANDS TO CONSIDER – SHOES

Like the clothing section, I researched brands on the GoodOnYou.eco website. I found many brands rated "It's A Start," the mid-rating on the website. Other brands didn't have a rating on the site but are mentioned in many discussions about eco-friendly shoes. Those are included here without a rating. Below is a summary of both mainstream brands and those that are lesser known.

Mainstream Brands – Those you have heard of and relatively easy-to-find locations in the US. These only carry casual shoes. I found it difficult to find mainstream brands with dress shoes actively working on sustainability. You will find dress shoes in lesser-known brands.

- **Nike**: Nike's sustainability program is called "Move to Zero." They are focused on materials, circular design, and reuse/recycling of their products. Currently, they do not include materials on their website's product detail pages. Rated It's a Start and $$. www.nike.com
- **Adidas**: Adidas is focused on three areas, materials, process, and reducing plastic waste and their carbon footprint. They have partnered with brands like Allbirds (information below) to co-create products. Rated It's a Start and $$. www.adidas.com

Lesser-Known Brands – These brands you may not have heard of but are ones I found that I think should be on your consideration list. I'm honestly surprised that these brands are rated the same as mainstream ones. As I look at the information about what they are doing, it feels much more advanced and progressive than what I saw with those above.

- **Cariuma**: This men's and women's brand is B Corp Certified and focused on sustainability and fair working conditions. The website has information on the materials they use, manufacturing, and other eco-topics like packaging efficiency. They show the materials in each product, like bamboo, cork, sugarcane, and recycled plastics. Rated Good and $$. www.cariuma.com
- **Able**: This brand focuses on its impact on people and the planet. They carry not only casual shoes but also heels and booties. In addition to the shoe line, Able has clothing, purses, and jewelry. Rated Good and $$. www.ableclothing.com
- **Nisolo**: This is a B Corp ethical footwear and accessories brand for men and women. They have a sustainability facts label that has a transparent production breakdown. They use leather in some of their

products, so keep that in mind if you are looking for vegan alternatives. Rated Good and $$. www.nisolo.com

- **Nae**: This vegan Portuguese footwear ranges from casual to dress styles for both women and men. Their work makes the world more sustainable and animal friendly. Rated Good and $$. www.nae.vegan.com
- **Allbirds**: This casual footwear brand is a B Corp focused on becoming carbon neutral and using natural materials like wool, plant sugar, wood, recycled plastics, and castor oil. They have a wide product range of shoes for men, women, and children. Rated It's a Start and $$. www.allbirds.com
- **Rothy's**: This brand aims to achieve a closed-loop production model by 2023. They use recycled, natural materials in their products and focus on the well-being of their people and the community. Products are available for men, women, and children. Rated It's a Start and $$. www.rothys.com

BRANDS TO CONSIDER – BAGS AND PURSES

When considering purses, bags, backpacks, and totes, it's all about the materials. Leather is still preferred by many but is not preferred by the planet. However, many leather-like alternatives are emerging, made from natural materials like cacti and apples. Recycled plastics and upcycled materials like tarps and feed bags are also used. I've tried to include various options below to give you choices on both price and style.

To begin, we have two brands that were included in the shoe section above, **Rothy's and Kokolu.** Rothy's (www.rothys.com) also carries a full line of bags and purses made from recycled water bottles with 3D knit technology. Kokolu (www.kokolu.eco) has one multi-purpose daily tote that is cute and looks like it would be very functional. Below are additional options:

- **Gunas:** The Gunas brand is 100% vegan, making products that look like leather. The primary materials used are vegan leather, recycled plastic bottles, and metals. Products are produced by hand in small artisan studios in Seoul, Korea, Rated $$. www.gunasthebrand.com
- **Alchemy Goods:** This brand upcycles old materials like bicycle tubes and advertising banners into bags and accessories. They are produced in Seattle and source all their used materials from around the US. Rated $-$$. www.alchemygoods.com
- **Uashmama:** This brand uses washable paper, organic cotton, and vegetable-tanned leather to create unique totes, purses, backpacks, and more. Rated $$-$$$. www.us.uashmama.com
- **Santos by Monica:** This brand started with bags and purses and expanded into clothing. The handbags are made of cactus leather which is long-lasting and partially biodegradable. They focus on made-to-order and small-batch production. Rated $$$. www.santosbymonica.com
- **Etsy:** Many brands on Etsy feature upcycled materials to make purses and bags. You could find a unique piece that you love. $-$$$. www.etsy.com
- **Allegorie:** This brand uses waste from mangos and apples to create leather-like handbags, backpacks, and wallets for women and men. The bags are produced to minimize environmental impact and ensure health and fair wages. $$$. www.allegoriedesign.com

BRANDS TO CONSIDER – JEWELRY AND ACCESSORIES

When considering jewelry, materials and processing are the two areas of focus. When possible, buying vintage or secondhand is always preferred. If you are buying new, below are three brands to consider:

- **Article22**: This brand uses many eco-friendly materials, including some recycled ones. They limit the number of chemicals and water used in production. They trace their entire supply chain and ensure living wages are paid. Rated Good and $$. www.article22.com
- **Two Days Off** This brand was featured as a clothing brand, but it also has jewelry, scarves, and bags that follow the same sustainable practices. Rated Great and $$. www.twodaysoff.com
- **Etsy**: I have found many pieces on Etsy that are either made of natural materials like wood or are upcycled, such as rings and bracelets from forks and spoons, necklaces from bottles/bottle caps, upcycled scarves, natural materials, and more. You can find something uniquely your style that creates a great conversation piece. www.etsy.com

FAST FIVE IN THE CLOSET

Five steps you can take quickly to make an impact and begin to celebrate some wins!

1. **Shop Secondhand** – The best way to start reducing our dependency on fast fashion is to shift to less purchasing and buy secondhand when you do. You might find you love the thrill of the hunt for the perfect piece to add to your closet.

2. **Recycle** – Once you don't wear pieces anymore, move them on to someone who will. Sell them secondhand or donate them to a good friend or cause. Letting them sit idly doesn't make sense for anyone. If they are beyond donation because they have been so well loved, find a location that recycles clothing to drop them off.

3. **Shop with Intention** – Know your style, your colors, and what your closet truly needs every time you go out or online to shop. Keep your purchases to this small list and purchase things you love; focus on quality over quantity.

4. **Find New Brands** – This chapter is full of lesser-known brands for clothing, shoes, and accessories. Spend time online checking them out and see if you can find a few that fit your personal style and price points. Then, you'll have them top-of-mind when needs arise.

5. **Create a Personal Challenge** – Consider the current state of your closet and the challenges you face. Could you challenge yourself to move toward the curated closet you want? For an over buyer, maybe it's a month wearing only thirty pieces you own or a year shopping only secondhand? For an under buyer, perhaps it's setting a vision for a curated style and shopping for a few pieces secondhand. Define your challenges and set a goal.

THE LAUNDRY ROOM

The average household runs 392 loads of laundry annually in the United States. (*Homemade Laundry Detergent Can Save Money*, n.d.) That's about 7.5 loads and 50 pounds of laundry per week. On the surface, the laundry room is small, and we should be able to cover the space quickly. However, this room can have a lot of positive or negative impacts on your home's environmental friendliness and your family's health.

The chapter will start with my story and then move into three focus sections: Energy Consumption, Products, and Dry Cleaning. Each focus area will dive deeper into the category and provide ideas on reducing your environmental impact.

MY ONE SHADE GREENER STORY

I started making changes in my laundry room in 2008 when I purchased Energy Star appliances, including a front-load washing machine. At the same time, I was beginning to experiment with alternative laundry products with less harsh ingredients.

The most significant change I made in using the machines was to shift to washing everything in cold water. Before the switch, I washed every load on warm or hot settings. I can honestly say that after nearly 15 years, I do not see any difference. While there are occasions that I still use warm or hot water, that happens maybe 4-5 times a year.

As I pulled the information together for this chapter, I realized that my product starting point years ago may have been lighter than many people. I've never used fabric softener or laundry whitener, and I rarely use any stain remover. Over the years, I've tried different detergents and primarily landed on Method products. While researching this book, I found the Dropps brand, which eliminates plastic packaging. I ordered some, and while I've only been using the brand for a short time, I like it and plan to repurchase. On the dryer side, I shifted from dryer sheets to dryer balls, and they work great. Sometimes I add essential oils, and sometimes I don't. It just depends on whether I remember.

As the kids have grown and moved out on their own for most of the year, the volume of laundry has decreased dramatically. We typically have just 2-3 loads per week. I don't do laundry all in one day like I used to. Instead, I run the machine when I have enough for a full load. When the kids were still living here full time, the number of loads of laundry was much higher. I'm sure that now they are doing their own laundry, they are much more conscious of the number of loads!

At the end of this chapter, we will cover dry cleaning. As I've continued to learn more on my journey, I have been working hard to remove the need for dry cleaning. At this point, I'm going to the cleaners a maximum of 1-2 times a year. This is lighter on both the planet and my pocketbook!

UP NEXT IN MY HOME – I will continue to try new laundry products as mine run out, and I aspire to try more DIY products. I think it would be fun to make my own, and I just need to dedicate the time to try making my own.

ENERGY CONSUMPTION

The washer and dryer are the sources of all energy used in the laundry room. In fact, according to a study by the Journal of Integrative Environmental Sciences, laundry cycles were responsible for 8.29% of all residential emissions from running the machines and heating the water in the washing machine (Golden et al., 2010).

OVERALL ENERGY ASSESSMENT

For those who are interested in the general energy costs of doing a load of laundry, you can get an estimate quickly by answering two questions:

1. **Are your appliances Energy Star?** You should be able to just look at the front and see the logo. You likely do not have an Energy Star machine if there is no logo.
2. **Is your washing machine a front load or a top load?** This is important because the loading method determines how much water is squeezed out during the spin cycle, cutting energy used in drying.

Below are the summaries for both washing and drying. You can see that the Energy Star ratings have significant impacts on cost. The numbers are based on average energy costs in the United States.

Cost to Wash Your Clothes: There are two costs with washing –electricity, and water. The annual prices below are based on 392 loads of laundry per year.

- Non-Energy Star Top Load costs $0.84/load or $328/year
- Energy Star Top Load costs $0.53/load or $210/year
- Energy Star Front Load costs $0.52/load or $205/year

Cost to Dry Your Clothes: Like the washing machine, many factors come into play with your energy use per load. However, the Energy Star rating is also the main factor for drying. Costs are for 392 loads of laundry per year.

- Non-Energy Star costs $0.29/load or $113/year
- Energy Star costs $0.08/load or $31/year

REPLACING THE WASHER AND DRYER

While I realize that you aren't going to rush out and buy appliances today, or likely even this year, here are some things to consider when replacement time comes. The energy efficiency of washing machines and dryers has increased significantly in the last 20 years. This is great for any model you select.

For those in the US and Canada, the Energy Star logo is the first thing to look for when shopping for new appliances. You can go to www.energystar.gov to search for and compare the washing machines and dryers you are considering. In addition to finding the most efficient appliance for you, the site will also tell you if there are any rebates in your area by typing in your zip code.

Washing Machines: The Energy Star-certified washing machines use about 25% less energy and 33% less water than regular washers. Selecting a front-load washing machine will save around 6000 gallons of water a year compared to a top-loading machine. While that won't save a great deal of money, the switch will significantly impact your overall water use, and the spin cycle is more effective at getting water out of the clothes, making the dry time shorter and more efficient.

Dryers: Selecting an Energy Star dryer will save about 20% of your energy usage or cost. The dryer also has the added complexity of buying gas or electric. The answer to this question is a bit complex. Gas dryers are more efficient than electric, so the monthly operating costs may be lower. However, gas dryers are a bit more expensive up front, and not all homes have a gas line in the laundry room.

SAVE ENERGY - DO LESS LAUNDRY

Aside from buying more efficient appliances, the first tip to save energy in the laundry room is to do less laundry. This reduces your carbon footprint, saves you money, and cuts the time you spend doing laundry. Think about the loads you wash each week. Are there ways you could reduce one load per week? Even one less load makes an impact over the year.

OPTIMIZE THE SIZE OF LAUNDRY LOADS

In the average home, more than 6000 articles of clothing are washed each year. This means that each load typically contains about 16 items (Jaeger, 2019). Waiting until you have a full load of laundry before running the washing machine can be another way to ensure maximum efficiency. Carbon dioxide emissions are estimated to be reduced by 99 pounds per household yearly by only running full loads of laundry.

On the dryer side, the optimal range for a load is to fill the dryer at least 1/3 of the way full but not over 3/4 of the dryer capacity. This range will enable the dryer to run most efficiently.

WASH IN COLD WATER

According to TreeHugger, almost 90% of the energy used to wash clothes comes from water heating. Research has shown that about 50% of households wash in warm water, 15% in hot, and 35% in cold (Verchot, 2019). If you are one of the 65% washing in warm and/or hot water, consider trying cold as an alternative. TreeHugger suggests that 34 million tons of carbon dioxide emissions would be saved if every US household only used cold water for washing clothes.

If shifting all your loads to cold water isn't feasible, consider moving from hot water to warm. You can use up to 40% less energy by switching your washing machine from 104 degrees (recommended) to 86 degrees (Delaney, 2011). Spend a few minutes to determine how this temperature change is made on your washing machine.

MAXIMIZE DRYER EFFICIENCY

Of all the appliances in your home, the dryer uses the most energy in a year, even more than the refrigerator. Finding ways to be more efficient with your dryer can quickly reduce your environmental impact and save money. Below are ideas to maximize efficiency.

Use the Washer High Spin Setting: The best way to save drying time and costs is to use the high spin speed on your washer to get as much water out as possible. Check out your washing machine's current settings and ensure you know how to leverage the high-spin cycle.

Moisture Sensor: Using the moisture sensor will be the quickest way to ensure you are running the dryer for the appropriate amount of time. If your dryer does not have a sensor, try different dry times to find the optimal setting.

Mix of Materials: If you have heavyweight and lightweight pieces in the same load, they will take longer to dry. Cotton requires a higher temperature to dry than materials like polyester and acrylic. Sorting your clothes ahead of time can help ensure the right balance.

Remove Clothing Early: For clothing that you plan to iron, pull the pieces out while they are still slightly damp, as over-dried clothing is harder to iron.

Add a Towel: Add a dry, fluffy towel to the dryer load. Pull the towel out after about 15-20 minutes, let the towel air dry, and the rest of the load will finish in much less time.

Clean Out the Lint: Clean out the lint filter after each load to keep the dryer running more efficiently and take less energy, adding life to the machine.

Fold Right Away: Folding right away ensures fewer wrinkles and can often remove the need for ironing. The other benefit of folding and putting laundry away right after the cycle finishes is that you don't have the lingering mental load of laundry piles sitting around the house ready to be folded and/or put away.

TRY LINE DRYING

In the US, nearly all wash loads are put in a dryer. Going one level greener, you could consider shifting one load per week to line dry. According to The Green Book, naturally drying one load per week—outside on a line in nice weather or on racks indoors—would save the same energy required to run your refrigerator for two months.

Another alternative is to damp dry items by getting them mostly dry by line drying and then finishing them off in the dryer. This can significantly cut dryer times, and this process has the added advantage of extending the fabric life of your clothing.

LAUNDRY PRODUCTS

As we move from energy use to the products used in the laundry room, we will focus on three key areas, i.e., ingredients, packaging, and attachment.

Ingredients: The ingredients in many products used in your laundry negatively impact the environment and the health of the people in your home. In fact, in all our households, laundry products are among the harshest household chemicals we use. Our clothes, sheets, and towels are directly touching our skin, and we breathe in these products' ingredients all day, every day. We want our clothes to be clean. However, shifting our laundry product choices can be healthier for both planet and people.

Packaging: Another impact in the laundry room is the product packaging. Most households have multiple laundry products, including detergents, fabric softeners, bleach, stain removers, dryer sheets, and more. Each of these comes in different types of packaging, and many are in plastic containers that are challenging to recycle.

Attachment: A final challenge in the laundry room I hear from many people is a deep, emotional connection to the products used. We often use the same laundry products we grew up with, the ones our mothers and possibly even grandmothers selected. Using these products has a familiar rhythm (we know how to use them) and nostalgia (they remind us of our youth). We are reluctant to try something new because these products have always worked well and "smell right." This is a challenge that is a bit more difficult to overcome. However, the fact that you are reading this book tells me you are willing to try some new options to see if you can find the right alternative for you.

The goal is to find an alternative product that is the perfect solution for you. The advantage of changes in laundry products is that you don't have to commit forever. Laundry room products are used up in a few months, and you can cycle through a few options to find the perfect one. If you buy something that doesn't work, use it up and try something else.

LAUNDRY DETERGENT

There are many ingredients in popular laundry detergents that are not healthy for the earth or your family. Most laundry detergents are petroleum-based, which depletes a nonrenewable resource. The ingredients to watch out for include sodium lauryl sulfate, phosphates, chlorine bleach, fragrances, and dyes. Below are alternatives and brands to consider.

Light Green: These detergents have better ingredients but still have traditional packaging.

- **Puracy Natural Free & Clear Laundry Detergent** – This detergent is plant-based and cruelty-free. The product comes in a concentrate which uses less plastic packaging. www.puracy.com
- **Method** – Method has both liquid and pod alternatives. The liquid packaging is plastic but can be recycled. The pods are better as they come with less packaging. www.methodhome.com
- **ECOS Hypoallergenic Free & Clear Liquid** – This brand is plant-based, 100% biodegradable, and free of chlorine and petroleum-based ingredients. The detergent is also doubly concentrated, so you use half as much as traditional brands, saving plastic packaging. www.ecos.com

Dark Green: These brands have better ingredients and packaging.

- **Dropps Laundry Pods** – They have pods for regular and small loads. The website has a lot of transparent information on ingredients. They are packaged in compostable cardboard, so there is NO plastic! www.dropps.com

- **Blueland** – Blueland starts with a tin to hold their laundry pods. You purchase the pods in a recyclable pouch to drop into the tin. www.blueland.com
- **EarthBreeze** – Earth Breeze uses laundry sheets that dissolve in water. The packaging can be torn into pieces and buried in the ground, where it will decompose. www.earthbreeze.com
- **Tide PureClean** - Tide has introduced PureClean, which has removed many ingredients, is packaged in a recyclable box, and is manufactured with clean energy. www.tide.com

DIY Green: Laundry detergent is relatively straightforward to make. Here's how you do it:

1. **Purchase** 1 box of Arm & Hammer Washing Soda (55oz), 1 box of Borax (65oz), and three bars of Fels-Naptha soap.
2. **Prep the Fels-Naptha**: Cut the bars into smaller pieces and then microwave for 2-3 minutes. This makes the soap easier to turn into powder. After it cools, you can crumble it with your hands. If the powder isn't fine enough, use a food processor to grind it into a fine powder.
3. **Mix**: Mix the Fels-Naptha with the boxes of washing soda and borax in a large sealable container. You could use a plastic storage bin and keep it in this container for refills.
4. **Use**: Fill an air-tight glass or ceramic container with the mixture. For each load of laundry, scoop out 1-2 tablespoons. The batch lasts a LONG time and is light on your pocketbook.

If you don't want to make such a large batch at once, you can use 1 bar of Fels-Naptha with 1/3 of each of the boxes of washing soda and borax.

FABRIC SOFTENER

Fabric softener is a product used by some, but not everyone. These products soften our clothes, help with static and wrinkles, provide a fresh smell, and help fade prevention. The easiest fabric softener alternative is to skip it. If going without is not for you, below are alternatives to consider.

Light Green: These fabric softeners have better ingredients and traditional packaging.

- **Method** – They list all the ingredients on the website's product page and come in recyclable plastic bottles. www.methodhome.com
- **Frey** – This company is a B Corp and PETA certified. Their product is made with natural ingredients and essential oils. Also, for every order, the brand plants a tree. www.frey.com

Dark Green: Better ingredients, better packaging.

- **Dropps** – These fabric softener pods use natural ingredients, and even the pod covers are completely biodegradable. www.dropps.com
- **Soap Nuts** – Soap nuts reduce static and soften your clothes. Etsy is a great source for soap nuts with instructions on use and small bags for washing. Soap nuts can be used on their own without detergent or as an addition to the detergent as a fabric softener.

DIY Green: There are several do-it-yourself options to replace fabric softeners in your laundry. Two alternatives to consider include:

- **Vinegar**: Pour ¼ to ½ cup white distilled vinegar into the fabric softener cup on your washing machine. It provides a great fabric softener and does not cause your laundry to smell like vinegar.
- **"Crystal" Fabric Softener**: Mix 1 cup Epsom salt with ¼ cup baking soda and 10-15 drops of the essential oil of your choice. Seal the

container and shake to mix. Add 2 tablespoons of the mixture directly into the washer for each load.

LAUNDRY WHITENERS

When it comes to brightening your whites, the go-to solution for many is bleach or other harsh cleaners. In researching, I was surprised to find that there are different types of "bleach." You want to ensure you avoid chlorine bleach as it harms your skin, the water system, and wildlife. The alternative form of bleach is oxygen-based and is often referred to as hydrogen peroxide. I had no idea!

Light Green: These alternatives have better ingredients and traditional packaging.

- **Seventh Generation Chlorine Free Bleach – Free & Clear** – This product fights stains, whitens whites, and is color safe. The biodegradable formula uses hydrogen peroxide to fight tough stains and is free of fragrances and dyes. www.seventhgeneration.com
- **Nature Clean Oxygen Liquid Bleach** – This brand is chlorine-free and formulated from hydrogen peroxide. The product is hypoallergenic and not tested on animals. www.natureclean.ca

Dark Green: These brands have better ingredients and packaging.

- **Branch Basics** – This brand is EWG-certified, biodegradable, and plant-based. www.branchbasics.com
- **Dropps** – Dropps has an oxi booster pod product with no chlorine and eliminates the plastic packaging. www.dropps.com

- **Grab Green** – The bleach alternative pods remove the chlorine. While the packaging isn't as good as that from Dropps, it's less than the mainstream brands. www.grabgreenhome.com
- **Molly's Suds** – Another bleach alternative, but this time, a powder that is chlorine free. Like Grab Green, the packaging is less than mainstream. www.mollyssuds.com

DIY Green: When whitening your laundry, there are many DIY alternatives. They include things from the kitchen, like baking soda, lemons, and vinegar. Here are a few ideas to consider:

- **Baking Soda**: Add to the wash cycle to maximize the effectiveness of your detergent.
- **Vinegar**: Use the same way you would add bleach to your laundry.
- **Lemon Juice**: Add one cup to your wash to brighten up the laundry.
- **Sunshine**: Put the item outside in the sun while still very wet, and before you know it, the discoloration will fade away.
- **Hydrogen Peroxide**: This can be added to the bleach dispenser on your washing machine or in the rinse cycle. DO NOT pour directly on clothes, or it will cause spotting.

STAIN REMOVERS

When we head through the aisles of our local stores in search of something to remove the stain that just appeared on our favorite shirt, the product choices are full of unknown ingredients that can be harmful. Below are some brands to consider as alternatives.

Light Green: These options have better ingredients and traditional packaging.

- **The Laundress Stain Solution** – This product is made of a concentrated blend of plant-derived surfactants and is free of petroleum, phosphate, and artificial coloring. www.thelaundress.com
- **Molly's Suds Stain Spray** – This product uses a unique blend of enzymes to provide stain-fighting power. The ingredients are listed on their website. www.mollyssuds.com
- **Seventh Generation Free & Clear Laundry Stain Remover** – This brand is a certified B Corp and has 97% plant-based ingredients. www.seventhgeneration.com

Dark Green: These brands have better ingredients and packaging.

- **Etee Laundry Stain Bar** – This is exactly as described, a bar of soap-like stain remover wrapped in very minimal packaging around the center of the bar. www.shopetee.com
- **Meloria Stain Stick** – Another stain stick alternative with a bit more packaging, but no plastic and easy to recycle. www.meloriameansbetter.com
- **SoulShine Laundry Stick** – Made in the owner's kitchen in small batches, this alternative is close to DIY and packaged with minimal wrap material. www.soulshinecompany.com
- **Ingredients Matter Laundry Soap Stain Stick** – This product is made of all-natural ingredients and rated by EWG. www.ingredientsmatterclean.com

DIY Green: When it comes to removing stains, there are many recipes online. You can search for the ones that are right for you. Below are a few tips to get you started:

- **General Stain Remover** – Mix ½ cup hydrogen peroxide with ¼ cup Thieves Dish Soap (or an alternative eco-friendly liquid dish soap) in a glass spray bottle. Shake well and spray on.

- **Grease Stains** – Mix cornstarch and water to make a paste, place the mixture on the stain, let it sit for 10-15 minutes, and then wash normally in cold water.
- **Fresh Blood Stains** – Vinegar, hydrogen peroxide, baking soda, and lemon are all effective cleaners for blood. Treating the stain right away is key.
- **Sweat or Yellowing** – Mix lemon juice and salt on the stain, let it soak through, and rub.

DRYER SHEETS

When it comes to dryer sheets, the ingredients include chemicals and fragrances that can irritate skin and be dangerous to the water system. In addition, they can leave a coating of residue inside the dryer, which can interfere with the sensors that allow the automatic dry cycle to work properly. The final issue with dryer sheets is that they are one-time-use products that end up in landfills. Below are some alternatives to consider.

Light Green: These options have better ingredients and traditional packaging.

- **Seventh Generation** – This brand is a USDA-certified biobased product without dyes or fragrances. www.seventhgeneration.com
- **Mrs. Meyers** – These dryer sheets have natural ingredients, including scents derived from plant sources, to add a fresh smell. www.mrsmeyers.com

Dark Green: Dryer Balls – A great alternative to dryer sheets, dryer balls will remove the static from clothes and shorten drying time. You can add essential oil for a fresh scent. A few brands are below:

- **Free the Ocean** – These dryer balls are sold in sets of six and are adorable! There are nine styles, including penguins, ladybugs, and bees. www.freetheocean.com
- **Smart Sheep** (www.smartsheepdryerballs.com/) – This brand is rated highly on many websites and is also sold in sets of six. There is a cute sheep design or plain white and multi-color.
- **Etsy** – Etsy is full of handmade, fun dryer balls and essential oils at reasonable prices. The two searches that worked for me were "dryer balls" and "dryer ball scent." Remember to read the fragrance ingredient list to ensure you know the formula and look for only essential oils. www.etsy.com

DIY Green: When it comes to replacing dryer sheets, there are options for creating your own "sheets" as well as making your own dryer balls:

- **Dryer "Sheets"** – For a make-your-own and reuse dryer sheet, you can cut up squares of an old t-shirt and add essential oils.
- **Dryer Balls** – The simple option is to fill old socks with flaxseed and add essential oils for scent. If you want to explore making felted wool dryer balls (like those you would purchase), there are directions online to demonstrate this more complex solution.

DRY CLEANING

The laundry room isn't always in our house; sometimes, we outsource to the dry cleaner.

When considering dry cleaning, the biggest challenge is eliminating perchloroethylene, often referred to as "PERC." According to a report from Frontiers in Public Health, this chemical has been linked to many health issues, from a skin irritant to a potential occupational carcinogen. In addition, the report indicates that PERC can contaminate natural resources and is potentially toxic to wildlife. When the report was written in March of 2021, 60-65% of all dry cleaners in the United States were using PERC in their cleaning process (*Frontiers | Perchloroethylene and Dry Cleaning: It's Time to Move the Industry to Safer Alternatives*, n.d.).

There are two alternative cleaning methods to look for: carbon dioxide cleaning and professional wet cleaning. These will both get your clothes clean and remove the PERC.

These alternatives won't remove the amount of packaging waste like metal hangers and plastic covering that comes from taking your clothes to a service. If you have clothing dry-cleaned, return the wire hangers for reuse. You could also ask your dry cleaner if they would not place the plastic covering on your clothes to eliminate the waste.

At-Home Alternatives: A great resource for washing anything at home can be found at www.thelaundress.com/pages/how-to/#. This website has tips, advice, and tutorials on how to wash nearly any fabric at home. If you scroll down the page, you will see an A-Z material listing. Just click on the material you want to wash; all the advice you need is there.

Below are additional ideas to adjust your dry-cleaning habits to lessen the environmental/health impact:

- **Reduce**: As you purchase new clothing, look for items that do not require dry cleaning.
- **Hand Wash**: Consider hand washing the dry clean only items. Many of them can be cleaned carefully at home. Looking online will provide directions for hand washing.

- **Delicate Cycle**: Another at-home alternative is to place dry clean clothing in a mesh bag in your washing machine on the delicate cycle and then lay them flat to air dry.

FAST FIVE IN THE LAUNDRY ROOM

Five steps you can take quickly to make an impact and begin to celebrate some wins!

1. **Reduce Number of Loads** – The best way to lighten your laundry load (literally) quickly is to find ways to reduce the number of loads per week. Two ways to reduce the number of loads include ensuring your loads are full and thinking twice before putting something in the laundry bin; do jeans really need washing after a single wear?

2. **Use Cold Water to Wash** – Most of the energy used by your washing machine is attributed to heating the water. A simple switch to cold will save you both energy and money.

3. **Discover a New Detergent** – Laundry detergents have some of the harshest chemicals of any products in your home. Switching to a product without toxins and plastic packaging can significantly impact. Glance at the detergent section in the chapter for some ideas.

4. **Try Dryer Balls as an Alternative to Dryer Sheets** – Wool dryer balls can be purchased from various sources online at very reasonable prices. They will eliminate the need for dryer sheets, and essential oils of your choosing can be added to give a scent to your laundry.

5. **Limit/Eliminate Dry Cleaning** – Reducing or eliminating dry cleaning will save money and protect the planet. If you have clothing you aren't comfortable treating at home, look for a wet cleaner in your area as an alternative. They do not use PERC in their process.

THE BATHROOM

The bathrooms in your home are filled with A LOT of products. Many of those products, such as soap, lotion, shampoo, makeup, and deodorant, are all placed directly on your skin. Unlike products in the kitchen that the FDA evaluates, there are few to no personal care product regulations.

The chapter will start with my story and then move into seven focus sections: Cleaning Products, Shower and Personal Care, the Medicine Cabinet, Skin Care, Makeup, Hair Care, and Nail Care. Each focus area will dive deeper into the category and provide ideas on reducing your environmental impact.

As mentioned in the introduction chapter, always check with a doctor before using any new product or DIY recipe to ensure the ingredients won't adversely impact you and your current health.

MY ONE SHADE GREENER STORY

We have bathrooms that serve different purposes in our home—a half bath for guests, the master bath which includes all my personal skincare and makeup, a "medicine cabinet" with most of the items residing in a kitchen cupboard, and the kids' bathroom that has cycled through a lot of different products as they moved from babies to adults. Because many of the products in these rooms last just a few months vs. years, I've been able to try a lot of different things over the last fifteen years. Some I liked, and I'm still using today, while I have purchased other items that just weren't right for me.

Adjustments in shower products like soap and shampoo were also made long ago. I experiment with different brands because I enjoy finding unique and new alternatives. In the last six months, I've shifted to bar shampoo and conditioner instead of liquid to remove packaging. I'll admit the change is still taking me a while to get used to (without the suds of traditional shampoo), but I've stuck with it.

Shampoo transitions nicely into the broader area of hair care. On this topic, the COVID lockdown took me down a whole new path with my hair, discovering my natural curls. I found a lot of information online about the Curly Girl Method (based on the book by Lorraine Massey) (Massey, 2011) and decided to try it. In addition to my natural shampoo, I purchased t-shirt towels, learned how to "scrunch" my hair, stopped using a brush daily, and just used my fingers to "comb" my hair instead. This change has cut out daily blow drying, flat ironing, and hair spray. I should also mention that when I shifted from "letting my hair air dry with curls" to the Curly Girl method, I started getting compliments on my curly hair. It really works!

Hair coloring is where I haven't made progress and want to investigate more. I started getting highlights when I was about thirty years old and have continued ever since. I used to highlight every 4-6 months, but as the grey has started to creep in, the frequency is now every 3-4 months. The research from this chapter has given me some good information to have a conversation with my stylist to see if we can try some eco-friendly alternatives.

While I've tried new skincare products that I've liked, I don't know that I've found a brand that is my new favorite. I continue to try brands as what I have runs out. I can't say the same for two other beauty areas, makeup and nails.

I've used a popular makeup brand since high school and have just started down the path of making changes here in the last three years. You might think to yourself, "She has been working on becoming one shade greener for fifteen years, and she hasn't changed her makeup?!" This is a good example that we each have our own journey and priorities. There are two makeup changes I have made. The first was shifting from a liquid foundation and concealer to an eco-friendly concealer and powder foundation. The second change is wearing less makeup. I only use powder foundation, lip gloss, and mascara most days.

On the nails front, I don't go to a salon for manicures, but I do my own at home once a week. I use a popular brand of polish, base coat, and topcoat. On the Environmental Working Group (EWG) website, my various products are rated between a two and a six (on a 10-point scale, with one being the best). So, while they aren't great, at least they aren't on the worst end of the scale. I will likely start adding some greener alternatives as polish runs out.

The area I didn't mention is the medicine cabinet. While we had many of these products as the kids were growing up, this isn't an area I personally purchase or use very much. When I need something, I look for a brand with healthier ingredients for our family and the environment.

UP NEXT IN MY HOME – In researching this chapter, I have found several brands and products I want to try as supplies run out, especially some dark green cleaning products, as mine are currently light green. The other areas I'm ready to try some changes are in my makeup and nail care products. I found several of the companies included in this chapter to be ones that could be a right fit for me. In addition, I want to use some of the books I purchased a couple of years ago on DIY skincare and bath products.

BATHROOM CLEANING PRODUCTS

As we get to the bathroom, we've had cleaning information in other chapters. So, we will touch quickly on product recommendations for countertops, mirrors, windows, and floors. Then, we will dive deeper into products specifically focused on cleaning the tough spots of the bathroom, like showers and toilets.

Below are products found in other chapters of the book that may be used in the bathroom:

- **Windows and Mirrors**: Two alternative cleaners to use with microfiber cloths are Truly Free (www.trulyfree.com) and Aunt Fannies (www.auntfannies.com). Refer to the family room chapter for additional details, brand alternatives, and DIY solutions.
- **Tile Flooring**: Two brand alternatives are Aspen Clean (www.aspenclean.com) and Aunt Fannies (www.auntfannies.com). For DIY and other floor types, refer to the family room chapter.
- **General Cleaner**: For the countertops and sinks in your bathroom, you could consider all-purpose countertop cleaners such as Aspen Clean (www.aspenclean.com), Method (www.methodhome.com), and Mrs. Meyers (www.mrsmeyers.com). DIY solutions and other brand alternatives can be found in the kitchen chapter.

TOILET BOWL CLEANER

Traditional toilet bowl cleaners contain many toxins that are not recommended. Alternatives are found in the sections below.

Light Green: These alternatives have better ingredients and traditional plastic packaging.

- **Seventh Generation** – Toilet Bowl Natural Cleaner in Emerald Cypress & Fir. www.seventhgeneration.com
- **ECOS** – Toilet cleaner in Cedar. www.ecos.com
- **Greenshield** – Organic toilet bowl cleaner. www.greenshieldorganic.com

Dark Green: These options have both better ingredients and better packaging.

- **Blueland Toilet Cleaner** – These are tablets you drop in the toilet; let them soak, scrub, and flush. The first order comes with a container and then refill packaging. www.blueland.com
- **Mama Suds Toilet Bombs**: Drop in the toilet, scrub, and flush. The product comes in a cloth pouch with a drawstring. www.mamasuds.com
- **Seventh Generation Zero Plastic Toilet Bowl Cleaning Powder**: The powder is packaged in a pouch and thus gets rid of the plastic packaging. www.seventhgeneration.com

DIY Green: In a glass bowl, use a wooden spoon to mix 2 cups baking soda with 1 teaspoon tea tree oil and break up the clumps. Store the mixture in a glass, airtight container. When it's time to clean the toilets, drop 1 tablespoon into the bowl, rubbing on the sides with your toilet brush. Pour ½ cup of 20% vinegar (not your regular kitchen vinegar) into the bowl and watch it fizz. Use the toilet brush to scrub, and then wait 10-15 minutes before flushing.

BATH AND SHOWER CLEANER

Finding eco-friendly shower cleaners is complicated, as many products use harsh chemicals. Two light green options and a few DIY solutions are below. There are no dark green options in this category, as I could not find alternatives with reduced packaging.

Light Green: These alternatives have better ingredients and traditional packaging.

- **ECOS Bathroom Cleaner – Tea Tree** – This plant-based cleaner can also be used for general purposes in the bathroom. The formula works on soap scum and stains. www.ecos.com
- **Sensitive Home** – This brand has a tub and tile cleaner and a daily shower spray. Both products are plant-based and come fragrance-free. www.sensitivehome.com

DIY Green: As with all DIY solutions, many recipes are online. You can use baking soda on a damp sponge for general tub and shower cleaning. For tougher cleaning, use vinegar first and follow with the baking soda. In addition, below are some other combinations for specific cleaning challenges:

- **Grout** – add lemon juice to 1 or 2 teaspoons of cream of tartar, apply with a toothbrush and rinse.
- **Shower doors** – apply 2-4 drops of lemon oil twice a month to protect them from buildup.

- **Mold** – mix one part hydrogen peroxide (3%) with two parts water in a spray bottle. Spray on areas with mold. Wait at least one hour before rinsing or showering.

CLEANING TIP: I have started keeping cleaning supplies under the sink in each bathroom (countertop cleaner, toilet bowl cleaner, cleaning cloth, etc.). This way, when I clean, I don't have to bring the supplies with me. The slight change has made the process much more convenient and saves time when I'm ready to tackle cleaning a bathroom. I'm not sure why it took me so long to figure this one out!

DRAIN CLEANER

There are very few eco-friendly drain cleaner alternatives. Like shower cleaners, I couldn't find any products that I would classify as dark green. Light green and DIY options are below.

Light Green: These alternatives have better ingredients and traditional packaging.

- **BioKleen Bac-Out** – Treats slow drains and can be used to eliminate odors in pipes. This product uses live enzyme cultures that break down buildup into tiny particles. www.biokleenhome.com
- **Drainbo All-Natural Drain Cleaner** – This product is made with natural ingredients and certified safe and all-natural by the Natural Products Association. www.drainbo.com
- **Oanie Drain Hair Cleaner Tool** – This alternative is made of plastic but is very effective and can be reused many times. The product is a long piece with sharp edges that helps literally cut and pull out hairballs clogging your bathroom sink and shower drains. You aren't using any liquid product, so there are no worries about chemicals

getting into the water. Available at major retailers like Amazon, Walmart, and Target.

DIY Green: Mix ½ cup baking soda and ½ cup vinegar together, pour down the drain, cover with a damp cloth for 5 minutes, and then flush with hot water.

THE SHOWER AND PERSONAL CARE

This focus area will concentrate on the shower and the products used in and just after showering. We will start with water use in the bathroom and provide some ideas on how your family can conserve water in their daily hygiene routines. From there, we'll dive into products, including soap, shampoo, razors, deodorant, lotions, toothpaste, and toilet paper.

REDUCING WATER USE

Much water use occurs in the bathroom with baths, showers, face washing, teeth brushing, and toilet flushing. In fact, toilets alone use about 30% of all indoor water (*Residential Toilets | US EPA*, 2016). The most popular tip for reducing the water used when flushing the toilet is to add a brick to the toilet tank in each bathroom. This will reduce the amount of water used with each flush.

When it comes to the shower, you can consider installing low-flow showerheads to reduce the water used. If you are wondering if it is better to take a bath or shower, the short answer is "It depends." If you take long showers, the bath could be better. However, in most cases, the shower will use less water—about seventeen gallons for an eight-minute shower (Schwartz, n.d.). If you opt for a bath, a bubble bath will keep the water warm longer by insulating the surface.

Another way to conserve water in the bathroom is to turn off the water flow while doing other things like washing your face, brushing your teeth, or shaving. Keeping the water running while doing other things is just letting water run down the drain with no purpose

One final tip for the bathrooms (and other water sources in the home) is to ensure nothing is leaking. A leaky sink can waste a lot of water in a short period. When you see a leak or a drip, address it immediately; this stops the water and provides peace of mind without having a nagging "to do."

> **The Navy Shower** – A water-saving shower technique to try is the "Navy Shower," inspired by the method used to conserve water on Navy ships. You get in the shower, get wet, and then turn the water off. You soap and shampoo from there and then turn the water back on to rinse off. According to TreeHugger, this method can reduce water use from 60 gallons to 3 gallons per shower (Alter, 2008)!

SOAP

When considering the soap you use daily, some alternatives remove the harmful ingredients and are better for both people and the planet. In addition, the soap category is an easy one to get rid of unnecessary plastic packaging by using bar soap. Below are some light green liquid and dark green bar soap options.

Light Green: These brands have better ingredients and traditional plastic packaging.

- **Dr. Bronner's Pure Castile Soap** – This concentrated liquid can be diluted for daily use. There are several scents available. This soap is also an ingredient in many DIY recipes for other cleaning uses around the home. www.drbronner.com

- **Everyone Brand 3 in 1 Soap** – Everyone carries an unscented soap and six scent alternatives. The soap has three uses: shower gel, shampoo, and bubble bath. They also note it can be used for shaving. www.eoproducts.com
- **Honest Shampoo and Body Wash** – This brand can be found at many popular retailers and can do double duty as a body wash and shampoo. www.honest.com

Dark Green: These brands have better ingredients and little or no packaging.

- **Makes 3 Organics** – This brand offers six scents of bar soap (including unscented) and sells a natural cotton soap bag that ensures you can use every last drop. www.makes3organics.com
- **Attitude Leaves Body Bar** – These bars have four scents available and come to you packaged in a recyclable cardboard box. www.attitudeliving.com
- **Dr. Bronner's Bar Soap** – Eight scents (including unscented) are available. This is not only a good soap but has a good price point compared to others. www.drbronner.com
- **Wildland Organics Super Bar** – This alternative is touted as an "all-in-one" body, shampoo, and conditioner. Lather up with no need to reach for different bars for different uses. www.wildlandorganics.com

DIY Green: As with all DIY solutions, there are many recipes online, in this case, hundreds and thousands! You first decide if you are making liquid or solid soap and then explore alternatives. Because of all the options, I've included a soap-making book in the resources at the end of this chapter for those who want to dive in deeper and give soap-making a try.

SHAMPOO AND CONDITIONERS

Shampoo is like soap; the light green options are liquid and arrive in plastic packaging, while the dark green options are in bar form.

Light Green: These brands have better ingredients and traditional plastic packaging.

- **Avalon Organics** – These products use organic botanicals and essential oils to create safe and effective plant-based shampoos and conditioners. www.avalonorganics.com
- **Alaffia** – This brand has many haircare products. While packaged in traditional bottles, the ingredients are healthier for use by the people in your home. www.alaffia.com
- **Juice Organics** – These haircare products use plant sudsers and conditioners. All products are free of harmful ingredients and are both vegan and cruelty-free. www.juicebeauty.com
- **Odylique Tea Tree & Herb Shampoo** – This shampoo is specifically targeted at those who struggle with dandruff. www.odylique.com

Dark Green: These brands have better ingredients and little to no packaging.

- **Lush Cosmetics** – Lush has over ten bar shampoo alternatives, regardless of your hair type or what you want the shampoo to achieve. They note that shampoo bars will get you around eighty washes, making it more economical than most liquid shampoos. www.lushusa.com
- **Superzero** – This brand also has many options for different hair types (including a dandruff bar). Their website has a hair quiz to determine the right product for you. www.superzero.com

- **Love Beauty and Planet Shampoo Bar** – This product is found at many popular superstores, has a great price point, and is good for color-treated hair. www.lovebeautyandplanet.com
- **HiBar Shampoo & Conditioner** – This brand has many different formulas and sells sets of shampoo and conditioner, including one for natural and curly hair. www.hellohibar.com
- **Be Green Bath & Body Dry Shampoo** – Dry shampoo is an alternative that enables you to skip days of washing your hair. This brand comes in an aluminum bottle that can then be refilled with a product that comes in a paper pouch. www.begreenbathandbody.com

DIY Green: The basic ingredients for DIY shampoo can include items like Castile soap, various oils, and then "extras" for fragrance and unique benefits (dry hair, curly hair, etc.). Those extras include essential oils, molasses, coconut milk, and more.

Here is one recipe to try: Whisk together 1-13.5oz can of full-fat coconut milk, 2 tablespoons raw honey, 2 tablespoons apple cider vinegar, 1 teaspoon jojoba oil, 1 teaspoon castor oil, and 1 teaspoon essential oil (if desired). Put in a squeeze bottle and shake well before each use.

A Little Treat – I found some brands with great and eco-friendly offerings in researching bath products. The challenge was that their prices were a bit higher than I wanted to feature. So, if you are looking to spend a little more on bath and personal care, I would recommend checking out: Soap for Goodness Sake (www.soapforgoodnesssake.com), Manos Soap Company (www.manossoap.com), and Codex Beauty Labs (www.codexlabscorp.com). In addition, don't forget to check out Etsy for makers worldwide focused on eco-friendly products.

RAZORS

Disposable razors significantly impact the environment as they are typically made of plastic, used for just a few weeks, and then thrown away. In fact, the EPA once estimated that two billion disposable razors end up in landfills yearly (*Landfill Waste: How to Prevent Disposable Razor Plastic Pollution*, 2019). This section will look at light green alternatives that lessen the impact, like reusable razors and dark green options that eliminate razor use completely.

Light Green: Razors that are reusable and lessen the impact of disposables. When moving to a more permanent razor solution, the razor is called a safety razor, and you have a choice of double-edged or butterfly. You will want to decide which is right for you before purchasing the razor. While the upfront investment in the razor is higher, you will stop buying disposables several times a year. In the long run, you will likely save money with this shift.

Many options are gender-neutral, so men and women can use the same brands and products. Below are some alternatives to consider:

- **Detox Market Safety Razor K**it - Includes a brass safety razor and five-blade replacements. This razor has a weighted handle, so you can shave without applying pressure that can irritate. www.thedetoxmarket.com
- **The Leaf** – The leaf razor has a pivoting head that moves smoothly over your skin. The blade design helps eliminate razor burn and irritation. www.leafshave.com
- **Hanni** – This metal razor has a powder-coated handle that won't rust when wet. So, this is a good one to consider if you shave in the shower. www.heyhanni.com

- **Eco Roots** – This brand has a rose gold safety razor that provides a more feminine look. www.ecoroots.us
- **Electric Razors** – An electric razor is a better option than a disposable, but not as good as a safety razor because it uses electricity and won't last a lifetime. The other issue is that it is more difficult to dispose of/recycle at the end of life. If this option seems best for you over disposable razors, brands to consider include Philips Norelco, Braun, Bevel, Remington, and Panasonic.

Dark Green: These are alternatives that eliminate the razor.

- **Sugar Waxing** – Please note the word "sugar." This is an alternative form of waxing that leverages a mixture that includes sugar, lemon, and water. Because of these ingredients, the impact on the environment is lower than shaving. This is not the case with traditional "strip" waxing. You can go to a salon for the sugar waxing procedure and do DIY at home. This type of waxing can be done on any area of the body.
- **Laser Hair Removal** – This option can potentially eliminate hair removal for good. There are now options for having the removal professionally done and products sold for use at home. If you go the at-home route, remember that you will end up with a product you need to donate or figure out how to dispose.
- **Bleame Hair Eraser** – This is marketed as an alternative to waxing or laser hair removal. You run the product over your skin, and the hairs are removed. They also suggest that the product helps exfoliate and make your skin feel smoother. www.bleame.com

DIY Green – Shaving Cream: Here is a recipe you can try if you use shaving cream. Melt 1/3 cup shea butter and 1/3 cup coconut oil on low heat. Once melted, pour into a bowl, and stir in ¼ cup olive or sweet almond oil. Place the mixture in the refrigerator and let it harden. Once it's solid, whip it with a mixer for 2-3 minutes until it becomes creamy. If you want the scent of essential oils, add them now.

TOOTHPASTE, TOOTHBRUSH, AND DENTAL FLOSS

Brushing our teeth is a daily activity that uses three products: toothbrush, toothpaste, and floss. First, let's talk about the toothbrush. According to the American Dental Association, one billion plastic toothbrushes are thrown away yearly in the United States (Racovites, 2020). The good news is that there are alternatives to single-use plastic. Below are some materials and brands to consider:

- **Bamboo**: This material is popular as bamboo replenishes quickly, and the toothbrushes (minus the bristles) are compostable and biodegradable. Brands to consider include:
  - **Brush with Bamboo** – www.brushwithbamboo.com
  - **The Humble Company** – www.thehumble.co
  - **Olas** – www.olaswellness.com
  - **Isha** – www.ishalife.com
  - **Goodwell Company** – This product works like an electric toothbrush but is "charged" by twisting the handle. www.goodwell.co
- **Beechwood**: Georganics – www.usa.georganics.com
- **Charcoal**: Hello Charcoal (www.hello-products.com) and Me Mother Earth (www.memotherearthbrand.com)
- **Recycled Plastics**: These alternatives are made from disposed plastics. Brands include Unilever (www.unilever.com) and Preserve (www.preserve.eco).

As we move from the brush to the toothpaste, the light green alternatives have better ingredients, and the dark green provides alternatives with better ingredients and eliminates plastic packaging.

Light Green: These toothpaste brands have better ingredients but still use traditional packaging.

- **Davids** – This brand specializes in toothpaste with six products (two of which are sold in travel sizes). They are made in and sourced from the US with natural ingredients. www.davids.com
- **Attitude** – This brand has multiple kinds of toothpaste and sells bamboo toothbrushes. www.attitudeliving.com
- **Tom's of Maine** – This mainstream brand is rated well by EWG and can be easily found. www.tomsofmaine.com

Dark Green: These brands have improved both the ingredients and the packaging.

- **Happy Tooth Powder** – This tooth powder is in a glass bottle and is made with just six ingredients described in detail on the website. www.naturaltoothhealth.com
- **Olivia Care Tooth Powder** – These tooth powders are also made with a short list of ingredients listed on the website. www.oliviacare.com
- **Crush & Brush Toothpaste Tablets** – This brand leverages tablets you chew, packaged in a glass jar. The ingredients are all listed on the site. www.nelsonnaturalsusa.com

DIY Green: If you want to try your own toothpaste, here is a quick recipe to try. Combine 3 teaspoons of baking soda with 1 teaspoon of sea salt. Add ¼ cup of MCT oil and stir to combine. If you want the mixture a little thicker, add 1 teaspoon of arrowroot powder. Store the mixture in a cool, dark place for up to three weeks.

Dental Floss: Eco-friendly dental floss is typically made of bamboo and comes in a refillable glass jar for storage. A few brands to consider include Treebird (www.treebirdeco.com), Etee (www.shopetee.com), EcoRoots (www.ecoroots.us), Georganics (www.usa.georganics.com), and Dental Lace (www.dentallace.com).

DEODORANT

When considering deodorants, there are several ingredients to avoid, including parabens, aluminum, and artificial fragrances. There are a lot of natural alternatives out there, and a few are listed below:

Light Green: These brands have better ingredients and use traditional packaging.

- **Schmidt's** – Schmidt's deodorants come in sprays, sticks, and creams to let you find the formula that fits you best. The products are free of aluminum salts and parabens. www.schmidts.com
- **Weleda** – These deodorants come in roll-on and spray options. www.weleda.com
- **Think** – This brand is a B Corp and has products in multiple categories. There are eight deodorant options to select from. www.gothink.com
- **Type A Cream Deodorant** – This non-toxic, cruelty-free cream deodorant comes in seven different scents. www.typeadeodorant.com

Dark Green: These brands have improved both the ingredients and the packaging.

- **Tom's of Maine** – This brand has many deodorant choices and can be found at many retailers. They have traditional plastic packaging and a non-plastic alternative. www.tomsofmaine.com
- **Native** – The Native brand deodorant is available in many retailers and has plastic-free and plastic options. There are also many scents and formulas available. www.nativecos.com
- **Meow Meow Tweet** – This lesser-known brand has both tubes and creams available in several scent options. The tubes are made of compostable material, and the jars holding the cream are refillable after you've used the product. www.meowmeowtweet.com
- **Peach by Grove Collaborative** – The peach brand of deodorant within the Grove Collective has a refillable deodorant product. You purchase the container in the first purchase and then buy refillable tubes after that. www.grove.co

DIY Green: A recipe to try making your own deodorant takes just a few steps. Mix ¼ cup baking soda and ¼ cup cornstarch or arrowroot powder in a glass bowl. Then, add 1/3 cup of coconut oil and 10-15 drops of your favorite essential oils like lavender or grapefruit. Pour the mixture into an airtight glass jar. To use, scoop out a small amount (the size of a dime) with a spoon or stick and apply.

For the Men in Our Lives – While men can use any products and brands featured in this chapter, Boyzz Only is a brand focused 100% on eco-friendly products for men. The brand carries shampoo, body wash, hand sanitizers, and more. The two products I think would be a great addition to their offerings are deodorant and bar soap (all the body washes are liquid). www.boyzzonly.com

BODY LOTION

When considering body lotion, the alternatives to consider are below.

Light Green: These brands have better ingredients and use traditional packaging.

- **Just the Goods** – This brand has lotions featuring grape seed oil to keep costs down. The lotions are available in four scents and various packaging sizes/materials. www.justthegoods.net
- **Everyone Nourishing Lotion** – The Everyone brand has lotions in two sizes and six different scents. The company is a B Corp and has many certifications. www.eoproducts.com
- **Sea Kind Lotion** – This lotion contains a proprietary blend of four sustainable sea plants. www.sea-kind.com

Dark Green: These brands have improved both the ingredients and the packaging.

- **Plaine Products** – This brand offers refillable vegan products. The body lotion is in a reusable aluminum bottle that can be shipped back to be cleaned and refilled. www.plaineproducts.com
- **Corvus Botanicals** – Corvus offers a variety of low-waste options with a lotion bar and stick available. The sticks come in a compostable cardboard tube. www.corvusbotanicals.com
- **Amazon Aware Lotion** – This product by Amazon comes in a refillable aluminum container. The lotion is made in the US and is EWG certified. www.amazon.com

DIY Green: Some DIY lotions can be rather involved to make. Here's an easy recipe to get you started and determine if you want to explore other options. In a glass bowl, combine 1 cup of aloe vera gel, ¼ cup of coconut oil, 1 teaspoon of vitamin E oil, and 10 drops of essential oils of your choice. Whip with a hand mixer for a minute or two and place in airtight jars. The lotion lasts about three months.

TOILET PAPER

In 2020, the NRDC (National Resources Defense Council) updated its scorecard on toilet paper sustainability (*Toilet Paper and Climate Change: NRDC's Updated "Issue With Tissue" Ranks Brands on Sustainability | NRDC*, n.d.). Brands that many use daily, like Charmin, Scotts, Kirkland, Cottonelle, and Quilted Northern, all received F Ratings. The primary reason for these ratings is that these brands are made with virgin materials instead of recycled content.

Light Green: These brands are produced using at least 60% recycled content.

- **Seventh Generation** – This brand has a 100% recycled alternative available. www.seventhgeneration.com
- **Marcal** – This brand is Green Seal Certified and uses 60% post-consumer recycled content. www.marcalpaper.com
- **EverSpring** – This brand is 100% recycled and FSC Certified. Available at major retailers.

Dark Green: These brands are produced with alternative materials.

- **Betterway** – This brand is made of 100% bamboo and rated soft, absorbent, and effective. In addition, it's free of dyes, chlorine, and BPA. www.gobetterway.com
- **Cloud Paper** – This brand is made from FSC-certified bamboo and arrives direct from the manufacturer without any plastic packaging. www.cloudpaper.co
- **Who Gives a Crap** – This brand provides a subscription service, and the toilet paper arrives at your door when needed. The product is made from 95% recycled materials, although they also have a bamboo alternative. The company is a certified B Corp and donates 50% of its profits to communities needing toilets. www.us.whogivesacrap.org

DIY Green: DIY is a bit odd here, but the way to move away from needing toilet paper is to consider purchasing a bidet. This toilet sprays water to clean you instead of using toilet paper. While it is an upfront investment, you will save hundreds each year by not buying toilet paper. I do not have a bidet, so I can't advocate for or against it, but many worldwide believe this is a better alternative.

TISSUES

Tissues are like toilet paper, with mainstream brands using virgin materials that have a negative impact on the environment. Below are some light green options to consider for both recycled and sustainable alternatives. Some brands are the same as those with toilet paper. In addition, the dark green options are shifting from disposable to reusable tissues.

Light Green: These are made with recycled or alternative materials.

- **Seventh Generation** – 100% recycled tissues.
  www.seventhgeneration.com
- **Who Gives a Crap** – 100% bamboo tissues that are compostable.
  www.us.whogivesacrap.org
- **Grove Collaborative** – 100% bamboo tissues. www.grove.co

Dark Green: These brands have reusable options instead of disposable ones.

- **Last Tissue Box** – This brand sells organic cotton tissues in a reusable container. You wash the tissues in a special bag, and the container can be put in the dishwasher. www.lastobject.com
- **Hankybook** – This brand has machine-washable organic cotton "pages" and is easy to take on the go. If you need another tissue, flip the page for a new sheet. www.hankybook.com
- **Etsy Handkerchiefs** – Etsy is full of shop owners with organic cotton and vintage handkerchiefs. You can find the perfect match for your personality. www.etsy.com

DIY Green: The at-home solution would be to repurpose old t-shirts or sheets and make your own handkerchiefs. If you love to sew, this could be a fun activity.

MENSTRUAL PRODUCTS

Menstrual products have come a long way in the last 5-10 years, developing more eco-friendly alternatives. From mainstream brands, pads are almost 90% plastic, and nearly all tampons contain plastic.

Light Green: Below are a few brands to consider with organic cotton tampons, pads, and liners. Many of these tampons are applicator free. If you prefer an applicator, try the Dame Reusable Tampon Applicator.

- **TOP: The Organic Project** – Tampons, pads, and liners. www.toporganicproject.com
- **Veeda** – Tampons, pads, and liners. www.veedausa.com
- **FLO** – Biodegradable and Organic tampons. www.hereweflo.co

Dark Green: These are reusable for months and years to come.

- **Reusable Cloth Pads** – Period Aisle (www.periodaisle.com) and Rael Organic (www.getrael.com).
- **Period Underwear** – Thinx (www.thinx.com), Knix (www.knix.com), and Saalt (www.saalt.com).
- **Menstrual Cups** – Diva (www.divacup.com), Saalt (www.saalt.com), Real (www.getreal.com), and Lunette (www.store.lunette.com).
- **Menstrual Discs (like cups, but inserted further)** – Intimina Ziggy Cup (www.intimina.com) and Nixit Menstrual Cup (www.nixit.com).

THE MEDICINE CABINET

Of all the areas in the bathroom, the medicine cabinet is the most challenging to find eco-friendly products. The EWG doesn't rate these products, and many others online don't provide thoughts or evaluations on what is out there. Always check with your doctor to ensure new brands and DIY recipes don't contain ingredients that wouldn't be right for you.

The two category exceptions are sunscreen and bug spray, which have received much attention over the last ten years on the need to remove toxic ingredients. Those two categories will have a bit more detail in this section.

There are a few brands I found that offered multiple medicine cabinet products. If you are looking for something that isn't featured, check out these brands to see if they provide what you are looking for.

- **Forces of Nature Medicine**: First aid, cold and flu, pain relief, skin care, and sleep products. They are the first company to manufacture USDA Certified Organic and FDA-registered medicines. www.forcesofnaturemedicine.com
- **Badger**: Sunscreen, bug spray, wellness products, skincare, and more. A B-Corp located in rural New Hampshire. www.badgerbalm.com
- **Hilma**: Digestive, respiratory, and sleep products. The company has many certifications, and the products are made in the US. www.hilma.co
- **Traditional Medicinals**: Teas, lozenges, and capsules for pain, sleep, digestive issues, and more. This brand is a certified B Corp and is in California. www.traditionalmedicinals.com
- **Asutra**: Pain relief, sleep support, exercise recovery, and rest and relaxation. The company is based in Chicago and is focused on organic ingredients. www.asutra.com
- **Etsy**: There are many great small makers focused on all-natural products. Type in what you are looking for, and several alternatives will pop up. www.etsy.com

The next few sections highlight the products by the brands above in each category and others that focus more on one area. There are also some ideas for DIY alternatives.

PAIN RELIEF

Pain relief products come in many forms and types of packaging. I would recommend going to several of the brands mentioned below to find the product that is the right fit for you. Brands to consider:

- **Forces of Nature**: Products for headaches/migraines, joint/back/muscle/nerve pain, and gout. www.forcesofnaturemedicine.com
- **Badger**: Joint, muscle, and headache balms. www.badgerbalm.com
- **Hilma**: Tension relief. www.hilma.co
- **Asutra**: Lotions, sprays, and bath salts. www.asutra.com
- **Traditional Medicinals**: Hemp & Herb Joint Health tea. www.traditionalmedicinals.com

DIY Green: Essential oils, including lavender, rosemary, and eucalyptus, have been used to relieve pain. Online, you can find recipes to make sticks and balms for your particular need that you would have on hand for when the pain hits.

DIGESTIVE SYSTEM

Digestive challenges can vary widely from indigestion to bloating and hemorrhoids. Below are some brands that offer products for specific ailments.

- **Forces of Nature**: Hemorrhoids. www.forcesofnaturemedicine.com
- **Hilma**: Digestive aids, gas and bloating, and heartburn relief. www.hilma.co
- **Traditional Medicinals**: Smooth move capsules, belly comfort lozenges, and gas relief tea. www.traditionalmedicinals.com

DIY Green: A quick mixture of 1 tablespoon apple cider vinegar, 1 tablespoon honey, and a cup of warm water helps with indigestion, gas, and heartburn. Many other alternatives can be found online, including chamomile tea, peppermint, and a heating pad.

COLDS, COUGHS, AND ALLERGIES

These creep up on us when least expected. So, it would be good to look at alternatives and get some products before the season for colds and allergies starts.

- **Forces of Nature**: Cold and flu, allergy, and sinus options. www.forcesofnaturemedicine.com
- **Badger**: Aromatic chest rub. www.badgerbalm.com
- **Hilma**: Immunity and respiratory support. www.hilma.co
- **Traditional Medicinals**: Throat coat lozenges and cold care tea. www.traditionalmedicinals.com

DIY Green: Products like ginger tea, honey, and cinnamon sticks are popular for soothing a cough or cold. Search "DIY cold (or allergy) remedy recipes" to find a mixture that relieves your symptoms.

SLEEP, FOCUS, AND ANXIETY

There continue to be more products developed and launched to support sleep, focus, and anxiety. Below are a few brands to consider:

- **Forces of Nature**: Sleep, calm, and focus products. www.forcesofnaturemedicine.com

- **Badger**: Sleep, stress, calm, focus, and other aromatherapy products. www.badgerbalm.com
- **Hilma**: Sleep essentials. www.hilma.co
- **Traditional Medicinals**: Teas for sleep, calm, mental focus, and more. www.traditionalmedicinals.com
- **Asutra**: Sleep support lotions and aromatherapy. They also have eye pillows. www.asutra.com

CBD Alternatives: While I haven't personally tried these for sleep and anxiety, I've heard many people have succeeded with CBD products to help with sleep and anxiety. These brands include products for both humans and pets. Below are a few to consider:

- **Extract Labs**: This brand is certified USDA organic and carries tinctures, topicals, gels, and gummies to relieve various issues. www.extractlabs.com
- **CBDistillery**: This brand also carries CBD in many forms and has many certifications. They have an area where it's easy to sort by benefits. www.thecbdistillery.com
- **Joy Organics**: This brand has a wide range of products and is very transparent with the manufacturing process. They also have carbon-neutral shipping. www.joyorganics.com

DIY Green: Using a diffuser in your room and adding essential oils just before bedtime helps some with relaxation and sleep. Some essential oils that promote sleep and relaxation include lavender, frankincense, bergamot, and cedarwood.

CUTS AND SMALL BURNS

We reach for the bandages and ointments when getting a small cut or burn. Many traditional bandages are made of plastic. The eco-friendly bandages are made from bamboo. A few brands I would consider dark green (with good ingredients and packaging) to consider are below:

- **Patch** – This brand features bamboo bandages, wraps, and organic anti-bacterial wipes. www.nutricare.co
- **FEBU** – They carry bandages and body tape made of bamboo. Available on Amazon.
- **Essence of Life Organics** – Biodegradable bamboo bandages. www.essenceoflifeorganics.com
- **Forces of Nature Medicine** – Fissure ointment. www.forcesofnaturemedicine.com

When shifting to ointments, many alternatives can be used for more than just cuts and scrapes. They are described as being good for many skin challenges.

- **All Good Goop** – This is an all-purpose ointment. www.allgoodproducts.com
- **Green Goo** – The skin repair healing salve comes in a glass jar, travel tin, or rub-on stick. www.greengoo.com
- **Essence of Life Organics** – The brocco fusion ointment can be used for various needs. www.essenceoflifeorganics.com

DIY Green: The natural remedy I use frequently is to cut a leaf off my aloe vera plant, rub the juice on the wound, and cover it with a bandage. There are many recipes online if you are looking for an alternative to the plant. They contain ingredients like beeswax, coconut oil, tea tree oil, and calendula.

SUNSCREEN

There are many natural ways to lessen the need for sunscreen, including wearing clothes that cover you well, staying in the shade vs. the sun, and limiting time outside during the strongest sun hours. However, we can't avoid the sun and should wear eco-friendly sunscreens when we go out.

You can look your current product up on the EWG website and see how it's rated. If you look for an alternative, some ingredients to avoid would be anything that has Oxybenzone, Octinoxate, Avobenzone, Homosalate, and Octisalate, to name a few. Zinc oxide and titanium dioxide are the two active ingredients that are both safe and non-toxic.

To not overuse sunscreen, you only need one ounce (one shot glass full) to get enough protection from the sun. Below are some sunscreen alternatives that you could consider.

Light Green: These brands have better ingredients and traditional packaging.

- **Two Peas** – They have two SPF levels, 30 and 50, have no chemicals, and are biodegradable. www.twopeasorganics.com
- **Kokua** – This brand is produced in Hawaii with locally grown ingredients. www.kokuasuncare.com
- **Solara Suncare** – There are options, including body, face, and lip formulas. www.solarasuncare.com

Dark Green: These brands have improved both the ingredients and the packaging.

- **Raw Elements** – This plastic-free packaging alternative comes in tins and bio-resin tubes. There are many formulas available, and they include sunscreen for lips and hold many certifications. www.rawelementsusa.com

- **All Good** – SPF 50 Sunscreen butter in a metal tin. www.allgoodproducts.com

DIY Green: There are two types of DIY alternatives online; those you make from scratch and those you make by adding a couple of ingredients to an eco-friendly lotion. For the simpler version, you take your lotion and mix in non-nano zinc oxide. I'm not sure how I feel about the DIY solutions; they are out there, but there is no research on the SPF and effectiveness.

DIY SELF TANNER – When it comes to DIY, you can even find recipes for self-tanning!

The ingredients are simple—black tea bags, boiling water, and a spray bottle. You boil the tea for 10-15 minutes, put it in a spray bottle, shower, and spray on. Wait until you are fully dry before getting dressed. The other DIY tanning tip is to eat more sweet potatoes, which have lots of carotenes that can warm your natural skin tone.

BUG SPRAY

When considering bug sprays, like many other products, look for ingredients you understand, not complex chemicals, especially DEET. You may see eco-friendly ingredients, including citronella, eucalyptus oil, and rosemary extract.

Light Green: These brands have better ingredients and traditional packaging.

- **Murphy's** – This brand is B Corp certified and offers sprays, balms, and candles. www.murphysnaturals.com
- **Natrapel** – Long-lasting bug sprays made of plant-based ingredients. www.natrapel.com
- **Sawyer Products** – This company offers insect repellents, sunscreen, and first aid. www.sawyer.com

Dark Green: These brands have improved both the ingredients and the packaging.

- **Aunt Fannie's** – While this brand has traditional packaging, they also offer biodegradable mosquito repellant wipes. www.auntfannies.com
- **Badger** – This brand has traditional sprays and a bug balm in a metal tin. www.badgerbalm.com

DIY Green: The extremely simple DIY solution is to spray on a mixture of water and vinegar. A more complex recipe is to put the following into a spray bottle; ½ cup apple cider vinegar, ½ cup witch hazel, and 40 drops of essential oil. The essential oil can be any combination of tea tree, citronella, rosemary, lemongrass, eucalyptus, peppermint, or bergamot. Just spray on before going outside.

FUNGUS, WARTS, AND MORE

I wanted to mention this as a category because there were products from Forces of Nature (www.forcesofnaturemedicine.com) for athlete's foot, nail fungus, ringworm, and warts. I found two other brands for athlete's foot: Gotucream (www.gotucream.com) and Foot Cure (www.gofootcure.com) tea tree oil foot soak.

DIY Green: Because these situations are a bit different, I recommend doing the searches online rather than listing possible ingredients here.

> RECYCLING MEDICINES – Some people have grown up flushing unused medicines down the toilet. Today that is NOT a recommended practice as the ingredients in the medicines then make their way into our groundwater and can harm our health. Instead, do a quick search for your community's drop-off days or find a year-round drop-off location on www.Earth911.org. This process will also ensure that those unused drugs aren't accidentally taken by someone else in the home.

HAIR CARE

Beyond washing, the number of products and the associated impact on hair care varies dramatically. Some get out of the shower, let their hair air dry, and are completely natural. On the other end of the spectrum are those that color their hair every six weeks, blow it dry every day, use a flat/curling iron, and add mousse and hair spray. Many of us fall somewhere in the middle of the two extremes. We will cover hair coloring, electronic products/use, and styling products in this focus area.

HAIR COLORING

Traditional hair coloring products contain toxic ingredients that aren't recommended on your skin or in the air you breathe. Some conventional dyes have up to twenty-two coal-tar-based ingredients and include PPD (Paraphenylenediamine) to increase longevity, ammonia to open the hair cuticle, and proteins to keep the hair shaft healthy.

If you go to a salon to have your hair colored, ask questions about the brand your stylist is using. You can then research that brand and see if there are better alternatives that you might be able to ask them to try. Some organic brands you could have them investigate include Wella, Matrix, Kevin Murphy, Goldwell, and Schwarzkopf. For those who color their hair at home, below are some light green alternatives to consider and one dark green option:

Light Green: These brands have better ingredients and traditional packaging.

- **Light Mountain** – This brand has 100% botanical hair colors that developed a non-chemical 2-step program to color gray hair. They offer 12 shades and 8 formulas for covering grey hair. www.light-mountain-hair-color.com
- **Desert Shadow** – This brand is certified organic and offers 12 shades. In addition, they have a line of hair masks, shampoos, and conditioners. www.desertshadoworganic.com
- **Henna Color Lab** – This brand is certified organic and cruelty-free. In addition to hair color, they feature a beard coloring line and shampoos, conditioners, and other hair products. www.hennacolorlab.com
- **Green Hare** – 100% natural hair dye made from ground herbs, walnut shells, and flowers. The dyes are vegan and cruelty-free and will cover grey roots. www.greenhare.com
- **Brite** – This brand is available at many mainstream stores. They have a line called Naturally Brite Hair Color Made from Plants. This line, not their mainstream line, is an eco-friendly alternative. www.briteorganix.com

Dark Green: These brands have improved both the ingredients and the packaging.

- **Lush** – Lush makes henna hair dyes in four shades that come in a bar-like soap. You melt the bar to create the dye. These products are vegan and cruelty-free, with two synthetic ingredients. www.lushusa.com

DIY Green: There are recipes online for achieving some hair coloring with items around the house, like lemon in sunlight for blondes and a coffee mixture for brunettes.

HAIR SPRAY, GELS, MOUSSE, AND MORE

When considering hair products, the light green brands below have improved ingredients. I didn't find any dark green alternatives with improved packaging.

Light Green: These brands have better ingredients and traditional packaging.

- **John Masters** – John Masters Organics creates hair products that are clean, cruelty-free, and sustainable. Products include sprays, de-frizz, and more. www.johnmasters.com
- **Carina Organics** – This brand has products free of chemicals and synthetic ingredients. They have a full line of haircare products, including hair gel and spray. www.carinaorganics.com
- **QET Botanicals** – This brand was born in a small Midwest town. They have many certifications, and all their products are 100% natural and organic. There is a hair spray and serum. www.qetbotanicals.com
- **Nature's Brands** – This brand carries many certifications, including USDA-certified organic. The products include styling gels, hair sprays, and hair treatments. www.naturesbrands.com

- **Shaz & Kiks** – This company is focused on sustainability and drawing insights from generations of beauty rituals of Indian women. They have a line of prewash, repair, and cleanser products. www.shazandkiks.com

DIY Green: The hair product recipes are abundant online. You can find homemade hair spray, mixtures to make your hair hold its curls, and some to reduce frizz. Just search for the challenge you are trying to solve, and alternative recipes will be available to find the one that's right for you.

BRANDS FOR PEOPLE OF COLOR WITH NATURAL HAIRSTYLES

While I won't profess to be an expert on what is important in hair care for people of color with natural hairstyles, I do know how to vet recommended brands and provide a summary of those focused on healthy ingredients for the planet and people.

Overall, I feel like this category of hair care did not have as low (good) ratings on EWG as the previously listed haircare brands. However, the ones I selected were all in the low to low-moderate range for the brand, and after reading the information on their websites, I felt comfortable including them here.

Light Green: These brands have better ingredients and traditional packaging.

- **Sienna Naturals** – This brand is vegan, cruelty-free, and responsibly sourced. They have an extensive haircare line with shampoo, conditioner, styling, hair and scalp oils, and more. The packaging is all curbside recyclable. www.siennanaturals.com

- **Suki Suki Naturals** – This brand is cruelty-free and contains products from mineral oil, preservatives, parabens, sulfates, and more. They provide full ingredient lists for each of their products on their website. www.sukisukinaturals.co.za
- **Melanin** – This brand has a smaller product line and sells head wraps and t-shirt towels. They have positive EWG ratings and provide a full ingredient list. www.melaninharecare.com
- **Mixed Chicks** – This brand lists that they are paraben, sulfate, and cruelty-free. I enjoyed their origin story, and they received mid-ratings on EWG. www.mixedchicks.net
- **AfroShe** – While this brand had no ratings on EWG, there were good reviews online, and the website lists all ingredients used in detail. The products are handmade with natural and certified organic ingredients as well as vegan and cruelty-free www.arfoshe.com
- **Soultanicals** – This brand makes toxin-free, vegan hair and body care by hand. They have an extensive product line and list all ingredients for each product on their site. www.soultanicals.com
- **Carol's Daughter** – This brand has an extensive product line and is easy to find in stores like Target. The ratings on EWG go from as low as a 3 (good) to as high as 10 (the worst). So, once selecting a product, go to the EWG website to check the rating. www.carolsdaughter.com
- **Canviiy** – This brand formulates with ingredients to build safe products for its customers. The products are free of sulfates, parabens, artificial fragrances, and color. www.canviiy.com

Dark Green: These brands have improved both the ingredients and the packaging.

- **Kreyol Essence** – This brand focuses on planting and harvesting its raw ingredients and caring for people and the planet. They are working to shift their packaging out of plastic. Some are packaged in glass and rated favorably by the EWG. www.kreyolessence.com
- **Wonder Curl** – Wonder Curl sources its ingredients from vendors who share their values. The products are vegan and cruelty-free, and the jars are made from 100% postindustrial resin. They ask customers to please recycle empty jars and bottles. www.wondercurl.com

HAIR DRYERS, CURLING IRONS, FLAT IRONS, AND MORE

Regarding the electronics in your haircare routine, the two planet impacts are the product materials and electricity use. In addition, the heat from the products hurts the health of your hair. The following sections include tips and ideas for your electronic hair products.

Use Less Styling Equipment

The best solution for the environment and your hair is to go natural and not use electronic products. You could start experimenting with your natural hair on days off work, on vacation, or any day when you aren't worried about how it might turn out. You may be pleasantly surprised at how good your hair can look without all the products and styling. One idea for reducing the drying time is to let your hair partially dry before you start to dry with a blow dryer. This will save energy and time and be kinder to your hair.

Purchasing Electronics

I will not recommend any specific brands here, as products in this category change frequently. When you are in the market for something new, look for alternatives made with less plastic and more natural materials. Also, consider the wattage and electric use of the device and strive to find the most efficient device that will still meet your needs.

COMBS AND BRUSHES

As you style your hair, combs and brushes may be integral to your routine. Below are four brands that offer a line of eco-friendly brushes and combs for many hair types and purposes:

- **Henna Color Company** – They carry various combs and brushes for multiple purposes. Many are made of bamboo with wood brush pins. www.hennacolorlab.com
- **Saya** – This brand is focused on "products that serve you and give back to the environment." They have brush options as well as hair accessories like sticks and forks. www.sayadesigns.com
- **Bass Brushes** – This company carries brushes for any need you can imagine. They are transparent with the materials used in all the products. Many feature bamboo handles and have different alternatives for the bristles. www.bassbrushes.com
- **Redecker** – This brand has been making natural brushes since 1935. They have brushes for hair, cleaning, nail care, and the body. You can't purchase the products on their website, but they are available on Amazon. www.amazon.com

ECO-FRIENDLY HAIR TIES – We might not automatically think of looking for a greener hair tie, but these small items are often made in a way that isn't environmentally friendly. Next time you need new hair ties, consider purchasing from Terra Ties (www.terraties.com) or Kooshoo (www.kooshoo.com).

SKINCARE

Skincare and makeup are two categories with many environmental concerns. In fact, according to the Environmental Working Group (EWG), the FDA has only reviewed 11% of the 10,500 cosmetic ingredients that are cataloged. The unreviewed ingredients are used in more than 99% of all available products (*FDA Warns Cosmetics Industry to Follow Law on Untested Ingredients | Environmental Working Group*, n.d.).

In addition to the ingredients, plastic packaging is of equal concern to the environment. In this focus area and the following (makeup), we'll look at companies making strides in the ingredients and the packaging. I hope you will find some new brands on the list that make sense for your skincare and makeup routines.

Light Green: These brands have better ingredients but still use traditional packaging.

- **QET Botanicals** – This brand was born in a small Midwest town. They have an extensive line and many certifications, and all products are 100% natural and organic. www.qetbotanicals.com
- **Carina Organics** – This brand has products free of chemicals and synthetic ingredients. They have a full product line, including moisturizers, cleansers, & toners. www.carinaorganics.com
- **John Masters** – John Masters Organics creates high-performing skincare products that are clean, cruelty-free, and sustainable. Products include cleansers, serums, and moisturizers. www.johnmasters.com
- **Nature's Brands** – This brand carries many certifications, including USDA-certified organic. The skin care products include face wash, toners, masks, serums, and wrinkle creams. www.naturesbrands.com

- **Sea Kind** – This brand uses Atlantic Ocean elements to create skincare formulas. Many of the products are verified by the Environmental Working Group. www.sea-kind.com
- **Tata Harper** – This higher-end luxury brand focuses on its products' ingredients and is completely free of GMOs, toxins, synthetic materials, and artificial fragrances. www.tataharperskincare.com
- **Paul Penders** – This brand provides 100% Vegan Certified Natural Skincare & Cosmetics and holds many certifications. In addition to skincare, they have hair care, makeup, suncare, and more. www.paulpenders.com

Dark Green: These brands have improved both the ingredients and the packaging.

- **Provence Apothecary** – This brand makes products with 100% plant-based ingredients. In addition, they have a recycling program for all their packaging. The brand has skincare consultations, classes, and a broad product line. www.provenceapothecary.com
- **Eco Roots** – Eco Roots is vegan and cruelty-free, with packaging that is either reusable or recyclable. They have cleansers, creams, and masks and carry products beyond skin care. www.ecoroots.us
- **Just the Goods** – This brand offers products that are vegan and all-natural. Every product's ingredient is transparently listed on the site; many are EWG-verified. They have an extensive line of skincare products for all skin types. www.justthegoods.net
- **Juice Beauty** – This brand focuses on "Farm to Beauty," transferring organic ingredients into the products. They are vegan and cruelty-free. The product line has offerings for nearly any kind of skin need. www.juicebeauty.com

- **Meow Meow Tweet** – This brand is focused on vegan, low-waste, and small batches. There are various skincare products and a line for hair and body. www.meowmeowtweet.com

DIY Green: From cleansers to facemasks and everything in between, there are recipes online to create your own skincare products at home. In addition to online resources, if this is an area you want to dive into, there are entire books written with DIY recipes to follow. Check out some options in the resources section at the end of this chapter.

MAKEUP

As mentioned in the prior focus area of skincare, many brands use ingredients that haven't been evaluated. Because so many of the brands we use have harmful toxins, I've included many options for you here in hopes that you will find some that are right for you and your pocketbook. One item to note is that some makeup alternatives are so natural that they may have shelf lives of 3-6 months. Keep that in mind as you look at the options.

Light Green: These brands have better ingredients but still use traditional packaging.

- **Elate Cosmetics** – This brand is a certified B Corp and focused on all elements of sustainability—product ingredients, recycling/packaging, fair trade, cruelty-free, and more. Their products are formulated for all skin types and tones. They offer a wide range of foundations, lips, eyes, and blushes/bronzers. www.elatebeauty.com
- **Pacifica Beauty** – The Pacifica brand has an extremely wide variety of products for all skin types and tones. Products cross skincare, makeup, haircare, and fragrance. They are 100% vegan and cruelty-

free. Products are rated mid-range to good by EWG.
www.pacificabeauty.com

- **RMS Beauty** – This brand has a full line of skincare and beauty products for every skin type and tone. The founder is a makeup artist who wanted to produce cosmetics with better, safer ingredients. www.rmsbeauty.com
- **W3LL People** – This brand has a broad range of skincare and cosmetic products. They are produced without toxins, are cruelty-free, and have over 35 EWG-certified products. There are options for all skin types and tones. www.wellpeople.com
- **Antonym Cosmetics** – This brand was looking to develop a line of cosmetics with natural ingredients without compromising the integrity of the makeup. They carry many certifications and have a full line. www.antonymcosmetics.com
- **LYS** – This brand is vegan, plant-based, and cruelty-free. The products are focused on foundation and blush. They have products for all skin types and tones. www.lysbeauty.com
- **Ilia** – Ilia believes that not all natural ingredients are good and not all synthetics are bad. They push the limits with innovation to create natural beauty products that are safe for those who wear them. www.iliabeauty.com

Dark Green: These brands have improved both the ingredients and the packaging.

- **Clean-Faced Cosmetics** – This company is very transparent with ingredients and also offers products to be refilled. The packaging is plastic free. They have a full makeup product line. www.cleanfacedcosmetics.com
- **Izzy** – Izzy is a zero-waste beauty company that is carbon neutral, and the products are made with clean ingredients and are cruelty-

free. Products include mascara, lip gloss, and brow pencils.
www.yourizzy.com

- **Athr** – Athr is focused on both the ingredients and the packaging. For every product on the site, it shows the ingredients and details on the packaging, including how to recycle. www.athrbeauty.com

- **Fat and The Moon** – This brand is focused on self-care and self-love. They have products that cross many categories, including cosmetics, skincare, haircare, and bath. The products are handmade to order in small batches. www.fatandthemoon.com

- **Sappho** – This brand has a wide range of vegan and cruelty-free products. Ingredients are certified organic and listed for every product. They offer cosmetics for all skin tones. www.mysappho.com

- **Axiology** – This brand is 100% focused on lipsticks that can also be used for cheeks and eyes. The sticks come in recycled paper, and the boxes are also recycled. www.axiologybeauty.com

DIY Green: Makeup is a category with so many DIY recipes for so many different products; you are sure to find some that work for you if you are interested in making your own. If you want to dive in here, I've included a book in the resources section at the end of this chapter.

MAKEUP BRUSHES AND APPLICATORS

Several makeup brands also carry eco-friendly brushes and applicators. Three are shown below:

- **Antonym Cosmetics** – They carry a full line of brushes with bamboo and black aluminum handles. The bristles are made of synthetic material. www.antonymcosmetics.com

- **Ilia** – Their brushes are made from FSC-certified wood and aluminum with synthetic bristles. www.iliabeauty.com
- **W3LL People** – This brand carries a full line of makeup brushes. However, they don't disclose what the casing is made of; they refer to it as "eco-friendly and lightweight." www.wellpeople.com

NAIL CARE

Many products are involved in nail care, including clippers, files, and cuticle oils. However, for many, the center of nail care is the polish worn for the days and weeks between using the other products. I'll start this focus area with nail polish to introduce brands that should be on the consideration list. Then, in the other sections, you will see me mention some of those same brands offering broader nail care lines with other products that might fit your needs.

NAIL POLISH

Nail polish contains a LOT of chemical names on the ingredients list. Three are known as the "Toxic Trio"—formaldehyde, toluene, and dibutyl phthalate (DBP). Instead of focusing on what to avoid, below are some nail polish brands for you to consider that have fewer toxins to impact your health and the environment.

Light Green: These brands have better ingredients but still use traditional packaging.

- **Zoya** – If you are looking for variety, Zoya is the brand for you, with over 650 different shades. The polishes are vegan and free of 10 of the most concerning chemicals. www.zoya.com

- **Olive & June** – The Olive and June polishes are vegan and free of 7 of the most concerning chemicals. The full ingredient list is available on their website. www.oliveandjune.com
- **786 Cosmetics** – This brand was developed to serve the Muslim community specifically. The water-permeable nail polish is vegan, halal, and cruelty-free. www.786cosmetics.com
- **Sophi** – This brand carries an odorless, vegan, and cruelty-free water-based formula. www.sophinailpolish.com
- **Traditional Brands with New Lines** – If you want to stick with a brand you know, some are coming out with more eco-friendly lines. Two to consider are Sally Hansen Good Kind Pure (www.sallyhansen.com) and OPI Nature Strong (www.opi.com).

Dark Green: These brands have improved both the ingredients and the packaging.

- **Cote** –Cote has removed 10 of the most toxic ingredients, is vegan, and is cruelty-free. In addition, they have a bottle recycling program; you send back your used bottles and get 10% off your purchase. www.coteshop.co
- **TenOverTen** – This brand is vegan, cruelty-free, and eliminates ten toxins. They use a lot of recycled materials in their packaging and point out how to recycle the products. www.tenoverten.com
- **Kester** – Kester has removed the toxic ingredients and makes vegan and sustainable products. The company is B Corp certified and 100% carbon neutral. www.kesterblack.com
- **Dazzle Dry** – The company was started by a biochemist who wanted to create healthy yet effective products removing the toxins in traditional polishes. There are over 150 colors available. They are also very focused on eco-friendly packaging and shipping materials. www.dazzledry.com

- **Habit** – This nail polish is vegan, cruelty- and toxin-free. The polish is packaged in recycled plastic components with biodegradable bamboo over caps to keep plastic to a minimum. www.habitcosmetics.com

DIY Green: I wouldn't have guessed that nail polish was a product that had DIY recipes, but there are! The most straightforward is to purchase an eco-friendly clear polish or topcoat. Then, add mica powder or crushed eco-friendly eye shadow in the color of your choice. Shake to mix and paint away.

Recycling Nail Polish – If you are like many of us, you likely have unused nail polish at home that you want to get rid of. Because of the ingredients in the traditional polishes on the market, the jar in your cabinet needs to be treated like any other household hazardous waste. You could take the polish to the next hazardous waste day in your community or look up on www.Earth911.org a location that would take it. Another alternative would be to pour the polish onto cardboard or another surface, allow the polish to dry completely, and then dispose of it in your regular trash, like disposing of unused paint.

NAIL POLISH REMOVER

Nail polish removers are offered by some of the same brands that sell nail polishes. This way, you could make an order that includes both. The dark green section below provides options without plastic packaging and reusable alternatives to cotton balls or pads.

Light Green: These brands have better ingredients but still use traditional packaging.

- **Zoya** – This brand carries a 3-in-1 nail polish remover, nail prep, and nail conditioner product. www.zoya.com
- **786 Cosmetics** – This brand carries a soy-based formula that uses almond oil to moisturize nails. www.786cosmetics.com
- **Sophi** – They carry a liquid remover and a gel that uses a stick to remove tough areas. www.sophinailpolish.com

Dark Green: These brands have improved both the ingredients and the packaging.

- **Freon Collective Nail Polish Remover Pads** – This brand sells square pads that can be used, washed, and reused. They are black and grey bamboo squares sold in packs of six. These could be used with any polish liquids shown in this section. www.freoncollective.co
- **TenOverTen** – They carry removers in both liquid and biodegradable wipes. The liquid remover is packaged in a recyclable glass bottle. www.tenoverten.com
- **Cote** – They carry both liquid and wipes. The liquid is in a plastic pump bottle. However, they sell large refill containers to keep future packaging down. www.coteshop.co

DIY Green: Mix equal parts of vinegar and lemon juice. Put the mixture on your nails, hold for 20 seconds, and then wipe off. Repeat as needed to remove all the polish.

CUTICLE OILS, NAIL TREATMENT, AND PRIMERS

Again, some nail polish brands include these items in their overall nail care lines for primers, topcoats, and cuticle oils.

Light Green: These brands have better ingredients but still use traditional packaging.

- **Zoya** – Zoya carries a nail polish remover, primers, topcoats, and a nail repair kit. www.zoya.com
- **Olive & June** – This brand features their cuticle product as able to transform your nails. They also have nail primers and topcoats. www.oliveandjune.com
- **786 Cosmetics** – This brand carries cuticle oil, primers, and more. www.786cosmetics.com

Dark Green: These brands have improved both the ingredients and the packaging.

- **TenOverTen** – This brand has a full line of cuticle products. The packaging is made of recycled materials, printed with soy ink, and in FSC-certified paper. www.tenoverten.com
- **Kester** – They carry base coats, topcoats, and cuticle oil. With the B Corp and carbon neutral rating, I've included them as a dark green alternative. www.kesterblack.com

DIY Green: The DIY cuticle oil recipes are very straightforward, with many only having three ingredients—olive oil, almond oil, and essential oils like lavender. Here's one to get you started: Use a small glass bottle with a dropper. Add 1 tablespoon of sweet almond oil, 2-3 drops of vitamin E, and 4 drops each of lavender and rose geranium oil. Shake well to mix.

TOOLS - NAIL CLIPPERS, FILES, SPACERS, AND MORE

When it comes to the more permanent products for nail care, two of the sustainable nail polish brands do carry a variety of products. If you want to look beyond the two listed below or there is something you need that they don't carry, look for products made of materials that will last a long time and are easy to recycle when they no longer serve their purpose.

- **TenOverTen** – This brand has a full line of products to consider. www.tenoverten.com
- **786 Cosmetics** – Offer a crystal glass nail file that is longer lasting than traditional files. www.786cosmetics.com

Salon Manicures – When it comes to pampering at the salon, the most eco-friendly is to have a basic manicure with no polish. If you have polish, you might bring your own to ensure you know the brand and ingredients involved. When it comes to gel and acrylic nails, they may look great, but they damage your nails. In addition, they hurt the environment as they are non-biodegradable and considered toxic waste.

In fact, in a study published in the journal Environmental Science and Technology (February 2022), researchers from the University of Toronto found that nail salon workers' chemical exposure was ten times higher than that of electronic waste facility employees (Varanasi, 2022).

PERFUME

The perfume category is like skincare and makeup, with the complexity of the ingredients. According to the Environmental Working Group, most fragrances are synthesized from 3,100 stock chemical ingredients or are derived from petroleum or natural raw materials. There are a lot of brands out there with many choices of scents (*Not So Sexy | Environmental Working Group*, n.d.).

Two of the brands we introduced in prior sections— Paul Penders (www.paulpenders.com) and Pacifica (www.pacificabeauty.com)—have reasonably priced fragrances and are worth considering. Below are other brands for consideration broken into light green and dark green, just like in prior sections. One additional piece of information I've included here is the use of a $-$$$$ rating so that you know which brands are more or less expensive before looking them up.

Light Green: These brands have better ingredients but still use traditional packaging.

- **Abbott** – This brand carries nature-inspired, unisex fragrances. They are PETA-certified vegan, cruelty-free, and committed to using clean and sustainable ingredients. Rated $. www.abbottnyc.com
- **Lavanila** – Lavanila carries five fragrances in both spray and roll-on. They replace harsh chemicals with natural technology and include high-powered antioxidants, vitamins, and natural oils in their products. Rated $. www.lavanila.com
- **DedCool** – This brand is carbon-neutral, vegan, and cruelty-free. The fragrances can be layered to create additional, unique scents. Rated $$. www.dedcool.com
- **Phlur** – This brand carries eight fragrances. They describe their philosophy as modern and Intentional, leveraging a mix of natural and synthetic materials. They believe that sometimes synthetics can be better for allergies and the environment. Rated $$. www.phlur.com
- **Blade & Bloom** – This brand offers six unique fragrance blends. Their formulas are 100% natural, use plant-based ingredients, and

are handmade in small batches. They use recyclable or reusable containers, are vegan, and no chemical fillers or ingredients are used. Rated $$. www.bladeandbloom.com

- **The 7 Virtues** – This brand is both vegan and cruelty-free. They offer 16 products made with sustainably sourced ingredients from nations rebuilding after war or strife. Rated $$. www.the7virtues.com
- **Strange Invisible Perfumes** – This brand is headquartered in Venice, CA, and offers 12 mainstream fragrances and one fragrance for each Zodiac sign. The products are completely natural and botanical. Rated $$$. www.siperfumes.com
- **Heretic Parfum** – This brand works with naturally-derived botanical ingredients to create vibrant, non-gendered functional fragrances. The products are blended in organic non-GMO sugarcane alcohol and handcrafted in small batches. They are also vegan and cruelty-free. Rated $$$. www.hereticparfum.com
- **Cultus Artem** – This brand offers 16 fragrances crafted with intention in small quantities. Each fragrance is hand-formulated from natural, botanical, and rare ingredients at Cultus Artem's atelier. Rated $$$$. www.cultusartem.com

Dark Green: These brands have improved both the ingredients and the packaging.

- **Just the Goods Vegan Perfumes** – This brand offers an alternative to reliance on petroleum, other unhealthy chemicals, and wasteful packaging. There are eight unique blends packaged in recycled glass bottles. Rated $. www.justthegoods.net
- **Henry Rose** – The brand was founded by Michelle Pfeiffer and are the first fragrances to be both EWG Verified and Cradle to Cradle Certified. The bottles are 90% recycled glass and 100% recyclable,

and the caps are made of commercially compostable soy. There are ten fragrances to choose from. Rated $$. www.henryrose.com

- **St. Rose Fragrances** – This brand offers many vegan, cruelty-free, and circular selections. They have a recycling program encouraging customers to return their empty perfume bottles for disassembly and recycling. Rated $$$. www.st-rose.com

DIY Green: There is a lot of online information about making your own fragrances. The process appears very straightforward—a carrier oil plus essential oils. I'm sure the artistry is in the blend of the scents you select. I think this could be an interesting and creative DIY project.

FAST FIVE IN THE BATHROOM

Five steps you can take quickly to make an impact and begin to celebrate some wins!

1. **Order Some Soap** – The bathroom can be overwhelming with all the products and alternative brands to consider. So, start small; order some soap. There are many options, and it will be a fun and easy way to start your one shade greener journey in the bathroom.

2. **Plan a Replacement Process** – Because of the complexity, having a plan for your process when items run out will ensure that you start looking for alternatives. Maybe once a month, you scan what is running out and spend 30 minutes looking up those items in this book and online to find products to order. Or you may spend 5 minutes each time you realize you are out of a product. The process choice is yours, but I encourage you to develop one.

3. **Download and Bookmark the EWG Resources** – Having the EWG Skin Deep website bookmarked and having the app downloaded on your phone will help you look up products quickly when you are ordering at home or out and about purchasing in-store.

4. **Pick a Category** – If you could only work on one focus area in this chapter, which would it be? Dive into that focus area and create a plan for the products you want to purchase and try.

5. **Find Some Brands** – Spend 30 minutes online scanning the brands referenced in the chapter and looking for matches that feel right for you. Bookmark those brands for future purchases.

THE GARAGE

The "garage" varies from home to home, and the environmental impacts are broad. Some city dwellers may not have a physical garage or a car and have few tools with few considerations in this chapter. On the flip side, some homeowners may have many vehicles, a garage full of tools, cleaners, and even more to consider.

The chapter will start with my story and then move into seven focus sections: The Energy Efficient Garage, Tools and Equipment, Modes of Transportation, Purchasing a Vehicle, Driving Habits, Vehicle Maintenance, and Donating and Recycling. Each focus area will dive deeper into the category and provide ideas on reducing your environmental impact.

MY ONE SHADE GREENER STORY

We live in a home in the suburbs and have a garage full of all the things many US suburban homes have—cars and trucks, a motorcycle (my son's), lots of tools, car care products, painting supplies, a second refrigerator, lawn equipment (those will be covered in the backyard chapter), and much more.

I will start my story by saying that we are a car family. I worked for General Motors, and my husband worked at Ford for over half of our careers. Our son is very into vehicles as well. This chapter will discuss the move toward electric vehicles, and I will give perspectives on the positive elements of the shift to electrification. I will also mention areas that concern me where I don't think there is enough public conversation yet. Now, let's dive into my garage story.

Starting with the vehicles, I will focus on my choices. In 2010 when I left GM, I purchased a Ford Fusion hybrid. This was not a plug-in hybrid but had regenerative braking, which increased my previous fuel economy by about 10 mpg to an average of 40 mpg. Then, in 2014, I purchased a Chevrolet Volt plug-in hybrid. The vehicle had a range of 35-40 miles all-electric and then would convert to gas. I now have a 2016 Cadillac ELR plug-in hybrid (purchased secondhand) that has a similar range to the Volt.

My observation across all these vehicles is that I love driving a hybrid. While the lighter impact on the planet is why I tried my first one back in 2010, I REALLY grew to appreciate the convenience of not having to go to the gas station all the time. In addition, the financial savings of buying less gas was a great perk for my pocketbook. Honestly, I don't know if I spend less on electricity to charge vs. gas to fill the tank, but I don't see the electric costs the way I did at the gas station. I also like the peace of mind that I still have a gas backup if the electric charge runs out. This is the main reason why I'm reluctant to go to an all-electric vehicle.

The other vehicles in our home are a Ford Ranger (my husband's) and a Ford Focus (my son's). Both have performance packages that are important to them. As my husband and I continue to work from home a couple of days a week, the impact of our driving has been reduced from where we were in the past (pre-Covid). I would be surprised if the truck gets driven more than 100 miles per month.

Moving to the other aspects of our garage, we have a lot of tools and products. My son enjoys washing and caring for the cars, and he is always working on something. On the tools front, we have had most of them since we married nearly 30 years ago, and they are still in use today. We also have a refrigerator in the garage that holds beverages; this was important when the kids were in high school. With friends over, we always had drinks and snacks for them in there. Now, the need for a second fridge is starting to diminish.

Our garage always feels like the place where "stuff" gathers. We try to do a deep clean and clear everything out once a year, but somehow things build up. Each time we clean, we usually find at least one or two items that need to go to the community hazardous waste day. I would love to find alternative products to eliminate the need for this, but I haven't found the right options yet.

UP NEXT IN MY HOME – The refrigerator is probably something that we will likely sell or donate soon. On the vehicle front, I will be in the market to replace the ELR in the next year or two based on age and mileage. I'm torn on what to look for. As I mentioned, I'm nervous about going all-electric. In addition to the vehicle, I want to purchase a scooter or bike for around-town errands (like groceries). Michigan weather wouldn't allow me to use it all year round, but from April through November, this would be a great alternative for the environment. With a bike, it could be healthy for me as well.

THE ENERGY-EFFICIENT GARAGE

Our garage is an extension of our home. The more energy efficient the garage is, the less our indoor heating and cooling are impacted. I won't go into a lot of detail in this focus area, but I did want to provide some ideas if you want to increase your space's energy efficiency.

Insulation is the key improvement. Ensuring walls, ceiling, and even power outlets in the garage are well insulated keeps warmth in the winter and cool in the summer. To provide even more insulation, doors are next on the list. The garage doors will protect you from the outside heat and cold, while the door from the garage to the house is key to keeping the indoor temperatures from leaking out of the house. Regularly checking and maintaining the seals of both the indoor and garage doors to keep the seal as tight as possible is important.

Below are some additional areas that can improve the energy efficiency of your garage:

- **Garage Door Openers** – Depending on the age of your system, many advancements have been made that require less energy to raise/lower the doors.
- **Flooring** – Keeping cracks sealed will keep garage debris (salt and chemicals) from leaking into the ground below.
- **Refrigerator/Freezer** – Do you have one in the garage? Do you really need it? If you do, refer to the kitchen chapter for tips to ensure it's as energy efficient as possible.
- **Organization** – Keeping the garage organized helps ensure pests don't get in that could eat away at that new insulation you just installed!
- **Lighting** – Using LED lights will improve efficiency. For details about lighting, refer to the family room chapter.

RECYCLING – The garage is full of hazardous materials. Knowing the proper way to dispose of items and the locations available to recycle is important. As with all the other rooms in your home, Earth911 (www.earth911.org) is a great resource. Your local community hazardous waste days is also an option—leverage both as resources for disposing of items in the garage.

TOOLS AND EQUIPMENT

The tools and equipment in a garage can vary greatly depending on the home. Do you tend to take on projects around the house on your own, or do you have contractors come in and complete little handyman projects to more extensive remodel or lawn projects? If you do these things on your own, I'm guessing your garage has or needs more equipment than your neighbors.

SHOPPING SECONDHAND

If properly cared for, tools truly can last a lifetime. That makes this category a great one to consider for secondhand purchases. I've found many well-kept tools on eBay and Facebook Marketplace. As you look at the listings, ensure you are looking at secondhand or refurbished. Especially on eBay, the new listings will pop up first unless you select used.

If you are a parent, you could focus on high-quality equipment for your grown children. Search for tools and package them as a birthday, holiday, or housewarming gift. This could also be a unique category to consider for family and friends who are getting married or moving into their first home.

NEIGHBORHOOD SHARING – Often, there are products we purchase for our garage for a specific project, like a wheelbarrow for hauling dirt for a landscape project or a power saw to cut some large branches off a tree. For these occasions, you might ask your family or neighbors if you could borrow theirs rather than buying. Some neighborhoods have even created tool-sharing spaces where the community owns these products, and you check them out when needed. If your neighborhood doesn't have this system, maybe this is a project you would want to take on for the benefit of everyone in the community! You will all save money and some valuable space in the garage!

PURCHASING NEW

This is a category where many tend to purchase items for life and don't replace them very often. So, if you are in the market for anything new in the tools and equipment space, look for quality pieces that will serve your needs well for years to come.

Another area of consideration when purchasing tools is gas vs. electric. Lawn tools like mowers, trimmers, leaf blowers, and more will be covered in the lawn section. Many battery-powered models are available for small tools like drills, and the technology has advanced to a place where these are very effective and have sufficient battery life for most everyday home projects.

As I investigated garage tools and equipment, I didn't see the progress for eco-friendly alternatives like I saw in other industries. There weren't companies exploring options for wood handles using materials like bamboo seen in other chapters. There weren't alternatives to plastics being studied, and recycling products and/or transparency around working conditions and fair wages at the factories where the tools were produced is totally missing from product information.

One brand I did find that was developing tools with 50% recycled content was a partnership between Stanley Black & Decker and Eastman. The line is called Reviva and was scheduled to launch in 2022. I couldn't find anywhere online to purchase, but I'm hopeful that this might become an alternative to consider in the US soon. The brand appeared focused not only on the recycled content but also on the ability to return the tools for recycling after they were no longer in use.

CARE AND MAINTENANCE

The key to tools lasting a lifetime is taking the time for proper care and maintenance after you use them. Below are some tips to keep your tools at their best:

- **Cleaning**: While different tools require different approaches, ensure you wipe the dirt and dust off the tools each time you finish a project.
- **Storage**: To prevent tools from rusting or electrical components from corroding, tools are best stored in dry, clean environments; moist and dirty spaces will do tools no favors.
- **Sharpen and Lubricate**: Keeping tools properly sharpened and lubricated will extend their life and ensure they work efficiently. You know the saying, run like a "well-oiled machine!"
- **Inspect**: As you use your tools, now and then, take the time to inspect them to see if anything is wearing or needs attention. This will let you address issues before they become a problem.
- **Batteries**: The battery is key to your power tools. Many sources recommend they are stored in a location where temperatures remain consistent. This might be a good reason to keep them in a mudroom or inside the house instead of the garage.

> **REUSE TIP** – Those little silica gel packs that come in lots of items you buy are great at keeping moisture away. Instead of throwing them in the garbage, reuse them in tool drawers or boxes to keep rust at bay.

MODES OF TRANSPORTATION

In the US, the primary mode of transportation is a personal vehicle. According to Statista, 76% of Americans drive a private vehicle commuting to work and school (Richter, n.d.). Those passenger vehicles in the US consume 40% of the petroleum used and generate about 16% of greenhouse gas emissions (*US Passenger Cars | MIT Energy Initiative*, n.d.). When talking about reducing the environmental impact of vehicles, there are two components to consider—the gas that goes in and the emissions that come out.

DRIVING ALTERNATIVES

In addition to the high reliance on personal vehicles, a 2021 study from the Bureau of Transportation Statistics found that 52% of all trips by car are under 3 miles, with 28% of those under a mile (*FOTW #1230, March 21, 2022: More than Half of All Daily Trips Were Less than Three Miles in 2021 | Department of Energy*, n.d.).

Imagine how we could collectively reduce our environmental impact if we all considered walking an alternative for trips under a mile. When considering a trip in the car, check out the walking distance on your map app. If the walking route is less than thirty minutes, consider walking instead of driving.

For those trips between a mile and three miles, walking may not be an option. In these cases, especially in the warm weather months, you could consider biking to your destinations. With baskets on the bike, you could even do errands and shopping vehicle-free.

Depending on where you live, other modes of transportation like buses, subways, and trains may be more efficient alternatives than a car. If you are in a location with public transit, if you don't know much about them, I would encourage you to learn a bit more and consider these options.

RIDE SHARE – Waze Carpool and Uber Rideshare enable users to ride together and split the fares. This saves both money and reduces the environmental impact.

VACATION TRAVEL

When planning a vacation, there can often be a conversation determining if you should drive or fly. An analysis done by the International Council on Clean Transportation back in 2015 had some great information. They evaluated a 300–500-mile trip with different modes of transportation. On average, they found that a plane gets 43 miles per gallon per person, trains get 51 mpg/per person, and personal vehicles get 53 mpg/per person (Sunkara, 2020).

So, a family of four headed on a 500-mile trip would have less environmental impact driving than flying. Depending on the gas price, you might save some money, and there is no need to rent a car or find alternative transportation at your destination.

There are also opportunities to look for eco-friendly hotels, restaurants, and stores at your destination. Many hotels have started to do small things like not washing towels and linens daily unless a request is made, but others are diving deeper into changes that lessen their impact. I tried to find a good resource for locating eco-friendly hotels and destinations, but there doesn't seem to be one yet that covers a wide range of selections.

CARBON OFFSETS – When traveling (or for other areas of your life), you can consider offsetting your carbon usage by supporting companies planting trees to reduce carbon, supporting renewable energy, and more. Three companies focused on the US to consider in this space are:

The Conservation Fund www.theconservationfund.org – They plant trees to offset the carbon.

The Carbon Fund www.carbonfund.org – They plants trees and supports renewable energy.

Terrapass www.terrapass.com – They fund clean energy, biomass, and industrial efficiency projects.

Lifestyle offset programs start at less than $10/month, and enrollment is simple on their websites.

PURCHASING NEW VEHICLES

Purchasing new vehicles doesn't automatically require a new car or truck. We'll consider purchasing new cars, motorcycles, scooters, bikes, and more in this focus area. Before purchasing, I recommend considering the following two questions:

1. Do I need a new vehicle/bike/scooter **now**? Is my current model in good shape?
2. Do I need to purchase **new**? Purchasing secondhand may be a good alternative. You could buy a used plug-in hybrid vehicle, a new-to-

you scooter, or a secondhand bike. These will have a positive impact on both the planet and your pocketbook.

PURCHASING A CAR OR TRUCK

When purchasing a new vehicle, the one shade greener philosophy would suggest you look for something that has a lighter impact than the vehicle you are replacing. I'm not going to suggest you must buy a compact all-electric vehicle. If this is right for you, great. However, if you need a full-size truck for your lifestyle, then look for a full-size truck that is more fuel efficient than what you currently own. A newer model of the same product you have will likely be more fuel efficient and produce fewer emissions.

To better understand the fuel efficiency of your current vehicle and those you are considering, you can go to www.fueleconomy.gov. The website allows you to search vehicles and see the MPG and average annual fuel costs. I'm unsure how often they update the formulas to consider current gas prices. However, even if the cost per gallon is outdated, it's the same for all vehicles, so the calculator still provides a great comparison.

I'm not going to go into details here on what brands to consider, as all auto manufacturers have been focused for many years on improving fuel economy and reducing emissions. I will provide a quick summary of terms you might hear as we move to more electric vehicles on the market:

- **Internal Combustion Engine (ICE)**: This is the gas-powered engine most of us have driven all our lives. The vehicle runs on gas and does not have an electric battery.
- **Hybrid Electric Vehicle**: These vehicles have both gas and electric capabilities. If they require plugging in to charge the battery, they will be referred to as a plug-in hybrid. Vehicles without the "plug-in"

nomenclature are likely using some form of storing and using braking energy.

- **All Electric**: These vehicles run on 100% electric power without gas backup. They will require you to be at a location to charge the vehicle when the charge runs out.

As we move to more and more all-electric vehicles on the market, I have some concerns based on everything I've read and heard, especially regarding batteries. This includes the impact of producing them, charging them, and finally disposing of them after they no longer work. With battery production and recycling, I fear we may be replacing the petroleum problem with a battery problem.

We also have a long way to go on the infrastructure to support an all-electric world. I know many people and companies are working on these things. I believe they need to be resolved before we are ready for the large-scale adoption of non-hybrid electric vehicles. Here are a few of the challenges to be solved with the infrastructure:

- **Charging Stations**: There aren't charging stations everywhere like there are gas stations. Maybe an easy solution will be that gas stations will evolve into charging locations.
- **Time to Charge**: The charges aren't quick, so we need to wait to charge far longer than it takes to pump gas to be able to drive again.
- **Energy Sources**: According to the US Energy Information Administration, most (60%) of the electricity in the United States is still fossil fuel-based, i.e., coal and natural gas. Another 19% is from nuclear power. The remaining 20% are from renewable sources like wind, sun, and water (*Frequently Asked Questions (FAQs) - U.S. Energy Information Administration (EIA)*, n.d.). We have a long way to go before electric vehicles are powered by sources that don't hurt the environment.

I will end this section with the same thought I started with. As you look for a vehicle, consider the fuel economy of your current vehicle and what you can do to make the next product you purchase one shade greener.

TINTED WINDOWS – Tinting the windows of your new vehicle will reflect almost 80% of the sun's heat and enable you to use the AC less. This could be particularly beneficial in warm weather climates. However, check your state rules on legally how transparent the tint needs to be.

PURCHASING A MOTORCYCLE OR SCOOTER

This is a category that I don't personally own, so I did a bit of research before deciding where to take this section. While there are many options for gas-powered motorcycles with varying fuel efficiency levels, I decided to focus on featuring electric models. Below are brands I came across that I feel are solid alternatives to consider:

- **Zero Motorcycles**: This brand focuses on a superior riding experience and all the qualities of a traditional motorcycle powered by electricity. They look to balance value, performance, and fun. The average range is around 100 miles, and it takes 4-5 hours to charge. www.zeromotorcycles.com
- **VMoto**: This brand carries motorcycles and scooters with various looks, from street bikes to retro. The top speeds, range, and battery charging vary by bike but have many options. www.vmoto.com
- **Monday Motorbikes**: This brand offers four models that are a cross between a motorcycle and a bike. On their website, each bike shows the range, time to charge, and weight. www.mondaymotorbikes.com
- **Standing Scooters**: You could consider a stand-up for an electric scooter alternative for under $1000. Brands to consider include

Apollo City (www.apolloscooters.co), YVolution (www.yvolution.com), Segway (www.segway.com), InMotion (www.myinmotion.com), and Swagtron (www.swagtron.com).

- **More Expensive**: If you are willing to raise your price point to $10K or more for a bike, other brands to put on your list include Pursang (www.pursangmotorcycles.com), Livewire (www.livewire.com), and even Harley Davidson (www.harley-davidson.com) now has an electric offering.

PURCHASING A BICYCLE

If you have been considering a bike, a sustainability report released by Trek in 2021 suggests that you offset the carbon footprint of the bike's production after riding around 430 miles (*Rule of 430 | Trek Bikes*, n.d.). That may take a bit of time to reach the offset. Yet, you will immediately see the benefits to your pocketbook without fueling costs and to your health by getting some additional exercise.

When purchasing a new bike, considering how you plan to use it is important. Will you ride mainly on city streets? Will you ride offroad? Short distances or long? Answering how you will use the bike will be important in determining the right style for you.

I did a bit of research on bicycle brands. However, this is a product area where there aren't ratings and reviews to assess how eco-friendly the parts and manufacturing are. A few brands that are positively discussed include Detroit Bikes (www.detroitbikes.com), Bamboocycle (www.bamboocycles.com), Brooklyn Bicycle Company (www.brooklynbicycleco.com), and Boomers (www.booomers.com).

eBikes: Another alternative in the bicycle space is the eBike. These options are growing in popularity and allow the benefits of a bike and enable you to go further, faster. Some brands to consider include Rad Power Bikes (www.radpowerbikes.com), Cowboy (www.us.cowboy.com), Aventon (www.aventon.com), and Landry's (www.landrys.com).

ALTERNATIVES YOU MAY NOT HAVE CONSIDERED

Skateboards and rollerblades might be other "modes of transportation" to consider for getting around town or your neighborhood. When my kids were in middle and high school (pre-driving), they went everywhere on skateboards. The skateboards were faster than walking, not as bulky as a bike, and the small ones could be popped into a backpack if they wanted to go into a store or restaurant.

DRIVING HABITS AND MAINTENANCE

Many reports and articles have been published about how long Americans spend in their vehicles each day. While there is a range, many report roughly fifty minutes per day. This includes commuting, running errands, taking kids to school and sports, and much more. Some simple tips and techniques will reduce your impact on the planet and your spending on gas through better fuel efficiency. While these ideas focus on cars and trucks, some could apply to driving your motorcycle or gas-powered scooter.

AVOID IDLING

Many times in our day-to-day activities, we may be sitting idle. If you have children, you may frequently find yourself sitting and waiting in drop-off/pickup lines at school or a location for a sports practice to start or end. According to the US department of energy, if you are going to idle for more than ten seconds, you should turn your car off and back on (*Idling*

Reduction for Personal Vehicles, 2015). Another way to avoid idling while commuting would be to use a traffic app like Waze, which helps you avoid traffic. This will not only help your fuel efficiency but also help stem your frustration.

ERRANDS WITH A PLAN

Doing a bit of planning with your errands can be lighter on the planet while adding the benefit of saving you time and trips during the week. You could pick one "errand day" and run all errands at once. By thinking through the locations of your stops, you could discover the shortest travel route. The car would also get better fuel economy when it's warmed up.

DRIVE MORE EFFICIENTLY

When driving, being a less aggressive driver lightens your impact. According to the US Department of Energy, frequent braking and acceleration can result in 10-40% more fuel consumption (*What Is Good Gas Mileage? - Municibid Blog*, 2022). They also indicate that every five mph you drive over 50 mph is like paying $0.18 more per gallon of gas, based on the gas price of $2.63/gallon. With today's rates upwards of $4, the savings could be even higher (*Alternative Fuels Data Center: Techniques for Drivers to Conserve Fuel*, n.d.). Another great way to keep your driving more efficient and consistent is to use cruise control whenever possible.

VEHICLE MAINTENANCE

The two primary areas of vehicle maintenance that maximize fuel efficiency are keeping your tires properly inflated and using the manufacturer-recommended grade of motor oil. Check your manuals to ensure you know the proper tire pressure and recommended oil.

DIY FROST SOLUTION – Did you know that you can naturally fight the frost on your windshields? Just wipe the inside of the windows with salt water on a sponge. When the windows dry, the salt will remain and keep the frost at bay.

THE CAR WASH

Another impact of your vehicle maintenance is the car wash. In much of what is written, the discussion is around water use, and companies are now coming out with waterless car cleaners. However, the information isn't clear on the ingredients in these products, and when I looked for places to purchase them, many were out of inventory.

On the water impact, automatic car washes may use less water than washing at home as these systems often recycle and reuse the wastewater. If washing at home and using traditional soaps, the recommendation is to wash over the grass so that the soil filters the water and doesn't go directly into the drain system.

FAST FIVE IN THE GARAGE

Five steps you can take quickly to make an impact and begin to celebrate some wins!

1. **Consider Alternative Transportation** – For trips under 2 miles, consider walking or riding a bike instead of instantly jumping into the car out of habit.
2. **Consume Less Gas** – Consider purchasing a more fuel-efficient vehicle than you own today. Can you increase efficiency by ten mpg? Would an electric vehicle fit your lifestyle?
3. **Reduce Drive Time** – Look for ways to drive less; batch errands into one day, if your company allows, work some days from home, and ensure all trips have an intention and purpose.
4. **Purchase Carbon Offsets** – Check out a few carbon offset companies and find one that is a good fit for the next time you take a flight or just to offset your everyday lifestyle habits.
5. **Care and Recycling** – Tools in your garage can last a lifetime if properly cared for. Keep them clean in a moisture-free location and maintain them regularly. The garage is full of hazardous materials. When it's time to get rid of any of them, ensure you know where and how to recycle them and ensure they don't go in the trash.

THE BACKYARD

The backyard is a space that some have, and others don't have to worry about. Some of those with a backyard maintain their own, while others hire companies or have community associations that handle the care. In addition, some will have a pool, a deck, or a swing set that adds complexity and things to consider. So, just like all the other chapters in this book, you will need to evaluate your situation and determine the right adjustments that can make your backyard one shade greener.

The chapter will start with my story and then move into six focus sections: The Lawn, Softscapes, Hardscapes, Furniture and Accessories, Pool and Spa, and Pets. Each will dive deeper into the impacts and provide ideas on reducing your environmental impact.

MY ONE SHADE GREENER STORY

Our backyard has gone through waves of how eco-friendly (or not) we have been. Many aspects of our home aren't eco-friendly to start with, specifically, a large, maintained lawn and a swimming pool. We had a hot tub spa but stopped using that about three years ago. We also live in a subdivision community that puts restrictions and approvals around the outdoor spaces' appearance. These attributes offer opportunities and challenges in our journey to becoming greener.

We moved into this home twenty-two years ago. We had our daughter; our son wasn't born yet. The community was young and growing, and we loved the large yard for our kids to play in as they grew up. We immediately bought a lawn mower with all the tools, installed a sprinkler system, and built a deck. About four years later, we installed a pool with additional landscaping. While a few trees were added by the street, we haven't done any landscaping.

Over the years, we've tried different lawn treatments, watered the lawn and not, added furniture and firepits, stained the deck, and tried small gardening projects. The maintenance projects outside have always been a struggle as our lives got busy as the kids grew up. Weeds grow, we forget to water the flowers, and the project list sometimes seems overwhelming.

Fast forward to today, our lawn is still mowed weekly and treated occasionally, but we no longer water it. We still have the pool and try to do what we can to minimize the overall energy and water impact. We have a saltwater filter and don't run the heater regularly to keep the energy use down and as efficient as possible.

UP NEXT IN MY HOME: Creating this chapter has renewed my energy for projects in the backyard! I'm excited to take a space and convert it into a butterfly garden, and we are also considering the addition of a produce garden. As I write this, we are moving into fall, and the winter season will give us a good amount of time to plan things out. Another priority for the next year is to repair a retaining wall. The big project on the list in the next couple of years is replacing our crack-filled concrete driveway. Knowing the impact of concrete, the research for this chapter has given me some great ideas of alternatives we will consider as we make that big update.

THE LAWN

When considering our lawns, a great place to start is assessing the good they do for our environment. Lawns produce oxygen, have roots that hold soil and filter rainwater, absorb noise, trap dust, and can provide cooling to offset the heat of concrete and other hard surfaces.

With all the good they provide, how you care for your lawn can have significant negative environmental impacts. There are three key areas— mowing, watering, and treatments. Shifting habits in these areas can help maximize your lawn's benefits and lessen the environmental impact.

MOWING

In the US, over fifty million households mow their lawn each week, using 800 million gallons of gas and producing around 5% of the nation's air pollution (Marlow, 2020). In fact, according to the Environmental Protection Agency (EPA), a new gas-powered lawn mower emits more air pollution in an hour than eleven new cars being driving for that same hour (*Grass Lawns Are an Ecological Catastrophe – ONE Only Natural Energy*, n.d.)!

In addition to the lawn mower, lawn "accessories" like edgers, leaf blowers, hedge trimmers, and weed whackers are also significant polluters. A solution is to move to electric-powered equipment. Many popular manufacturers have already moved to offer electric models. Consider the available options for the size of your lawn, length of charge, and time to recharge. You want to ensure your choice can do the job without unexpected recharging in the middle!

In addition to the switch to electric equipment, below are mowing tips that are more eco-friendly and keep your grass healthy:

- **Mow Less Frequently:** Try moving from once a week to every one and a half to two weeks.
- **Raise the mower**: Keep your grass 2-3 inches tall to help retain moisture and require less water.
- **Keep the Clippings**: Let your grass clippings decompose on your lawn as a natural fertilizer.
- **Mow in the Evening**: The chemicals will lack the sunlight needed to form ozone more easily.

WATERING

During the summer seasons, around 30% of a home's water usage is outdoors, primarily due to lawn watering. The amount of water used depends on the lawn size and how often you water. The average irrigation system uses sixteen gallons/minute from **each** pop-up sprinkler head (*Your Water Usage | WSSC Water*, n.d.).

The best way to conserve water and money is to water less. Rather than having your system on a timer, consider turning it on only when needed between rain showers. Reducing the need to water down to once a week (or less) could provide significant savings.

While reducing water use is great for the environment, you also want to ensure there is enough water to keep the lawn, trees, and plants thriving. Finding the right balance to get the needed levels without overwatering is key.

One good practice for the lawn is to water deeply (one inch) when water is needed. The best time to do this deep water is in the morning so that the water doesn't evaporate in the heat of the day and doesn't sit on the lawn overnight, causing mold and mildew.

Adding moisture sensors to the lawn is a great way to ensure you are watering only when needed. This will let you know when the ground needs more water. Two brands to consider are the Nelson EZ Pro and Toro Wireless Rain Sensor.

TREATMENTS

The "keep off" signs on lawns after fertilization are a good indication that lawn treatments are not healthy for people and the planet. According to research by the University of Missouri, homeowners use ten times more chemical fertilizers, and pesticides per acre than farmers use to grow crops (*Yard and Garden Care: How It Affects Your Health and Environment (Fact Sheet) | MU Extension*, n.d.). Another challenge is that these chemicals can find their way into drinking water wells, lakes, and streams. The problem gets even worse when the soil gets washed away in storms.

A good first step in this area is to have your soil tested before applying any product. Knowing exactly what your soil needs enables you to purchase low nutrients vs. treating everything. You don't want to add nitrogen to the lawn if you don't need it. If the lawn doesn't absorb nitrogen, it converts to nitrous oxide, a greenhouse gas 300 times worse than carbon dioxide (Stanford University, 2020).

Many organic fertilizers are starting to emerge that provide nutrients from natural instead of synthetic sources. While this is a better choice, you still want to avoid adding unnecessary nitrogen or phosphorus. Natural products are made from plants like alfalfa, cottonseed, or even seaweed.

Using natural fertilizers may take longer and a bit more effort to see results. However, you eliminate the need to stay off the lawn after treatment, reduce the risk of burning the lawn, and there are no chemicals to leech into the groundwater. Brands to consider include Jobe's, Lawnbox, Espoma, and Scotts.

SOFTSCAPES

The softscapes in our backyard are comprised of our landscaping and gardens. These spaces can go in many directions and add personality to our homes. In addition, plants and trees lessen your impact on the environment and give back to the environment simultaneously. This section will provide tips to reduce negative impacts and amplify the positive benefits of a thriving landscape.

THE LANDSCAPE

When it's time to update or redesign a portion of your landscape, this is the perfect opportunity to think about the design and how to create a beautiful, eco-friendly environment. The goal is to eliminate the need for pesticides, fertilizers, and heavy maintenance to care for your outdoor environment. Below are some things to keep in mind as you reinvent areas of your landscape.

Choose Native Plants: Selecting plants that are native to your location enables them to be better able to handle pests, the local climate, and diseases as they grow. In addition to your local climate, also understand if plants thrive in the sun or shade so that you plant the right plant in the right location.

Learn Before You Plant: Understand your choices and what the plant will do throughout the year. Knowing how tall plants grow, when/if they flower, what color, and more, can ensure you consider what the space will look like during different seasons.

Minimize Water Needs: To create a landscape that requires less water, consider planting succulents, pathos, or snake plants if they will work well in your climate zone.

Leverage Trees: Plan to plant deciduous trees (oak, maple, birch, etc.) on the south side of your house. This will allow the trees to shade the house in summer and let the sunlight in during the winter. When planting evergreens, consider adding them to the west and north to act as a wind buffer.

Prioritize Maintenance: Learn how your plants, shrubs, and trees should be cared for. Do you trim them down before winter? Do they need to be covered under a certain temperature? Are there annual treatments you need to do? Understanding how to care for your landscape will help it retain its beauty.

Recycle Yard Waste: Grinding up leaves, twigs, and other plant matter from your lawn can turn this waste into compost and mulch that will be healthy for your landscape beds and help you avoid purchasing some mulch and compost each year.

BUTTERFLY GARDEN – One beautiful idea for your landscape could be creating a butterfly garden. Find a location with lots of sun and is protected from the wind. You want to plant both host plants—where they lay their eggs and caterpillars eat—and nectar plants, where the butterflies eat. A few host plants to consider are milkweed, dill, fennel, clover, and aster. Nectar plants include butterfly bush, purple coneflower, zinnia, and wild bergamot. A book to get you started is Butterfly Gardening with Native Plants: How to Attract and Identify Butterflies by Christopher Kline.

THE GARDEN

Growing your own produce can be both fun and rewarding. If a garden is something you would like to try, you could start small the first year and grow to a more permanent and planned space in the years to come. There are entire books written about organic gardening, and I would encourage you to buy one if this is an area you want to dig into. Below are a few pieces of advice for getting started and giving growing a try.

Pick a Location: The first choice for a garden is where you will locate the space in your yard. You want to find a sunny spot with at least six hours of sunlight daily. Two other considerations are the proximity to the house and the water source. You want to make it as convenient as possible to care for the garden.

Containers or Level: A second decision is the type of garden you want. You can have a traditional, flat plot of land or create a multi-level space with containers and pots. As you start, you might want a couple of containers on your deck or patio to see if you enjoy growing produce. Then, you could design and create a larger space in a future year.

Decide What to Grow: When deciding what to grow, the top considerations are what will grow well in your part of the world and what your family enjoys eating. A few products to consider that are good for beginners include tomato, cucumber, peppers, lettuce, radish, basil, blueberries, and strawberries.

Seeds or Plants: You can start your plants from seeds or purchase small plants that are already started. If you go the route of seeds, you can use old egg cartons to plant a seed in each egg space. Once the seeds begin to grow, you can transfer them to their permanent location.

Protecting Plants: You might encounter many issues when growing a garden that extend beyond the soil and water. Below are a few ways you can protect your plants as they grow:

- **Frost**: Protect plants by cutting an old milk jug in half and placing it over them to keep the warmth in.
- **Bugs**: A simple DIY spray to keep bugs off your plants is to add 1 ½ teaspoons of Castile soap to 1 quart of water, mix well, place in a spray bottle, and spray on plants.
- **Squirrels, Rabbits, and Chipmunks**: To keep these critters out of the garden, you could try a fine mesh barrier, although this will also need to be removed to get to the plants. Two other options are to place coffee grounds around plants (deters rodents and is a good fertilizer) or create a powerful-smelling spray. A simple DIY solution is to mash 5-10 garlic cloves with 1 cup of hot sauce and a pint of vinegar in a spray bottle. Let it sit in the sun, then spray it around plants.

COMMUNITY GARDENS – If you aren't interested in growing a garden at your home but would like access to a garden and fresh produce, you could consider joining or starting a community garden. These gardens are shared plots of land where people gather to grow fresh produce and flowers. Many of these gardens have been created by turning unused spaces into productive living plots. In the US and Canada, you can visit the site communitygarden.org to see if there is a garden in your area. If you don't find one, maybe this is an opportunity to champion a garden in your area.

FERTILIZING AND MULCHING

The advice provided in the lawn section earlier in the chapter also holds true when fertilizing your landscapes and gardens. Understanding and treating your specific soil is important. Two areas that are key for your landscape and garden spaces are mulch and compost. Below are some tips for using both.

Mulch – Mulch can be made from various organic materials like wood chips, sawdust, and compost. All the materials used are natural and don't contain chemicals. The mulch helps plants retain moisture which enables them to require less water. Mulch also helps discourage weed growth and makes your landscape beds look great. Each year, you should replenish the mulch in your landscape. The ideal level is 2-3 inches of mulch spread evenly around the plants.

Compost – Using compost in your gardens will enrich the soil, help retain moisture and minimize plant disease and pests. The compost will encourage beneficial bacteria that break down organic matter into humus, a nutrient-filled material. Many brands are now selling compost. You can also look for local composters to see if you can purchase direct. Another option is to compost yourself at home; this was covered briefly in the kitchen chapter. A simple trick in the garden is to use eggshells to accelerate growth. You sprinkle crushed shells on the soil for extra calcium and essential nutrients.

WATERING

Like fertilization, many watering tips were covered in the lawn focus area. The two additional considerations for your garden and landscape are plant maintenance and harvesting rainwater.

Plant Maintenance – If you are creating your landscape or garden space, plan to group plants with similar watering needs. This way, you don't over or under water specific plants in an area. In addition, pruning plants regularly causes them to need less water.

Harvesting Rainwater – You can create a rainwater catchment system to collect water for your plants. This process can be as complex or simple as you design. You can place large barrels (50 gallons or more) or small buckets (5 gallons) at the base of downspouts to collect water when it rains. This water can then be used to water your garden. There are systems online that can be purchased, or you can create your own with existing downspouts and buckets.

HARDSCAPES – DECK, PATIO, DRIVEWAY, AND WALKWAYS

Many of our homes have hardscapes for both function and entertainment. This focus area will dive into the considerations for your driveways, walkways, decks, and patios.

THE DECK

According to the US Census Bureau, just under 20% of single-family homes in the US have a deck (*Share of New Homes with Decks Drops Below 20 Percent | Eye On Housing*, 2021). For those homes that do, there are considerations around decking materials and the care and maintenance required each year. The sections below briefly overview deck materials, cleaners, and stains.

Deck Materials: The impact of your deck on the environment depends on the type of deck you have, whether it is wood or composite. If you are planning to replace your deck, both options have positive attributes and downsides.

A wood deck is made of natural and renewable materials. However, it will need to be treated annually with a stain or seal that may not be good for the environment. The composite decking may be made from recycled materials and will last a long time. However, the material is typically not recyclable or compostable at the end of use.

Deck Cleaners: Some deck cleaners have improved the ingredients. However, DIY solutions can also be made from ingredients you have around the home. Below are two light green options and two DIY recipes depending on whether your home has a wood or composite deck.

Light Green: These alternatives have better ingredients but still use plastic packaging.

- **Spray and Forget** – This brand can clean many things outdoors, from decks and patios to outdoor furniture and siding. The product is biodegradable, non-corrosive, and does not contain bleach, lye, acid, or other harmful heavy metals. As the name implies, you spray it on and don't have to rinse it off. www.sprayandforget.com
- **Simple Green Oxy Solve Deck and Fence Cleaner.** This biodegradable deck cleaner uses hydrogen peroxide as the active ingredient and is used manually or with a pressure washer. www.simplegreen.com

DIY Green: Wood Deck: Cleaning your wood deck with a homemade cleaner is simple with just two ingredients, oxygen bleach, and water. I would recommend Nellie's Oxygen Brightener Powder as this product is safe for the environment, biodegradable, and doesn't harm plants or pets. This product looks like it's for the laundry but works well for your deck.

Just spray the deck with water, scrub on the Nellie's/water mixture with a brush, let it sit for 10-15 minutes, and rinse off. If you have some dirty areas, you may need to re-treat those sections a second time with the same process. If you use oils to stain your deck, please check to ensure this cleaning method is compatible.

DIY Green: Composite Deck: For composite decks, the cleaner is a combination of baking soda, vinegar, and water. Just sprinkle baking soda on the deck, add 1 cup of vinegar to 1 gallon of water, pour onto the deck, and scrub with a brush. Like the wood deck, let it sit for 10 minutes and rinse.

Deck Stains and Sealers: Treating with stains and sealers is an annual project for wood decks. While there aren't DIY solutions, several brands on the market focus on ensuring the ingredients used are healthy for people, pets, and the planet. I would classify all these choices as light green with better ingredients and traditional packaging.

- **Earthpaint** – This brand carries many products for deck stains and sealers and treatments for other floorings like concrete and interior wood floors. The wood finishes and paints contain non-toxic, natural ingredients derived from plants, vegetables, and other elements. www.earthpaint.net
- **Vermont Natural Coatings** – Their PolyWhey Wood Finish was developed in collaboration with the University of Vermont and uses whey proteins, a byproduct of cheese making, as the differentiating ingredient. www.vermontnaturalcoatings.com
- **The Real Milk Paint Company** – This brand carries paints and wood oils. They have listed the ingredients of all products on their websites. In addition, they provide Safety Data Sheets for each product. If using oils on your deck, please check to ensure the DIY cleaners in the prior section work with the type of oil selected. www.realmilkpaint.com

PATIOS, DRIVEWAYS, AND WALKWAYS

Patios, driveways, and walkways are often made of concrete today. The material is strong and usually comes at a reasonable price. However, many environmental impacts of concrete aren't typically considered. The production causes a high level of greenhouse gas emissions, and because of the strength of the material, concrete is a strong contributor to the stormwater runoff problem.

For those of us who have concrete as part of their hardscape (like me), there is no need to run out and replace it today. However, when the time comes to replace a damaged concrete area, the options below are ones to add to your consideration list:

Porous Pavement: Porous pavement looks very similar to traditional concrete. The difference is that the surface has a higher-than-normal volume of air voids to allow water to pass through and penetrate the soil below. This prevents the problem of runoff associated with traditional concrete. This material is strong enough for applications from walkways to driveways.

Permeable Pavers: Like porous pavement, permeable pavers allow water to flow through the joints or holes. These pavers are often used for walkways, with the stones placed closely together with a sand-like material in between.

Open Concrete Grids: Another option that provides a unique look are square pavers with holes in the center. The holes can be filled with small stones or with small tufts of grass. Both alternatives can withstand weight loads like standard concrete.

Natural Stone: For walkways, you could consider using natural stepping stones. The gaps between can be filled with smaller stones, sand, or even grass.

Recycling: If you start a project to replace concrete with one of the materials above, it is good to know that concrete can be recycled into aggregate.   Check your local community and www.Earth911.org for recycling locations or pick-up companies.

> **UPCYCLED RETAINING WALLS** – When it's time to replace or add a retaining wall to your outdoor environment, some innovative and unique options exist.   Two difficult-to-recycle materials—old tires and used two-liter bottles—can be used to create an interesting conversation piece in your backyard.   These options are strong, and the look created is unique and interesting.   A quick search online will include photos of walls that have been completed as well as instructions for building.

FURNITURE AND ACCESSORIES

The best part of having an outdoor environment you love is enjoying the space.   As the environment comes together, it's time to shift focus to the furniture, firepits, and accessories to make the space perfect for everything from entertaining to hanging out alone with a good book.   This focus area will give some high-level thoughts about furniture and fire pits to fit your personality and design.

FURNITURE

Sustainable outdoor brands are just beginning to emerge.   I found in my research that many companies are doing great things with the base of furniture.   However, there is still work to be done to make the cushions and materials of the soft goods more eco-friendly.   I appreciate the direction, and they are following the philosophy that the companies are becoming one shade greener with each step.

Shifting to what you should consider in this space, I want to share two things I've learned after purchasing outdoor products for my own home for over twenty-five years.

My first lesson is that you get what you pay for. I never wanted to spend much on outdoor furniture, thinking that we only use it a part of the year, and even then, it isn't every day. My philosophy on this has changed. The pieces that I have spent more on have lasted for many years. The frames are solid and don't need to be replaced at the rate of the cushions. Rather than trying to furnish the entire space with lower quality pieces at once, spread the purchases and spending out over time to get pieces that will last for years.

The second piece of advice is to maintain the pieces you purchase; yes, it takes time, but this will extend their life. A few tips in particular: don't leave the cushions out all the time, bring the furniture out of the elements for the winter, and treat annually if needed (especially wood furniture). I've learned the hard way that when you ignore your pieces, they wear out quicker.

FIRE PITS

For many, a cozy night of smores by the fire is a vision of the relaxed outdoor living we aspire to have. Fire pits of any form do have an environmental impact. Wood fire pits emit smoke, release carbon dioxide, and pollute the air with particulate matter. Moving to a propane-powered fire pit will reduce some, but not all, of the issues.

If you are comfortable with either choice, I would lean toward the propane pit because it does have a lighter impact and the added benefit of less work—no wood to collect and nothing to clean up after. Some of the brands in the section below have fire pit options for wood and propane and outdoor heaters to consider.

BRANDS TO CONSIDER

The brands below have eco-friendly materials and fair-trade practices that demonstrate a focus on sustainability. As mentioned above, I think there is continued opportunity for innovation in this space.

- **Polywood:** The brand uses recycled plastic to create the bases of its pieces. The furniture resists stains and corrosive substances and isn't prone to splinter, crack, chip, peel, or rot. The pieces also come with a 20-year warranty. They recycle 99% of their manufacturing waste. www.polywood.com

- **Loll Designs:** This brand uses recycled HDPE, primarily from old milk jugs and shampoo bottles, to create furniture bases. They recycle more than 88% of their manufacturing waste, and when the product you purchase has run its course, the number 2 plastic can be recycled. www.lolldesigns.com

- **Yardbird**: This brand is focused on creating the world's most environmentally friendly outdoor furniture. They incorporate ocean-bound plastic into their hand-woven wicker and use recyclable materials and packaging whenever possible. In addition, many of their pieces can be recycled. www.yardbird.com

- **Made Trade**: This brand has a smaller outdoor collection than some of the other brands. However, the products are very transparent with materials and production practices. www.madetrade.com

- **Etsy:** Etsy is always great for looking for unique, handcrafted pieces. Because individual artists manufacture each product, you will have to assess the materials they use. Another positive with Etsy is that they offset their carbon emissions for shipping all products. www.etsy.com

- **West Elm**: This brand is focused on fair trade and organic materials. They have many outdoor products, including furniture, accessories, and heating. About half of their wood pieces are responsibly sourced. Look at the materials of each piece, as some pieces are more eco-friendly than others. www.westelm.com

- **Neighbor:** This brand has a collection of products produced from FSC Certified Teak and recycled plastic. They focus on craftsmanship, sustainability, and connection. www.hineighbor.com
- **Crate & Barrel**: This brand carries many wood products certified by the Sustainable Forestry Council (FSC). There is a wide range of products available. However, check each product's materials, as some use synthetic materials. www.crateandbarrel.com
- **Joybird:** This brand carries products made from responsibly sourced wood and waterproof teak. They also plant trees to offset those used in furniture production. www.joybird.com
- **VivaTerra:** This brand supports fair-trade artisans in over 20 countries. Their wood products are reclaimed or FSC-certified. There are fewer furniture options and more outdoor accessories. www.vivaterra.com

POOL AND SPA

Having a pool or spa at your home immediately adds to your impact on the environment. That said, there are many reasons people (myself included) have chosen a pool. We feel like we have a vacation space right out the back door. We don't take vacations in the summertime, so no flights, hotel stays, or driving. While I don't know if those trips' environmental impact balances out, we enjoy the space as part of our lifestyle and do what we can to minimize the impact and maximize enjoyment.

The areas to consider in your pool or spa are construction materials (if you are building), water use, energy for filtering and heating, and the chemicals needed to keep it clean.

CONSTRUCTION MATERIALS

Historically, most pools are made from concrete, fiberglass, or vinyl liners. The concrete and fiberglass are built to last for decades, while liners need to be replaced every 7-10 years. Challenges with these materials are both in the production and ability to recycle at the end of life.

Newer alternatives, including stainless steel and copper, are starting to emerge in the market. Both materials can be recycled without degradation, making them completely sustainable. If you are in the market to install a pool, I would recommend putting these options on your list to consider.

WATER USE

Obviously, the pool is full of water. The key is to retain as much water as possible during use to avoid the frequent need to add water. Suggesting that no one splash around or keep spray to a minimum when jumping in is likely not going to work, nor would I suggest dampening the fun! The best way to keep water in the pool is to protect it from evaporating into the air during the cooler night hours.

Considering a pool cover used during the summer when the pool isn't in use will help keep the heat and water where you want it—in the pool!

ENERGY USE

The pool uses energy in two places: the pump/filter and heating. Starting with the heating, the pool cover mentioned above will help keep the heat in and require less heating. Some covers are automatic, making them easy to put on and off.

To go a step further on the heating front, you could consider a solar system to keep the water warm. My parents had a system like this installed when I was young (back in the 1970s), and it worked wonderfully. While we don't currently have a solar system, I think it would be an alternative.

The other energy use is for the pump. Being conscious of how frequently and how long the pump runs will ensure you find the balance that keeps the water appropriately filtered but doesn't run more than necessary.

CHEMICALS

Getting the pool clear and beautiful for the summer season can require a mix of chemicals to get things in the right balance. Over the years, eco-friendly alternatives have emerged to reduce the need for high levels of chemicals. One relatively easy shift is to move to a saltwater pool. This can be done if you have an existing pool. A salt-chlorine generator takes salt that you add and converts it to chlorine. An added advantage to the more eco-friendly system is that the water feels silkier.

Another alternative that is just beginning to emerge is a "natural pool." These pools have a main swimming area and a second area filled with various hydroponic plants. The water is filtered into this zone to be cleaned and then back into the swimming area.

BRANDS TO CONSIDER – If you are looking for alternatives to the harsh chemicals you have been using in your pool, I found two brands that appear to be using natural ingredients in their products— Natural Chemistry (www.naturalchemistry.com) and Nature2 (www.nature2.com). There wasn't as much transparency in the ingredients as I would like. However, it appears that both companies have a philosophy of reducing environmental impact.

FAST FIVE IN THE BACKYARD

Five steps you can take quickly to make an impact and begin to celebrate some wins!

1. **Shift Lawn Chemicals** – Moving your lawn and garden treatments to organic approaches based on your soil needs will lessen the environmental impact and keep the lawn looking great and healthy.

2. **Reconsider Hardscapes** – Concrete has a lot of negative impacts on the environment. Check out the alternatives in this chapter to move to something that is both better for the environment and adds something unique to the personality of your home.

3. **Use Less Water** – Lawns, gardens, landscaping, and pools all need water to thrive. Create a plan to be intentional about water use and avoid the trap of set and forget.

4. **Purchase Quality Equipment** – When purchasing lawn equipment, consider electric alternatives and purchase equipment that isn't going to be worn out in just a couple of years.

5. **Try New Pet Food** – While many changes could be made in the pet space, take the first step by improving the quality of the ingredients in their food. This will make them healthier and happier. Next, tackle the poop to help the environment.

CONTINUE THE JOURNEY

The concept of this book has been in my mind for nearly ten years. As I come to the end of the journey to bring it to life, I am thankful for the experience. I started this book letting you know that I'm on my own path to a lifestyle and home that is one shade greener year over year. Throughout the book's development, I have learned more, purchased a few products I didn't know about, and have a list of things I want to explore next based on what I've learned.

As I set out to write the book, my goal was to provide you, the reader, with carefully curated information that enabled you to quickly cut through the clutter on what to look for when setting out on your own journey. I hope you are reading this feeling the same sense of accomplishment that I'm feeling, having learned new things, purchased a product or two and created your own list of topics to explore deeper. You can go back to the chapters here again and again for reference and ideas.

THE ULTIMATE FAST FIVE

As you finish the book, here are five actions to consider every day.

1. **Consume Less** – Always ask the question – do I need this? Bringing less into your home will be lighter on the planet, your pocketbook, and your peace of mind.

2. **Eat Less Meat** – Meat has one of the most significant impacts on the planet. Continue to move toward smaller meat portions and meals without meat.

3. **Avoid Plastic** – As you've seen, plastic is everywhere. Look for product alternatives that aren't made of plastic and/or don't come in plastic packaging.

4. **Embrace Secondhand** – Before automatically purchasing new, consider if the item could be bought secondhand or refurbished.

5. **Check the Label** – Throughout the book, we covered toxic ingredients to both the planet and the people in your home. Before making a purchase, ensure you know what the product is made of.

My journey doesn't end with this book, and I hope yours won't either. In addition to using the book as a reference, you can always find my latest updates, blog posts, and products on my website at www.oneshadegreener.com.

Congratulations on all you have accomplished!

I wish you the best on the next phase of your One Shade Greener journey.

ACKNOWLEDGMENTS

As the time comes to thank those who influenced this book, moving from a dream in my head to reality on the pages, I realize that so many contributed along the way. Some have advanced my understanding of the sustainability space, while others have supported me as I wrote the drafts to help me understand my future readers. My heartfelt thank you goes out to each of you with whom I've crossed paths on the journey, even if you don't see your name.

To the team at Saturn circa 2007 – My journey may not have begun without the Saturn VUE Green Line and our move into hybrid electric vehicles. From customer understanding to media partners, this is where my interest and passion began. We worked as a team to discover why protecting our environment was so important and learned from each other during this time. Thank you all for one of my career's most significant and fun times.

To Team Eco Etsy – Thank you for introducing me to an incredible global team of makers focused on products that protect our planet. As a team co-lead, I could see the products from our team that covered beauty, clothing, household goods, and much more. You introduced me to a whole new world of products and how to begin to look for and avoid toxins in the products I purchased.

To the Detroit Environmental Community – Over the years, I have met and learned from countless individuals in metro Detroit as we participated in Green Fairs and Conferences together. I thank all of you for expanding my understanding into the areas of energy/energy audits, architecture, and business considerations.

To The Carbon Almanac Community – I had the opportunity to join this awesome team a year ago. Seth Godin and the entire team reinvigorated my passion for making a difference in the sustainability space. I thank you for all the conversations and great work we have done in the last year. You expanded my knowledge to include more depth in many areas like Net Zero, regenerative agriculture, and the circular economy. I also have a deeper appreciation of why individuals need education so that we can drive toward the larger system change that needs to happen.

To My Early Readers – As this book came together, there are several people I want to thank for reading chapters and providing me feedback to make the final product stronger. Thank you to Michelle, Teresa, Anne, Laura, Tia, Jaclyn, Anne Marie, Dave, and Josie.

To My Book Coach – Linda Griffin. Without you, I wouldn't be here. I started this book writing journey with an idea and a loose structure. You were patient, insightful, and focused on helping me produce a book that is so much more than that original idea. Thank you for your contributions and your wonderful approach to giving me straightforward, encouraging feedback.

To My Family and Friends – I want to thank you for your encouragement and patience over the years. You listened to my stories and suggestions for change. You debated with me on points we weren't aligned with, which gave me a greater perspective. For Todd, Sydney, and Noah, you had the added layer of trying all kinds of new products and processes around the house. I appreciated you helping me test what worked and what didn't for our family.

REFERENCES

8 things to know about palm oil | WWF. (n.d.). WWF. Retrieved
   November 7, 2022, from https://www.wwf.org.uk/updates/8-
   things-know-about-palm-
   oil#:~:text=2.,%2C%20shampoo%2C%20toothpaste%20and%20l
   ipstick

10 Staggering Electronic Waste Facts in 2022 - ERI. (2022, August 22).
   ERI. https://eridirect.com/blog/2022/08/10-staggering-
   electronic-waste-facts-in-
   2022/#:~:text=Less%20Than%2020%25%20of%20E,waste%20wa
   s%20recycled%20in%202019

Alter, L. (2008, September 15). *How to Go Green: In the Bathroom*.
   Treehugger; Treehugger. https://www.treehugger.com/how-to-
   go-green-in-the-bathroom-4857311

Alternative Fuels Data Center: Techniques for Drivers to Conserve Fuel.
   (n.d.). EERE: Alternative Fuels Data Center Home Page.
   Retrieved November 8, 2022, from
   https://afdc.energy.gov/conserve/behavior_techniques.html#:~:te
   xt=Slow%20Down%20and%20Drive%20Conservatively&text=F

or%20light%2Dduty%20vehicles%2C%20for,by%207%25%E2%8
0%9314%25

Brodwin, E. (2014, June 16). *Scientists Say You Should Stop Using Your
Charcoal Grill Immediately*. Mic; Mic.
https://www.mic.com/articles/91303/scientists-say-you-should-
stop-using-your-charcoal-grill-immediately

Charles, K. (2021, September 13). *Food production emissions make up
more than a third of global total | New Scientist*. New Scientist;
New Scientist. https://www.newscientist.com/article/2290068-
food-production-emissions-make-up-more-than-a-third-of-
global-total/

D'Arcy, K. (2020, July 22). *Junk mail destroys 100 million trees every
year—and other alarming facts*. Document Management Blog |
MES; MES Hybrid Document Systems.
https://blog.mesltd.ca/junk-mail-destroys-100-million-trees-
every-year

Delaney, C. (2011, June 22). *Eco-Friendly Laundry Washing -
EcoFriendlyLink*. EcoFriendlyLink - Naturally Healthy Green
Living; https://ecofriendlylink.com/blog/eco-
friendlylaundrywashing/

Document Display | NEPIS | US EPA. (n.d.). EPA - Home Page . Retrieved
November 7, 2022, from
https://nepis.epa.gov/Exe/ZyNET.exe/P100JPPH.TXT?ZyAction
D=ZyDocument&Client=EPA&Index=2011+Thru+2015&Docs
=&Query=&Time=&EndTime=&SearchMethod=1&TocRestrict
=n&Toc=&TocEntry=&QField=&QFieldYear=&QFieldMonth=
&QFieldDay=&IntQFieldOp=0&ExtQFieldOp=0&XmlQuery=&
File=D%3A%5Czyfiles%5CIndex%20Data%5C11thru15%5CTxt
%5C00000011%5CP100JPPH.txt&User=ANONYMOUS&Passw

REFERENCES

ord=anonymous&SortMethod=h%7C-
&MaximumDocuments=1&FuzzyDegree=0&ImageQuality=r75
g8/r75g8/x150y150g16/i425&Display=hpfr&DefSeekPage=x&Se
archBack=ZyActionL&Back=ZyActionS&BackDesc=Results%20
page&MaximumPages=1&ZyEntry=1&SeekPage=x&ZyPURL

Earth911. (2020, October 29). *Infographic: Pens and Pencils by the Numbers - Earth911.* Earth911. https://earth911.com/home-garden/infographic-sustainable-pens-pencils/

Energy Efficient Cooking for The Holidays and Beyond | Consumers Energy. (n.d.). Home | Consumers Energy. Retrieved November 7, 2022, from https://www.consumersenergy.com/community/sustainability/our-hometown-stories/energy-efficient-cooking#:~:text=According%20to%20the%20U.S.%20Department,use%20occurs%20in%20the%20kitchen

FDA Warns Cosmetics Industry to Follow Law on Untested Ingredients | Environmental Working Group. (n.d.). Environmental Working Group. Retrieved November 8, 2022, from https://www.ewg.org/news-insights/statement/fda-warns-cosmetics-industry-follow-law-untested-ingredients

Food Waste and its Links to Greenhouse Gases and Climate Change | USDA. (n.d.). USDA. Retrieved November 7, 2022, from https://www.usda.gov/media/blog/2022/01/24/food-waste-and-its-links-greenhouse-gases-and-climate-change

Food Waste in America | Feeding America. (n.d.). U.S. Hunger Relief Organization | Feeding America. Retrieved November 7, 2022, from https://www.feedingamerica.org/our-work/our-approach/reduce-food-

waste#:~:text=How%20much%20food%20waste%20is,food%20t
hrown%20away%20each%20year

*FOTW #1230, March 21, 2022: More than Half of all Daily Trips Were
Less than Three Miles in 2021 | Department of Energy.* (n.d.).
Energy.Gov. Retrieved November 8, 2022, from
https://www.energy.gov/eere/vehicles/articles/fotw-1230-march-
21-2022-more-half-all-daily-trips-were-less-three-miles-2021

*Frequently Asked Questions (FAQs) - U.S. Energy Information
Administration (EIA).* (n.d.). Homepage - U.S. Energy
Information Administration (EIA). Retrieved November 9, 2022,
from https://www.eia.gov/tools/faqs/faq.php?id=427&t=3

*Frontiers | Perchloroethylene and Dry Cleaning: It's Time to Move the
Industry to Safer Alternatives.* (n.d.). Frontiers. Retrieved
November 9, 2022, from
https://www.frontiersin.org/articles/10.3389/fpubh.2021.638082/
full

Global daily social media usage 2022 | Statista. (n.d.). Statista. Retrieved
November 7, 2022, from
https://www.statista.com/statistics/433871/daily-social-media-
usage-worldwide/

Golden, J. S., Subramanian, V., Irizarri, G. M. A. U., White, P., & Meier,
F. (2010). Energy and carbon impact from residential laundry in
the United States. *Journal of Integrative Environmental Sciences,
1*, 53–73. https://doi.org/10.1080/19438150903541873

Grass Lawns are an Ecological Catastrophe – ONE Only Natural Energy.
(n.d.). ONE Only Natural Energy – Magazine on Sustainable
Energy, Climate Change, Innovation and Environment.
Retrieved November 9, 2022, from
https://www.onlynaturalenergy.com/grass-lawns-are-an-

ecological-
catastrophe/#:~:text=The%20EPA%20estimates%20that%20hour
,of%20toxic%20pollutants%20per%20year.

Greene, D. (2020, February 6). *The history of the wire hanger - Vox.* Vox; Vox. https://www.vox.com/the-goods/2020/2/6/21113481/wire-hangers-history-use#:~:text=Despite%20their%20seeming%20disposability%2C%20discarding,200%20million%20pounds%20of%20steel

Homemade laundry detergent can save money. (n.d.). Https://Www.Wafb.Com. Retrieved November 9, 2022, from https://www.wafb.com/story/9687193/homemade-laundry-detergent-can-save-money/

Household penetration rates for pet-ownership in the U.S. 2020 | Statista. (n.d.). Statista. Retrieved November 9, 2022, from https://www.statista.com/statistics/198086/us-household-penetration-rates-for-pet-owning-since-2007/

How Many Cars Are There In The World in 2022? Statistics by Country. (2021, June 24). Hedges & Company; Hedges and Company. https://hedgescompany.com/blog/2021/06/how-many-cars-are-there-in-the-world/

How Much Can You Save By Adjusting Your Thermostat | Direct Energy Blog. (n.d.). Direct Energy Blog. Retrieved November 7, 2022, from https://blog.directenergy.com/how-much-can-you-save-by-adjusting-your-thermostat/#:~:text=The%20Department%20of%20Energy%20estimates,savings%20of%20up%20to%2010%25

Idling Reduction for Personal Vehicles. (2015). Department of Energy. https://afdc.energy.gov/files/u/publication/idling_personal_vehicles.pdf

Igini, M. (2022, May 3). *10 Food Waste Statistics in America | Earth.Org.* Earth.Org; Earth.Org. https://earth.org/food-waste-in-america/#:~:text=Over%20240%20Million%20Slices%20of,every%20year%20across%20the%20country

Importance of Methane | US EPA. (2016, January 11). US EPA. https://www.epa.gov/gmi/importance-methane#:~:text=Methane%20is%20more%20than%2025,due%20to%20human%2Drelated%20activities

Is Energy Efficiency Cost-Effective? | EnergySage. (n.d.). Get Competing Solar Quotes Online | EnergySage. Retrieved November 7, 2022, from https://www.energysage.com/energy-efficiency/why-conserve-energy/cost-of-ee/#:~:text=The%20U.S.%20Department%20of%20Energy,amounts%20to%20over%20%242%2C200%20annually

Jaeger, N. (2019, September 25). *How Much Laundry Does the Average Person Do? | Laundry Butler For You.* Laundry On-Demand | Laundry Butler For You | Laundry Pickup; Natalie nhjaeger. https://www.laundrybutlerforyou.com/blog/how-much-laundry-does-the-average-person-

Kaja, A. (2021, December 10). *Meat Eaters Produce 59% More Greenhouse Gases Than Vegetarians - New Study - The Vegan Kind Blog.* TheVeganKind; The Vegan Kind. https://thevegankind.com/news/meat-eaters-produce-59percent-more-greenhouse-gases-than-vegetarians-new-study

Landfill waste: How to prevent disposable razor plastic pollution. (2019, August 7). USA TODAY; Associated Press. https://www.usatoday.com/story/news/nation/2019/08/07/landfill-waste-how-prevent-disposable-razor-plastic-pollution/1943345001/

REFERENCES

Lowe, L. (2018, January 15). *What Percentage of Your Clothes Do You Actually Wear?* LinkedIn. https://www.linkedin.com/pulse/what-percentage-your-clothes-do-you-actually-wear-lalita-lowe/

Marlow, A. (2020, May 23). *How do Lawn Mowers impact climate change? - EMSmastery.* EMSmastery. https://emsmastery.com/2020/05/23/how-do-lawn-mowers-impact-climate-change/#:~:text=An%20article%20on%20a%20US,the%20United%20States'%20air%20pollution

Massey, L. (2011). *Curly Girl.* Workman Publishing.

Mazzoni, M. (2018, August 22). *Recycling Mystery: Mattresses - Earth911.* Earth911. https://earth911.com/home-garden/recycling-mystery-mattresses/#:~:text=An%20estimated%2020%20million%20mattresses,difficulties%2C%20it%20can%20be%20done

McFarland, M. (2022, August 21). *Why you can't always throw AA batteries in the trash | CNN Business.* CNN; CNN. https://www.cnn.com/2022/08/21/business/aa-battery-disposal/index.html#:~:text=Seattle%20residents%20are%20encouraged%20to,year%2C%E2%80%9D%20the%20city%20cautions

Measuring biodegradability — Science Learning Hub. (n.d.). Science Learning Hub. Retrieved November 7, 2022, from https://www.sciencelearn.org.nz/resources/1543-measuring-biodegradability

National Overview: Facts and Figures on Materials, Wastes and Recycling | US EPA. (2017, October 2). US EPA. https://www.epa.gov/facts-and-figures-about-materials-waste-and-recycling/national-overview-facts-and-figures-materials#:~:text=Together%2C%20almost%2094%20million%20tons,percent%20recycling%20and%20composting%20rate.

Not So Sexy | Environmental Working Group. (n.d.). Environmental Working Group. Retrieved November 9, 2022, from https://www.ewg.org/research/not-so-sexy

Oxygen levels - Understanding Global Change. (n.d.). Understanding Global Change. Retrieved November 7, 2022, from https://ugc.berkeley.edu/background-content/oxygen-levels/#:~:text=Photosynthesizing%20algae%20in%20the%20ocean,of%20oxygen%20in%20the%20atmosphere

Polluted Pets | Environmental Working Group. (n.d.). Environmental Working Group. Retrieved November 9, 2022, from https://www.ewg.org/research/polluted-pets

Preventing Wasted Food At Home | US EPA. (2013, April 18). US EPA. https://www.epa.gov/recycle/preventing-wasted-food-home

Pulp and Paper. (n.d.). WWF. Retrieved November 7, 2022, from https://wwf.panda.org/discover/our_focus/forests_practice/forest_sector_transformation_updated/pulp_and_paper/

Racovites, N. (2020, September 14). *Brushing Away Plastic Waste - America's Plastic Makers.* America's Plastic Makers. https://plasticmakers.org/brushing-away-plastic-waste/

Report: Connected Devices Have More Than Doubled Since 2019 - Telecompetitor. (n.d.). Telecompetitor - Providing Insight, Analysis, and Commentary on the Evolving Telecom Competitive Landscape. Retrieved November 7, 2022, from https://www.telecompetitor.com/report-connected-devices-have-more-than-doubled-since-2019/

Residential Toilets | US EPA. (2016, October 14). US EPA. https://www.epa.gov/watersense/residential-

REFERENCES

toilets#:~:text=Toilets%20are%20by%20far%20the,wasted%20wa
ter%20in%20many%20homes

Richter, F. (n.d.). *Chart: Cars Still Dominate the American Commute |
Statista*. Statista Infographics. Retrieved November 8, 2022, from
https://www.statista.com/chart/18208/means-of-transportation-
used-by-us-commuters/

Rule of 430 | Trek Bikes. (n.d.). Trek Bikes - The World's Best Bikes and
Cycling Gear | Trek Bikes. Retrieved November 9, 2022, from
https://www.trekbikes.com/us/en_US/the-rule-of-430/

Schwartz, D. (n.d.). *How Many Gallons of Water Does a Shower Use?*
Don't Pour Money Down the Drain | The Water Scrooge; The
Water Scrooge. Retrieved November 9, 2022, from
https://www.thewaterscrooge.com/blog/how-many-gallons-of-
water-does-a-shower-use#:~:text=Flow%20Shower%20Fixtures-
,Shower%20gallons%20per%20minute,gpm)%20(7.9%20lpm)

Segran, E. (2022, January 13). *75 million gallons of paint is wasted each
year. This startup turns them into brand new cans.* Fast
Company; Fast Company. https://fastcompany.com

*Share of New Homes with Decks Drops Below 20 Percent | Eye On
Housing*. (2021, October 7). Eye On Housing | National
Association of Home Builders Discusses Economics and
Housing Policy. https://eyeonhousing.org/2021/10/share-of-
new-homes-with-decks-drops-below-20-
percent/#:~:text=Of%20the%20roughly%20990%2C000%20singl
e,and%20partially%20funded%20by%20HUD)

Smith, P. (n.d.). *Average number of clothing items purchased by women
U.S. 1996-2021 | Statista*. Statista. Retrieved November 9, 2022,
from https://www.statista.com/statistics/828040/average-
number-of-clothing-items-purchased-by-women-us/

Stanford University. (2020, October 7). *Why laughing gas is a growing climate problem | Stanford News*. Stanford News. https://news.stanford.edu/2020/10/07/laughing-gas-growing-climate-problem/#:~:text=In%20the%20industrial%20era%2C%20carbon,over%20a%20100%2Dyear%20period

State of Home Spending 2020: Year of the Home. (2020). Home Advisor; Home Advisor. https://www.homeadvisor.com/r/wp-content/uploads/2020/11/DP6355-StateOfHomeSpending-2020-R3.pdf

Study: Average Worker Spends 1,700 Hours In Front Of Computer Screen - CBS New York. (2018, July 31). CBS News - Breaking News, 24/7 Live Streaming News & Top Stories; CBS New York. https://www.cbsnews.com/newyork/news/study-worker-1700-hours-computer/#:~:text=Contact%20lenses%20manufacturer%20Acuvue%20sponsored,into%20the%20large%20glowing%20screens

Sunkara, L. (2020, September 7). *Which Is Worse for the Environment: Driving or Flying? | Reader's Digest*. Reader's Digest; Readers Digest. https://www.rd.com/article/which-is-worse-for-the-environment-driving-or-flying/#:~:text=According%20to%20an%20ICCT%20report,at%20152%20mpg%20per%20individual

Tax the Plastic. (n.d.). Penn State University. Retrieved November 7, 2022, from https://psu.edu

Textiles: Material-Specific Data | US EPA. (2017, September 12). US EPA. https://www.epa.gov/facts-and-figures-about-materials-waste-and-recycling/textiles-material-specific-data

REFERENCES

The MIT Press Reader. (2022, February 14). *The Staggering Ecological Impacts of Computation and the Cloud | The MIT Press Reader.* The MIT Press Reader; https://www.facebook.com/mitpress/. https://thereader.mitpress.mit.edu/the-staggering-ecological-impacts-of-computation-and-the-cloud/

The plastic waste problem explained. (n.d.). Alliance To End Plastic Waste. Retrieved November 7, 2022, from https://endplasticwaste.org/en/our-stories/the-plastic-waste-problem-explained?gclid=Cj0KCQjwwfiaBhC7ARIsAGvcPe6j9M76_oyNl IC7HNaoW6F_Vwa2JbjC0E_fxXGuJ1e3mvY4LvduOikaAiBGE ALw_wcB

Toilet Paper and Climate Change: NRDC's Updated "Issue With Tissue" Ranks Brands on Sustainability | NRDC. (n.d.). NRDC. Retrieved November 9, 2022, from https://www.nrdc.org/media/2020/200618-20

US passenger cars | MIT Energy Initiative. (n.d.). Main; MIT Energy Initiative. Retrieved November 9, 2022, from https://energy.mit.edu/news/us-passenger-cars/

Varanasi, A. (2022, February 13). *Nail Salon Technicians Inhale 10 Times More Chemicals Than E-Waste Workers.* Forbes; Forbes. https://www.forbes.com/sites/anuradhavaranasi/2022/02/13/nail-salon-workers-are-exposed-to-10-times-higher-chemicals-than-e-waste-workers/?sh=44e85f139ea2

Velasco, A. (2009, May 19). *Carbon Footprint of US Junk Mail Equivalent To 480,000 Cars - Matador Network.* Matador Network; Matador Network. https://matadornetwork.com/change/carbon-footprint-of-us-junk-mail-equivalent-to-480000-cars/

Verchot, M. (2019, September 20). *11 Ways to Green Your Laundry.* Treehugger; Treehugger. https://www.treehugger.com/how-to-go-green-laundry-4858690

Villazon, L. (2018, July 14). *The thought experiment: What is the carbon footprint of an email? | BBC Science Focus Magazine.* BBC Science Focus Magazine - Science, Nature, Technology, Q&As - BBC Science Focus Magazine; BBC Science Focus Magazine. https://www.sciencefocus.com/planet-earth/the-thought-experiment-what-is-the-carbon-footprint-of-an-email/

What is Good Gas Mileage? - Municibid Blog. (2022, March 17). Municibid Blog - Municibid Blog. https://blog.municibid.com/what-is-good-gas-mileage/#:~:text=According%20to%20the%20US%20Department,Drive%20the%20speed%20limit

Yard and Garden Care: How It Affects Your Health and Environment (Fact Sheet) | MU Extension. (n.d.). University of Missouri Extension | MU Extension. Retrieved November 9, 2022, from https://extension.missouri.edu/publications/eqm105f

Your Water Usage | WSSC Water. (n.d.). WSSC Water. Retrieved November 9, 2022, from https://www.wsscwater.com/understandusage

ABOUT THE AUTHOR

Lori Sullivan has been studying green living since 2007. Researching, trying many products in her personal life, and starting her company One Shade Greener in 2009.

Professionally, Lori has focused on sustainability in many forms starting with her first role working on lightweight materials at General Motors to improve vehicle fuel economy. During her time at GM, she also started an internal newsletter called "Lite News" and spent three years focused on the Saturn Green Line (hybrid electric vehicles). In 2022, she developed a sustainability strategy for MRM and was part of the core team developing a path to net zero as part of McCann Worldgroup. In addition, she was contributor to The Carbon Almanac – a book of simple facts about climate change – published in June 2022.

Lori is now a personal development coach and sustainability consultant. In her spare time, she enjoys reading, writing, and making upcycled jewelry. She is married with two grown children and lives with her husband in Plymouth, Michigan.

To learn more and sign up for her newsletters, please visit www.OneShadeGreener.com.

Made in United States
North Haven, CT
27 March 2023

34634456R00173